Memoir On The Language Of The Gypsies, As Now Used In The Turkish Empire

[FROM THE JOURNAL OF THE AMERICAN ORIENTAL SOCIETY, VOL. VII, 1861.]

MEMOIR

ON THE

LANGUAGE OF THE GYPSIES,

AS NOW USED IN THE TURKISH EMPIRE.

BY A. G. PASPATI, A.M., M.D.

TRANSLATED FROM THE GREEK BY REV. C. HAMLIN, D.D.,

MISSIONARY OF THE A. B. C. F. M. AT CONSTANTINOPLE.

Presented to the Society May 17th, 1860.

NOTE BY THE TRANSLATOR.

THE following memoir is a translation but in part. The learned author has written the whole of the Grammar and some other parts in English, which has needed very little correction. The original is written in so pure a Greek style, that any one who has studied the ancient Greek might read it, occasionally noticing an interesting change of meaning without a change of form, or the reverse. If all our Greek Professors should study the living Greek, in Greece, it would reanimate the dead language, and clothe it with a new power and beauty.

We are confident that this article will be acceptable to American scholars, both for its intrinsic merits and as a specimen of the present literature and learning of the Greeks.   C. H.

This memoir on the Language of the Gypsies will be divided into five sections, as follows: 1st. Introductory remarks on the history and present condition of the Gypsy race; 2nd. General explanation of the character and connections of their language, and a critical estimate of the works which have hitherto appeared upon the subject; 3rd. A vocabulary, with comparative etymologies from the Sanskrit and other languages; 4th. A comparison of the phonetical system of the Gypsy with that of the Sanskrit; 5th. A grammar of the language.

SECTION I.

HISTORY OF THE GYPSIES.

Most of the writings relating to the Gypsies have hitherto
been unsatisfactory and obscure. In various ways, laborious
and learned writers have endeavored to explain the origin and
affinities of these nomadic, wandering people, who dwell or roam
in the midst of us, but are generally regarded with aversion and
disgust.

The leading subject of this memoir will be the language and
origin of the Gypsies, and not their customs and history. A
few preliminary notices, however, may help the reader to appre-
ciate what we shall offer in regard to their language.

A valuable authority upon the Gypsies of Western Europe is
the Englishman George Borrow. His work, "The Zincali, or an
Account of the Gypsies of Spain," exhibits from beginning to end
a man thoroughly acquainted with this people, speaking their
own language with such facility, and with such a knowledge of
their habits and customs, that he was everywhere received as a
veritable Gypsy. His vocabulary of the language is invaluable,
although, as we shall see, his want of acquaintance with the
Sanskrit prevented his carrying forward his most useful labors
to the desired consummation.

In 1417,[*] in the reign of Sigismond, emperor of the Romans
and king of Hungary, the Gypsies first appeared in Europe, to
the number of about three thousand. They resided first in Moldavia, and thence spread through Transylvania and Hungary.
A part, led by Ladislaus their chief, having obtained leave to
settle upon the crown-lands, and living unmolested under the
protection of the autocrat, gradually adopted the religion of the
country which they inhabited. And, to the present time, such is
the very common custom of this race: everywhere they adopt
the common worship, caring little for its dogmas.

They received from Sigismond the privilege of having their
own chief, but this was taken from them in 1609. In 1782,
according to the census of that time, there were about 50,000
Gypsies in all Hungary, but their number afterwards diminished.
In vain did Joseph II. endeavor to civilize them.

It is worthy of remark that in Hungary, according to the
testimony of the Gypsies themselves, they have retained their
original language in the highest degree of purity.

They are now found scattered over Europe, and through
Russia, excepting the province of Petersburg, whence they were
long since expelled. They also prefer the extended and fruitful

---

[*] Bataillard, as we shall presently see, gives an ealier date than this.

plains of Interior Russia, where they find abundant pasturage for their horses, to the trade in which they are so much addicted. But nowhere have they been so fortunate as in the province of Moscow, where many of them have magnificent dwellings, splendid carriages, and near relationship with highborn Russians, preserving that singular good fortune, the sweet voice of the maidens, peculiar to their uncultivated tribes, and highly esteemed by the Russians.

About the beginning of the fifteenth century, says a French historian, the Gypsies appeared in Paris, to the number of one hundred and thirty-two. The French looked upon them as most satanic witches, and persecuted them with such severity that they fled into Spain.

In Spain they are numerous, in certain large cities, having quarters called *Gitanerie.* The fertility of the soil, and the mildness of the climate, were both favorable to this roaming race. The most part took refuge in Andalusia, where they live to this day, no longer nomadic, but laboring in the cities and villages.

A celebrated law of Charles III., who deceased in 1788, introduced a healthy and saving amelioration into the life of the race, which had become intolerable from its addiction to theft and robbery. What the civil arm and the severest laws were powerless to do, this wise law speedily effected. Charles repealed the inhuman laws which had been published against the Gypsies, invited them to dwell fearlessly with the native Spaniards, and secured to them the privileges of education and of participation in civil offices. While he threatened to punish the Gypsies who did not conform to the law, he invited the Spaniards to forget their ancient hatred, and live with them under the laws and government, as children of the same country.

This law, as also the philanthropy of the monarch, had a great effect upon the Gypsies. They collected into cities and villages, abandoned their thievish life, and, forgetting past evils, gave themselves up to the common labors of civilized existence.

But this law, the like of which Europe had not then seen, had the fate of many other laws, in not attaining its immediate design, which was to make the Gypsies forget their language, and become Catholic Christians and faithful Spaniards. No such result followed, and they remain to this day, in Spain, as elsewhere, a distinct race, and having a language common to all the branches dispersed through the world.

They appeared in England about three centuries ago, where they were mercilessly persecuted. Most of them were hung as magicians and satanic witches. A few survivors concealed themselves in dens and caves, and came out only in the night to beg their food. As the rage of the bigoted masses softened down, the starved and naked Gypsies reappeared, and, spreading themselves according to their national custom, remained in different places and cities of England.

It is worthy of remark that the foggy and sunless climate of England has given to the Gypsies more muscular strength and beauty than their fellow-countrymen have elsewhere, and more even than the English have in a similar rank of life.

Every where the Gypsy race is strongly marked by similar traits and customs.

They are celebrated dealers in horses, they are famous horse-doctors, their old women are noted fortune-tellers, and the young women drive a very profitable business in singing love-songs, decent and indecent, in the streets and public places.

They have no principles, they serve no God but the God of gain and fraud, they conform to all religions. They excite the voluptuous passions of others, but they rarely fall themselves into the sins which they lead others into. A merciless death hangs over the woman who has illicit intercourse, whether with a Gypsy or a foreigner.

I have followed Borrow in his general description of the Gypsies of Europe. As regards those in Turkey and in the Wallachian provinces, or rather in all those countries formerly known under the denomination of Dacia, I must refer the reader to other authorities, who have treated the subject more at length, particularly as my remarks upon their dialect may be elucidated by their history and social position in these countries.

The latest writer on the Gypsies is J. A. Vaillant.* This author resided for many years in the Danubian provinces, and paid particular attention to the history of the numerous Gypsies scattered over those countries. In describing the origin of these people, whose emigrations he makes coeval with those of the ancient world, he launches himself into such an ocean of crude and undigested learning, he unites such wild theories with positive facts, he distorts ancient history in such an unphilosophical manner, that the reader never knows where he is, or whither he is drifting. With the exception of his valuable remarks on the noble efforts of the Hospodars of Wallachia and Moldavia, to liberate from bondage and oppression so many Gypsies in those provinces, his work is of little value, either in a historical or a philological point of view. He appears to have studied these people for a long time,† and he would have bestowed an inestimable boon upon philology and ethnography, if, like Borrow, he had given us a vocabulary of the dialect of the Wallachian Gypsies, to which he appears to have paid little attention, though

---

* Les Rômes—Histoire Vraie des Vrais Bohémiens, par J. A. Vaillant, Fondateur du College Interne de Bucarest. Paris, 1857.

† "Je n'aurai point à regretter les dixhuit années que j'ai employées à la bible de leur science." p. 22.

he confesses that the foundation of their language is Sanskrit.[*] Though he confesses in another place that their language is the only criterion of their origin,[†] it appears strange that he has not based his work on this idea, by which their mysterious history would have been still farther elucidated.

Later writers on the social and political history of the Danubian provinces have followed Vaillant as an authority on the Gypsies, so numerous in those countries and in the provinces of Turkey south of the Danube. As no general persecutions ever took place against them, either on religious or political grounds, they have been suffered to live quietly in those provinces, and have multiplied to such a degree that they are superior in number to their fellow-countrymen in all the other states of Europe.

Those who are acquainted with the political state of Turkey are aware how difficult it is to give even an approximate estimate of its inhabitants. What confidence then can we give to Vaillant's statistics,[‡] who makes the number of Gypsies residing in Wallachia 125,000, in Moldavia 137,000, Turkey 200,000, Transylvania and the Banat of Temeswar 140,000—total 602,000?[§] According to the same author, the number of Gypsies scattered over Europe amounts to 837,000, so that nearly three fourths of all the Gypsies of Europe are to be found in Turkey and the provinces north of the Danube. Ubicini[||] has followed Vaillant, with slight variations. Regnault[¶] makes the Gypsy population of Wallachia and Moldavia 300,000, more numerous however in Moldavia than in Wallachia. He assigns 140,000 to Transylvania, Bucovina, and the Banat of Temeswar. All these numbers appear to me to be greatly exaggerated, and they may be owing in part to information from the Gypsies themselves, who by such mendacious accounts are inclined to give themselves importance and consideration in these provinces. Certain it is, that in Turkey proper, where the Gypsies are set down by Vaillant as 200,000, no census can be taken of them, even approximately; for a great part of the Gypsy population are continually roaming from plain to plain. Still, such information is valuable, as tending to show the great numbers of the Gypsy population in these countries, a fact remarked by travellers whose object has not been either the census or the history of this degraded people.

---

[*] "Mais il n'en est pas moins vrai, que, si la forme en varie, le fond en est toujours un partout, et pour tous, et ce fond est le Sanscrit." p. 13.

[†] "Leur langage, seul critérium de leur origine." p. 4:

[‡] p. 481.

[§] A late writer on Constantinople and Turkey, Louis Enault (Paris, 1855, p. 226), estimates the number of Gypsies in all the provinces of the Sultan at 214,000.

[||] Provinces d'Origine Roumaine. Univers Pittoresque. Paris, 1856, p. 11.

[¶] Histoire Politique et Sociale des Principautés Danubiennes, par M. Elias Regnault. Paris, 1855.

The Gypsies in the Danubian provinces are divided into three classes :*

1. The Laïesi, including artisans in works of wood and iron, musicians, exhibitors of bears, etc.

' 2. The Vatrari, employed in all the menial employments of the household. They are generally the servants of the servants. At times they have become head-cooks, coachmen, and *valets de chambre* of their wealthy masters.

3. The Netotsi, half savage, half naked, living by theft and rapine, feeding in times of want upon cats, dogs, and mice; they are the most degraded and debased of all the Gypsy population. This class, by their turbulent conduct and nocturnal depredations, have brought upon themselves dire persecution on the part of the local authorities, in which their more innocent fellow-countrymen have been in part sufferers. The Netotsi are of a darker hue, with short frizzled hair. Some are nearly black, and this difference of complexion may corroborate the statements of some authors, who make them the descendants of a separate immigration, and from a climate differing from that of the former two.

All the Gypsies in the Danubian provinces, like their fellow-countrymen in the rest of Europe, follow the religion of the people among whom they live. Here, as elsewhere, they seem indifferent to every external form of worship, and are considered by the Christian people in the same light as the Mohammedans view their Gypsy co-religionists in Turkey. The Turks, who are not particularly punctilious in the choice of their wives, often marry Gypsy women. Not so with the Christians, who have kept themselves aloof from family connections with the Gypsies, and will rarely have any intercourse with them. No Gypsy is ever permitted to enter into any of the sacerdotal offices of the Greek church.

A singular trait in the political history of the Gypsies residing in the Danubian provinces has been their state of bondage from time immemorial. Bataillard,† who has written on the Gypsies scattered over Europe, states that, from two charts discovered lately among the archives of the monastery of Tismana in Little Wallachia, it appears that they were to be found in Wallachia in the middle of the fourteenth century, and were then as now in a state of slavery. The long immunity from persecution enjoyed by the Wallachian Gypsies was probably owing to their state of slavery to the great landholders and the all-powerful monasteries, by whom their misdeeds were often concealed, and by whose power and influence, as interested masters, the iron rod of persecution was often arrested. As many of them passed to the

---

* Vaillant, p. 319.
† Nouvelles Recherches sur l'Apparition et la Dispersion des Bohémiens en Europe.

monasteries with landed property, on the death of charitable individuals, no doubt, from reverence to these asylums, such must have been protected in preference to those belonging to the state or to private proprietors, who at times suffered in the stormy periods of political disturbance.

Did these men subject themselves voluntarily to bondage? Were they driven to seek a shelter in slavery, to avoid ruthless persecution and impending death? Why did they not emigrate to other parts of Europe, where their countrymen are often suffered to roam, and in this manner avoid political and religious persecutions by flight and concealment? It is probably owing to a milder treatment on the part of the people among whom they came to dwell, and to the reports of heartless and bloody persecutions suffered by their countrymen in other provinces of Europe. Whatever the reasons may be which induced these despised people to subject themselves to bondage, in preference to a lawless and persecuted life, certain it is that in no part of Europe have they multiplied in such vast numbers as in these Danubian provinces.

Both in Wallachia and Moldavia a change has been lately effected in their condition. Alexander Ghika, Hospodar of Wallachia, and Stourja of Moldavia,* the former in 1837, and the latter in 1844, have both decreed the freedom of the Gypsies in their respective provinces, and this people, so long oppressed, enslaved in body and mind, will probably in a short time, as they rise in wealth and learning under the fostering hand of freedom, attain to some yet higher consideration.†

SECTION II.

LANGUAGE OF THE GYPSIES.

We come now to the principal subject of our memoir, the language of the Gypsies, which, with our present unsatisfactory knowledge of this people, is of paramount importance as a historical demonstration of their origin and nationality. The entire history of this race is in its idiom, and this point of comparative philology will, I hope, prove to the reader the inestimable advantages accruing to history from the comparative study of spoken idioms. It is wonderful that a race differing so widely from the races around them, so universally avoided, as foreign and barbarous, should have been so long in possession of indis-

---

* Vaillant, p. 435–442.
† The Gypsies are now allowed to intermarry with Wallachians, and such marriages are consecrated by the.Church. Formerly the price of a Gypsy was 150 to 200 francs. Ami Boué, Turquie d'Europe (Paris, 1840), iii. 325.

putable proofs of their origin and fatherland. History has not traced their mysterious migrations, or noted any sudden irruptions into more cultivated lands. It has marked, however, their notorious wickedness, their unconquerable propensity to roaming and pilfering, and their universal abhorrence of the customs and religion of the people amongst whom they roamed or dwelt.

Their origin has till of late been a mystery, and such it would have continued to be had not philologists undertaken the study of their spoken language, a study of extreme difficulty, owing to their long continued ignorance, and constant avoidance of a higher mental cultivation.

The study of the Gypsy language differs so widely from that of all other idioms, that the reader will excuse the following remarks upon the subject. Not only does it differ from that of other languages preserved both in writing and in the mouth of the people, but it is another thing, also, from the acquisition of unwritten dialects of savage tribes. In these latter, the language is one and the same, easily acquired by the laborious philologist who may mingle with the people, and from long colloquial usage fix their grammatical rules. But the Gypsies constantly avoid all who are foreign to their tribe, and, being universally abhorred, they shun intercourse, and suspect the most godlike benevolence shown to them. Acquainted as they are with the spoken language of the people among whom they dwell, they generally use it in the hearing of all, so that even here in Turkey, where they are so numerous, many do not even suspect the existence of any idiom peculiar to themselves.

Another consideration, extremely important in the study of this idiom, is the intermixture of foreign terms, generally borrowed from the language of the surrounding people, at times remodelled to the Gypsy forms of speech, and at times so distorted as to bear a very distant resemblance to the original word. Sheer ignorance, and long separation from those of their own tribe, have induced many Gypsies here in Turkey to make use of exotic terms, while many in their own neighborhood were constantly using well known and pure Gypsy terms. In such cases the student is extremely embarrassed, unless some one kinder than the others may direct him to a more learned Gypsy for farther information. It is, therefore, of the utmost importance that the student should possess a perfect acquaintance with the language of the people among whom they dwell, and particularly with the vulgar jargon, which can never be learned in dictionaries or books, words floating from mouth to mouth, extremely significant, and precisely of a stamp to please the low taste of a Gypsy in speaking to foreigners of similar education. This knowledge is of primary importance; otherwise he may introduce into his vocabulary, as vernacular terms, words which have no connection with the Gypsy language.* In this manner alone can we obtain a vocabulary of their language free from all words of foreign idioms, and capable of affording a solid historical basis for farther philological researches. This observation has often occurred to me in the course of this memoir, and such is the importance of it that its full weight can be felt only by those who have had the courage to undertake such an ungrateful task. Even in the composition of every Gypsy vocabulary, there should be a well-defined demarcation between foreign words and those native to the Gypsies, as a guide to others. Borrow is an illustration of this. In his vocabulary he has added a vast number of Spanish words, some pure, some mutilated, and every reader cannot but be perplexed with such a heterogeneous mass of terms, Spanish and Gypsy, without any guide as to their origin or etymology. Of what use, I ask, can a Gypsy vocabulary be, but as a foundation-stone to the history of the Gypsies? And in the vocabulary of Borrow, how can the student separate from the Spanish jargon the vernacular Gypsy? Who should have undertaken a similar work but a man like Borrow, who, moved by love to his fellow-men, went among the Gypsies, like a harbinger of peace, learned and spoke their language, and was perfectly conversant with the Spanish and with their jargon?

Even after all the learned works on the history and language of the Gypsies which I shall presently mention, a vast amount of treasure still lies hidden in the remains of their idiom which are scattered over their settlements in Europe. A comparative vocabulary, that should exhibit all the pure indigenous words preserved among all the Gypsies of Europe, to the entire exclusion of every foreign word, is still a desideratum, and would be a most precious acquisition to comparative philology, upon which might be finally based the true and undisputable theory of the origin of this people. Even as their language is now presented, most of the vocabularies exhibit a striking uniformity in all those terms which can be compared with the Indian languages, and which by common consent belong to the Gypsies. This, certainly, is a great incitement to farther labors.

The attempt to christianize the Gypsies, and to elevate them from their half-brutish state, by translations of the Holy Scriptures and other Christian works into their own idiom, I consider as perfectly useless. For by whom are such translations to be made, and by whom read? Here in Turkey, Gypsies roaming over the vast plains of Bulgaria, and speaking a purer Gypsy dialect, often cannot understand those south of the Balkans,

---

* The perusal of the Vocabulary will convince the reader of the truth of this proposition, and of the necessity of having some acquaintance with the language of those nations with whom the Gypsies have come into contact on their way to Europe.

and near Constantinople. Plain translations into the languages of the people among whom they dwell, Christian benevolence, and Christian oblivion of their misdeeds, may supply the want: they hate us as heartily as we hate them; they pilfer and injure us, because we persecute and despise them.

Before proceeding to give an account of my own labors on the language of the Gypsies, as preliminary to the understanding of the Vocabulary, I will succinctly describe to the reader the labors of the many learned men who have up to this day paid particular attention to the study of this idiom. As the subject is little known, many, no doubt, will be surprised to learn how much has been already done in this field of literature.

Pott, who in his admirable work on the Gypsies has laboriously collected every thing that had been said on the subject up to the date of his labors (1844–5), may serve as a guide in the history of Gypsy literature.[*]

The first writer on the Gypsies was Bonaventura Vulcanius, professor of Greek literature in Leyden, where he died in 1614. In his small treatise "De Nubianis Erronibus, quos Itali Cingaros appellant, eorumque Lingua"—published in the body of a greater work on the language of the Goths, at Leyden, 1597— he gives about sixty-seven Gypsy words, without any derivation, or plausible clue to their etvmology or relationship. Of course, before the study of the Hindu languages became common in Europe, no plausible account could have been given of their origin. Vulcanius makes the Gypsies come from Nubia, in doing which he appears to adopt the opinion of the famous Scaliger.

After Vulcanius, no historical or linguistic work of much importance appeared on the language of the Gypsies, till the great work of Grellmann: "Die Zigeuner—Ein Historischer Versuch über die Lebensart und Verfassung, Sitten und Schicksale dieses Volks in Europa, nebst ihrem Ursprunge; von M. H. M. G. Grellmann;" Dessau und Leipzig, 1783. An improved and enlarged edition of this work was published in 1787, and, about the same time, it was translated into French by Baron de Bock.[†] The work of Grellmann produced considerable impression at the time of its publication, and though as a work of comparative philology it is of little value now, still it can be usefully consulted for its historical observations, as the author has judiciously collected nearly every thing that was known of the Gypsies anterior to his time.[‡] Indian literature, then so little known, has made his work of comparatively little value to us now.

---

[*] Die Zigeuner in Europa und Asien. i. 3.
[†] Oriental Collections [by W. Ouseley]. ii. 386.
[‡] This author calculated the number of Gypsies in Europe as between 700,000 and 800,000, of whom 40,000 were in Spain, chiefly in the southern provinces.

In the Archæologia, or Miscellaneous Tracts relating to Antiquity, published by the Society of Antiquaries of London, vol. vii., London, 1785, are contained "Observations on the Language of the People commonly called Gypsies," in a letter to Sir Joseph Banks from Wm. Marsden. This learned author has made some observations on the relationship of the Gypsy language to the Hindustani, which had already been remarked by Ludolphus in 1691.* In this same work are contained the observations of Jacob Bryant on the Zingara or Gypsy language, transmitted to O. Salisbury Brereton, in a letter from the Rev. Dr. Douglas. Both these works contain a great number of Gypsy words. Pott however remarks that "the comparison with the Hindustani and Persian, etc., is weak."

In the work of Franz Carl Alter, "Ueber die Samskrd. Sprache," Wien, 1799, are contained some Gypsy words, extracted from Catherine's Comparative Dictionary.

"Zigeuner in Herodot, oder Neue Aufschlüsse über die Aeltere Zigeunergeschichte, aus Griechischen Schriftstellern, von Dr. Johann Gottfr. Hasse;" Königsburg, 1803. The author has been imitated in a still more unphilosophical spirit than his own by Vaillant, in his late work.

John Hoyland's "Historical Survey of the Customs etc. of the Gypsies;" York, 1816.† This author has made large use of the valuable work of Grellmann, adding also much of his own.

Another treatise, "On the Similitude between the Gypsy and Hindu Languages," in the Transactions of the Lit. Soc. of Bombay, 1819, was published by Irvine—"of no special value," according to Pott.

The next in order of time is the remarkable work of Anton. Jaroslav Puchmayer—"Romani Chib, d. i., Grammatik und Wörterbuch der Zigeunersprache, nebst einigen Fabeln in derselben. Dazu als Anhang die Hantyrka oder die Czechische Diebessprache;" Prague, 1821. This work is extremely valuable, and Pott frequently refers to it. Though I have not seen the work, the quotations often found in Pott, and the frequent references to it, amply prove the value which he set upon the labors of this learned author. There is a striking similarity between his Gypsy terms and those in my Vocabulary, so that I am induced to believe that Wallachian Gypsies must have afforded him his principal information.

"Deutsch-Zigeunerisches Wörterbuch, von Dr. Ferd. Bischoff;" Ilmenau, 1827—a work often quoted by Pott.

---

* Pott, p. 6.
† The full title of this work is given in the Penny Cyclopedia—" Historical Survey of the Customs, Habits, and Present State of the Gypsies, designed to develop the origin of this singular people, and to promote the amelioration of their condition."

"Travels in Hungary," by Bright. In this work are contained some views of the origin and language of the Gypsies. The orthography of Bright's Gypsy words differs widely from that of most other authors. Many of his Gypsy terms were collected in England, and comparisons are instituted between the forms of the language as spoken in Hungary, Spain, and England.

In the Transactions of the Royal As. Soc. of Great Britain and Ireland, vol. ii., London, 1830, is the following work: "Observations on the Oriental Origin of the Romnichal, or Tribe miscalled Gypsey and Bohemian. By Colonel John Staples Harriot, Bengal Infantry (read Dec. 5, 1829, and Jan. 2, 1830)." This work, according to Pott, is superior to every other one in English on the origin and language of the Gypsies. It gives a very plausible account of the progress of the Gypsies from India through Persia.

G. Louis Domeny de Rienzi's "De l'Origine des Tzengaris," in Revue Encyclopédique, Nov. 1832, p. 365–373; also his "Esquisse d'un Tableau Comparatif de la Langue Tzengare ou Bohémienne d'Europe, avec le Tzengare de l'Hindustan, et neuf Idiomes de l'Orient." Rienzi, as he himself confesses, was not profoundly versed in such philological studies. His work is not of much value.

"Geschichte der Zigeuner, ihrer Herkunft, Natur, und Art, von Dr. Theod. Tetzner;" Weimar und Ilmenau, 1835. It gives interesting notices on the Prussian mode of governing the Gypsies inhabiting that kingdom, and on the laws regulating their social position.

In 1835 was published at Erfurt, by Graffunder, "Ueber die Sprache der Zigeuner. Eine Grammatische Skizze." This work was reviewed in 1836 by the justly celebrated Bopp, in the Jahrbücher der Wissenschaftlichen Kritik, Nos. 38 and 39, and the relationship of the two idioms, Gypsy and Hindu, corroborated by the judicious remarks of this great Orientalist.* This work, together with that of Grellmann, forms the basis of the French work of Michel de Kogalnitchan, published at Berlin, 1837: "Esquisse sur l'Histoire, les Moeurs et la Langue des Cigains, suivie d'un recueil de sept cent mots Cigains."†

In 1841 was published the work of George Borrow: "The Zincali, or an Account of the Gypsies of Spain, with an Original Collection of their Songs and Poetry, and a Copious Dictionary of their Language;" London, in two volumes. Borrow, while in Spain as agent of the British and Foreign Bible Society, translated a portion of the Scriptures into the dialect spoken by the

---

* Bibliotheca Sanscrita, by Friedrich Adelung, 1837, p. 67.—Pott, i. 22.

† Vaillant is mistaken in saying that the work was published at Jassy, in Moldavia (p. 11). Pott (p. 23) remarks of the work: "The collection of words is not worthy of much commendation."

Spanish Gypsies. His work is well known, and is valuable for the historical information which it gives respecting the Gypsies in general; but its principal value is in the description of the numerous Gypsies of Spain, and in the vocabulary, the richest which had appeared up to his day. He has drawn largely from Grellmann and Marsden. To this author I shall have occasion frequently to refer in the course of this memoir.

Besides the above works, written expressly on this subject, notices of the Gypsies and their language are to be found scattered in different works on ethnography and comparative philology. In Adelung's Mithridates, continued by Vater, are some notices of the Gypsies and their language.* In 1818 was published, at Frankfort, the work of Chr. Gottlieb von Arndt: "Ueber den Ursprung der Europäischen Sprachen." The author gives some notices of the Gypsies, and their probable origin from India and the central parts of Asia. He gives at the end of his work some words of their language, which I have inserted in notes: they seem to belong to the Danubian Gypsies.

In 1841 was published at Milan the work of Francisco Predazi: "Origine e Vicende dei Zingari, con Documenti intorno le Speciali loro Proprietá Fisiche e Morali, la loro Religione, le loro Usi e Costumi, le loro Arti, e le Attuali loro Condizioni Politiche e Civili in Asia, Africa, ed Europa, con un Saggio di Grammatica e di Vocabolario dell' Arcano loro Linguaggio." This author seems to have borrowed largely from Grellmann and Kogalnitchan, and to have had little personal acquaintance with the language, which he terms "linguaggio arcano."

The most important work on the Gypsies is undoubtedly the German one of Dr. A. F. Pott, published in two octavo volumes, the first in 1844, the second in 1845, in Halle—"Die Zigeuner in Europa und Asien." To this work was awarded by the Institute of Paris, in 1845, the premium of comparative philology, originally instituted by Volney. It is a work of high character, showing unwearied application, and the most profound scholarship, in every department connected with its subject. Its author has collected and compared every thing written up to his time on the language of the Gypsies, so that the reader has in a single view every thing that had been gathered by many learned authors. He appears to have studied the subject for a long time, and no difficulty or dryness seems for a moment to have abated the courage of this learned and indefatigable author. It is the Thesaurus of the Gypsy language, and other dialects, better able to repay so much labor, might be justly proud of a similar grammar. The work of Pott is principally directed to the language and to its grammatical construction; his notices of the

---

* Bibliotheca Sanscrita, by Friedrich Adelung, p. 67.

Gypsies and their peregrinations are scanty and meagre. He has paid particular attention to the relation of the Hindustani and other spoken dialects of India to the Gypsy language, using as a reference the excellent work of John Shakespear on the subject.* His references to the present spoken Persian are very frequent, and often extremely judicious. The second volume contains a vocabulary, in which are inserted all the words found in the various vocabularies of the Gypsy language drawn up by preceding authors. Borrow's entire vocabulary is inserted, but no effort is made to separate what appears to be Spanish from Gypsy. Pott has had, however, the precaution to mark with an asterisk every word undoubtedly Sanskrit, and those of doubtful origin with a cross—the rest are left for farther investigation. The first volume is far from possessing the interest of the second, for the Gypsy language in its grammatical construction has lost nearly every mark of its Sanskrit character, and varies extremely in the different provinces of Europe, ingrafting upon itself very intimately the spirit and analytical character of the language spoken by the people. In this manner, the construction offers less interest than the primitive signification of the words. In his grammar, Pott gives nearly every author's construction, with numerous quotations for the elucidation of the subject, which render the work extremely voluminous.

It was not till I had completed nearly the whole of my vocabulary that I obtained this work of Pott, and I consider it as a very fortunate circumstance that I had not by me such a guide from the beginning, for so masterly a hand must have kept me in the path which he had already trodden. Left to myself, with what scanty help I obtained from Borrow's vocabulary, I have searched and researched for myself, and have assiduously examined the relation of the Gypsy to the Sanskrit, setting aside every term which to me appeared of other than Gypsy origin. Subsequently, I have compared many of my derivations with Pott's. There is a striking similarity in both, with this difference, that I have given in many of my derivations more attention to the Sanskrit than Pott. An example the reader may see in the definition of *yak*, 'fire,' which Pott refers to the Sanskrit *agni*, 'fire,' Lat. *ignis*, Pol. *ogien*. I have referred it to the root *yaksh*, 'to sacrifice,' since nearly all words in Sanskrit having the consonant *ksh*, in passing into the Gypsy, lose the final *sh*, and exhibit pure *k*. The reader will see numerous examples of this in Section IV. There is a marked difference in our derivations of *tav*, 'thread,' which Pott leaves doubtful, giving the Sanskrit *sthawi* (a weaver)?—while I have attempted to show its connection with the Sanskrit root *tap*, 'to heat, to torment,' a connection which be-

---

* A Dictionary Hindustani and English. 4to.

comes extremely probable from the occurrence of a similar word in the Persian language. Similar differences in our derivations I shall point out in the notes to the Vocabulary.

Pott's work contains all the words of Borrow's vocabulary, which to me appears rather a blemish, as many of them are the purest Spanish. Nothing should enter into a Gypsy vocabulary but what can be proved or shown to be pure Gypsy. It is on this account that I have eschewed nearly all borrowed terms, Greek and Turkish, from my own, inserting merely a few, in order to show the manner in which such words are mutilated and distorted. Whether Pott himself had much personal acquaintance with the Gypsies, with their language and pronunciation, it is difficult to say. For nearly every thing he refers to others.

No work on the language of the Gypsies has appeared since the publication of this great work of Pott. Vaillant, before the publication of his work, had given to some of the French periodicals dissertations on the Gypsies, but they are historical and descriptive. In his large work, of which we have already spoken, and which contains everything scattered in his other treatises, he has at the end a few Gypsy words, which I have inserted in notes, and which, with slight variations, resemble those in my Vocabulary, coming as they do from the Danubian Gypsies. No confidence can be placed in his derivations, even when he tries to his utmost to arrive at something like truth, for he is as wild here as in his descriptions of the Gypsy peregrinations. I give the reader a specimen. "*Ma-garu,* 'âne,' mot à mot, 'longue oreille;' *kar-pu,* 'melon,' mot à mot, 'fruit de la terre;' *kol-pu,* 'tour, golfe,' mot à mot, 'rond terre;' *kris'tal,* 'cristal,' mot à mot, 'transparente et solide surface.'" Now *magára* is a Bulgarian word, signifying 'a donkey;' *karpu* is the Turkish *karpúz*—probably from the Greek καρπός, 'fruit'—a name now given to the watermelon by the Turks; *kolpu* is the Greek κόλπος, 'a harbor,' pronounced by the Turks *kiorfúz; kristal* is the Greek κρύσταλλος, 'glass, ice,' etc.

I come now to my own labors, a notice of which is necessary to the understanding of the Vocabulary, and of the few grammatical observations inserted in Section V. I have remarked already, how widely the acquisition of the Gypsy language differs from that of every other language. The reader therefore should perfectly understand it, in order to judge of the accuracy of the author's observations, and the truth of every point in dispute.

About four years ago, Mr. John P. Brown, the learned Orientalist, and dragoman of the American Embassy in Constantinople, gave me a short vocabulary of the Gypsy language, which he had collected in his excursions in the suburbs of Constantinople. Up to that time, I had given little attention to this idiom, and knew not much of it, except what at times I met with in the course of my Sanskrit studies. Most of it had been collected from Moslem Gypsies, a few words being added by a Christian Gypsy. There was nothing in the vocabulary but the simple definitions in English. All the words, together with a few numerals, were about seventy. As the subject became extremely interesting to me, from the relationship so palpable in many words, I determined to continue the work, and to corroborate Mr. Brown's definitions by other Gypsies, adding whatever else I could obtain from other sources. After many months' assiduous labor, after repairing to different Gypsy haunts in Constantinople and its suburbs, and mingling with the people in search of more intelligent Gypsies, I collected about one hundred and fifty words, which I attempted to explain, unassisted by works on the subject. My observations were published, in the fall of 1857, in the excellent Greek periodical of Athens, the New Pandora. These studies, extremely imperfect, were praised by the learned editors, and kind words of commendation were forwarded to me by some friends and literati of Athens. All this was a farther incitement to proceed with my labors, and ever since I have been assiduously employed in collecting materials, in making acquaintance with Gypsies, and in awakening their interest for their native idiom. This has tended to flatter their vanity; and so I have been able to obtain abundant materials for a more perfect work: up to the present time they come forward with new words, frequently transmitting them to me by correspondence. These materials I kept scrupulously by me for future use, hoping to have occasion to add whatever I collected to a new edition of the Greek article. Precisely at this point of time, towards the latter part of last year, the Rev. Cyrus Hamlin, missionary of the A. B. C. F. M., offered to translate my little work into English, for the American Oriental Society. In this I acquiesced with all my heart, persuaded that this eminent and laborious friend of long years, perfectly conversant with the polished Greek of the present day, would make a faithful translation of the whole. I have reviewed the whole translation in company with Mr. Hamlin, and can testify to its accuracy.

In this manner has originated the present memoir, which is presented to the public enriched with all the additional materials collected by me since the first publication of my researches in Athens—additions which render it essentially a new work.

My first method of acquiring the language was to give a word to the Gypsies, either in Greek or Turkish, and to obtain from them the corresponding term in their language. This method, pursued for some time, is tiresome and extremely fallacious—for they may give you another word, in order to cover their ignorance, or this same word, with pronouns, in the plural, and often united to a verb. This, at first, is extremely perplexing, and the student cannot properly understand his position, or feel any degree of confidence, until he has in some manner fathomed the depth and breadth of their brutal ignorance. They will do their best, particularly when incited to such uncouth and unknown martyrdom by the exhibition of money as a spur to their sluggish memory. They will torment themselves, look at heaven and earth, scratch their heads, or put their fingers upon their temples, to recall the lost term, which, according to their expression, is sticking at the tip of their tongue. I have frequently pitied the poor fellows, since they seemed so in earnest to satisfy my curiosity; and I have desisted from farther demands for a particular word, which they professed they knew, but could not possibly recall.

With the Moslem Gypsies I have had great difficulty, for they are fast losing their idiom, and few of the new generation know any thing of it.* The Christian Gypsies, however, still retain it, with an incongruous mixture of Greek and Turkish terms, and from them I have obtained nearly all the materials contained in this memoir. The profound hatred of the Moslem Gypsies, or rather their contempt of every thing pertaining to a Christian, inherited from the genuine Moslems, makes them shy, and very poor guides in such matters.

This process of collecting words from single individuals soon disheartened me, on account of its imperfections, and the great difficulty of obtaining by it even a scanty knowledge of Gypsy terms. I therefore, after numerous trials, resorted to dialogues, which succeeded admirably, and which I can recommend to any individual in similar circumstances. One can hardly keep pace with their volubility. Words flow as in a torrent, while the elements and combinations of which it consists can afterwards be arranged in a systematic manner by the student, and easily elucidated one by the other. I cannot but make this remark, and say how much trouble might have been saved, had I begun with this plan, which has cleared up wonderfully all my notions and views of this very interesting idiom. I have permitted my Gypsy masters to add whatever came into their heads, in the course of the dialogue. In this manner a rich treasure of knowledge resulted from our studies.

It was my good fortune, however, in prosecuting these studies, to make the acquaintance of a Greek Gypsy, Andrea George, living twenty miles distant from Constantinople. His amiable character had induced a Greek gentleman, some years ago, to

---

* They strive to show zeal in their new religion, and consider their vernacular idiom as partaking of christian heresy, and of course avoid speaking it as much as possible.

3

put him into a Greek school, where he went through the first elements of the Greek grammar. To this young man, to whom education has imparted feelings nobler than those of his fellow-countrymen, the subject became very attractive, and to his kindness I am greatly indebted for the help he has rendered me in the latter part of my studies. He has, in his short excursions to the neighboring villages, collected from different Gypsies, coming from the north of Turkey, many terms unknown to him, which he has given to me, and which I have examined and inserted in the Vocabulary. We have reviewed together all the Vocabulary, and all the dialogues, collected from different quarters, which have served as the basis of it. I have noted with the greatest accuracy his accents, and the sounds of his voice in the pronunciation of the various consonants, and I have every reason to put entire confidence in his information. It coincided with whatever I had previously collected from numerous sources, and which I continually submitted to his examination. He himself was often unable to give me the desired information except in the form of dialogue, and by degrees he was induced to write for me dialogues in his vernacular idiom. In this way he acquired for himself a great number of terms, ascertained my wants, and with kindness of heart entered into my views, and has even attempted to collect whatever of his native idiom is known among the Gypsies dwelling in the villages near Constantinople, or roaming in tents, and coming from the distant plains of Bulgaria and Servia. Having become extremely interested in these labors upon his own language, Andrea still continues his observations, and submits them to me, often demanding whether such a word should be pronounced in such a manner, and not in another. He asked me once, for example, whether the word for 'he sells' should be *biklél* or *biknél:* I told him that the latter was the proper form, and that he should always avoid *biklél.*

In this manner have been collected and arranged all the materials which enter into the Vocabulary. There is nothing borrowed from any work on the Gypsies, and I am warranted in saying that all the terms are in constant use among the Gypsies dwelling around Constantinople and in the Roumelian villages, up to the skirts of the Balkans. My long intercourse with them has rendered me somewhat familiar with their idiom, and in the present state of my knowledge I offer this Vocabulary as exhibiting the actual condition of their spoken language, the result of four years' constant application and study. It is my earnest hope that it may prove of some utility to students in ethnographical science, and in all those scientific and philosophical pursuits that have for their object to ascertain the true origin of tribes and nations.

In the definitions, I have often inserted quotations from my dialogues, as pronounced by the Gypsies, quotations which in numerous cases serve to illustrate the term under consideration. They are extremely important, and may serve as points of illustration to those who shall desire to make farther researches upon this interesting subject. The reader may put implicit confidence in their accuracy, for they have been repeatedly sifted and examined.

The object of this memoir is to demonstrate the relation of the Gypsy language to the Sanskrit; and in this part of my work, as I have said before, I was perfectly unassisted. What I have done I humbly submit to the public. Though persuaded of its near connection with the Sanskrit, more intimate than that of any other spoken language of Europe, I confess that I have not always succeeded in pointing out the relationship of Gypsy terms to the Sanskrit, even in cases where their structure would seem to bear an undeniable stamp of Hindu origin. But I feel no discouragement; and when I consider that our immortal Coray has been able by long and unwearied study to define and trace to the ancient language most of our pure modern Greek jargon, and thus to explain so many obscure passages in ancient Greek authors, what cannot we hope to effect by a similar process, when Sanskrit shall be better known, and its etymologies better defined? I have no doubt, as I have remarked in the Vocabulary, that, as the modern Greek has vastly elucidated the ancient, so the Gypsy, which is so closely related to the Sanskrit, will impart the same advantage to Sanskrit, when the relation of the two is fully established and universally acknowledged. It will then become evident that Sanskrit verbs, most of which remain unaltered in form in the Gypsy, but have different significations, may have originally possessed these significations. Coincidence of original meaning becomes undeniably apparent in the case of many adjectives and nouns.

As the language of the Gypsies has been thoroughly permeated by the spirit of the modern Greek and Turkish, as spoken in and around Constantinople, I have derived considerable assistance from both these languages, in elucidating many points under discussion. Pott himself often makes reference to modern Greek words, with a judgment and an accuracy worthy of all praise. The reader will see the opportunity for similar references in the course of the Vocabulary.

As to the orthography of the Gypsy language, it is well to inform the reader that I have adopted for the vowels that of the Italians, as the most perfect, and least liable to error: *a* should be pronounced as *a* in *far—e*, as in *met—i*, as in *pin—o*, as in *no —u*, as in *bull.* As to the consonants, I have retained the ordinary notation of orientalists, writing *ch* for the sound of those

letters in *child, chime,* Italian *cima—j,* which by common consent
corresponds to the Sanskrit *j,* I have constantly written *j—*for
example, *janáva,* 'I know' (written by others *djanáva*)—as better
suited to English readers. The strongly aspirated Sanskrit palatal I write *chh,* the guttural *kh,* and the aspirate *h.* The Gypsies
in these countries have no sound corresponding to that of the
English *th* in *this, that,* Greek *ð.* The lingual and palatal sibilants of the Sanskrit I have represented by *sh* and *ç;* to both
belongs very nearly the same pronunciation, that of the English
sh, as in *shall, shore.*

There is such a softness in the pronunciation by the Gypsies of
some consonants, that I am at a loss how to write them. The
word *puró,* 'old,' is an example. It is not *puró,* nor *furó,* nor
phuró, nor *pfuró.* I cannot pronounce it; the sound is like blowing from the mouth, as in blowing out a candle. As to writing
or expressing it by Roman characters, there is a difficulty similar
to that which Europeans experience when trying to represent
the *ghain* of the Arabs. This word by some is written *puró,* by
others *furó;* still, to me, all are wrong, and do not give the true
pronunciation of the word. But I have preserved *furó,* generally
adopted by others. The same difficulty occurs in the pronunciation of *mindó,* 'mine,' which at times is heard as though pronounced *minró.* I have pronounced it in both ways, in the hearing of Gypsies, and they have made no remark. But I could not
pronounce it as they do themselves. Their manner is like an
imperceptible breath, passing upon a word *mindró,* so gentle that
both consonants are heard, while one is at a loss to say which
predominates. It must be heard to be appreciated. So with
their pronunciation of soft *k*—the Turkish *kef*—which at times
appears like a pure *t,* particularly when in the middle of words.
Utkiaváva, 'I mount, I hang,' at times appeared to me as though
it should be written *utiaváva,* and at times *ukiaváva;* so gentle
is the sound of *k* in similar cases, that with some Gypsies it is not
heard at all. I have followed the more general usage, and have
often been guided by the aorist in determining the proper orthography of the present of the verb. These delicacies in the
pronunciation I have noted in the Vocabulary. Some Gypsies,
and particularly the Moslem, pronounce the gently aspirated *p*
as a pure *p,* saying always *puró,* 'an old man.' The reader will
see farther notices of the pronunciation of the consonants in
Section IV, where their mutation in passing from the Sanskrit
to the Gypsy language is spoken of.

I have pointed out all the Persian words found in the idiom,
as they are an important element in the history of the Gypsies.
It is evident that a people using so many pure Persian words
must have formerly had close connection with the Persian people. They could not have borrowed them from the Turks, who

make no use of these particular words. The reader will observe them in their proper place.

Less interest is attached to the Slavonic terms, for the Gypsies are still found scattered among the numerous Slavonic tribes of the banks of the Danube.

All Mr. Brown's terms are inserted in their proper places, and marked "Br.," to distinguish them from Borrow's, marked "Bor."

Mr. Hamlin's remarks upon the Armenian language I have inserted in notes, and marked "Tr."

SECTION III.

VOCABULARY.

A.

To ABANDON—*mukáva.*—This is probably connected with the Sanskrit root *much*, 'to release, to let go.' The change of a palatal into a guttural, and *vice versâ*, is common in all languages. *Kamukáv tút,* 'I shall leave thee ;' *nápalal mukélaman bizoraló,* 'afterwards it leaves me weak.'

To be ACQUAINTED with—*pincharáva.*—This seems to be a compound verb, formed from the Sr. root *char*, 'to go, to proceed,' and the particle *vi*, which, joined to the verb, imparts to it in the causative the meaning of 'to pass back and forth in one's mind, to consider, to meditate upon.' *Pincharáva* shows the addition of a euphonic *n* after *vi*, and the change of *v* into *p*, so common among the Gypsies. *Méya pincharávales,* 'I also am acquainted with him :'—though transitive in form, it has here a neuter signification.

AFAR—*dúr;* Bor., *dur.*—From the Sr. *dúra*, 'distant.' *Kett dúr isi chin ti Silivri?* 'how far is it to Silivria?' *Durál,* 'from a distance :' *durál allián?* 'have you come from a distance ?'*

AFFIRMATION—*vá;* Br., *nangar;* Bor., *unga.*—I think there is an error in the definition of Mr. Brown, as it seems to me impossible that such an affirmative particle should have the negative *na* in its first syllable. Still, it is valuable as tending to elucidate Borrow's word. *Va* is the Sr. indeclinable *vái*, a particle of asseveration or confirmation. The Gypsies in these quarters know of no other particle, and will acknowledge no other, but most of the Moslem Gypsies use the Turkish or Greek. Borrow's form, although to appearance obscure, may be referred to a pure Sr. origin ; namely, to the word *angá*, itself also an asseverative or assenting particle, 'yes, truly.'

ALL—*sarró, sarvó, sárrore, sávvore, sárvolo ;†* Br., *sarvilles;* Bor., *saro.*—Almost unchanged from the Sr. *sarva*, 'all, the whole, entire.' As concerns the final syllables *lee* and *lo*, I do not know whence they come. *Te dikél sarré,* 'should he see all ;' *sarré o manushé isi khokhavné,* 'all men are liars ;' *sávvore o róm*, 'all the Gypsies ;' *keti isánas sávvore?* 'how many were you all ?' *sarvénghe te penésles*, 'to declare

---

* Armenian *dar, dara*, in composition ; as *darateainel*, 'to sound abroad.'—Tr.

† "*Sarĕ*, 'tous.'" Vaillant, p. 456.

(lit. 'to say') it to all.' It is a very common word, and understood by all the Gypsies, wherever they are to be found.

ALMS—*lachipé;* Bor., *lachipén.*—This is an abstract noun, from *lachó,* 'good,' and the common suffix *pe* or *pen;* it signifies 'goodness, benevolence.' It is used, however, by the Gypsies, in the sense of 'alms.' They have followed in this respect the usage of the Greeks, who frequently, in the place of ἐλεημοσύνη, 'alms,' use the term ψυχικὸν, 'contribution for the salvation of the soul.' Compare Turk. ṣadaḳá, 'alms,' lit. 'goodness, righteousness.' *Kamáva to lachipé mó chavó,* 'I desire thy happiness, my child.'

ALWAYS—*ghéles.*—Possibly connected with the Sanskrit *kâla,* 'time.'

AND—*tá, té.*—This conjunction may be identified with the Sr. *tu,* in preference to *cha,* which is more usual among Sr. authors. The following colloquial phrases amply illustrate its signification. *Tá é chavén,* 'and the children;' *tá penéna,* 'and they say;' *tá ná penéna chachipés,* 'and they do not speak (say) the truth;' *tá isi kodróm but chiká,* 'and there is in the road much mud (muds).' In the following examples it can be rendered 'also': *teréla ta yek dúlon* (Gr. δόυλον) , 'he has also a servant;' *teréla ta khelta,* 'it has also figs;' *kamésa tá mól?* 'dost thou wish also wine?' This conjunction is frequently pronounced *te,* particularly when it is not at the beginning of a sentence.

ANVIL—*amúni;* Br., *ammunee;* Bor., *amiñi.*—From the Greek ἄκμων, 'anvil,' pronounced by us now ἀμμόνιον and ἀμμόνι.

APPLE—*papai, hapai.*—This term, like many other denominations of plants and fruits, is obscure, and difficult to be explained.

ARMFUL—*angáli.*—This is the Greek term ἀγκαλιὰ and ἀγκάλη, meaning 'whatever can be held between the arms.' Cf. ἀγκάλη χόρτου (Xenophon). *Yék angáli chár,* 'an ἀγκάλη of hay.'

To be ASHAMED—*lajáva;* Bor., *lacha.*—From the Sr. root *lajj,* 'to be shamefaced or ashamed.' This is the term to which the Gypsies of Spain attach so high an importance, (Bor., ch. vii.) meaning by it as a substantive 'the unblemished chastity of the unmarried female.' With the Gypsies in these countries the signification of the word is simply 'shame,' and they translate it by the Greek ἐντροπή, or the Turkish 'ayb, 'shame.'—*Lachanó,* 'shameful.'

ASHES—*práhos.*—This is the Slav. *práh",* 'dust.' Among the Bulgarians, however, the term *pepál* is in common use for 'ashes,' from the ancient Slav. *pepél",* 'ashes;' Gr. παιπάλη, 'the very finest of flour,' and 'whatever is rubbed to extreme fineness.' *Kaló práhos,* 'black ashes;' *e bovéskori práhos,* 'the ashes of the baker;' *ketí práhos kamésa?* 'how much ashes dost thou wish?' *ketí práhos resélatut?* 'how much ashes suffices thee?'*

To ASK—*pucháva.*—From the Sr. root *prachh,* 'to ask, to inquire, to desire to know.' The liquid *r* has been dropped, as in other similar examples (Section IV). This verb is at times pronounced *pachára* and *pecháva. Sóske puchésa mánder?* 'why dost thou ask (from) me?' *kapucháv léstar,* 'I shall ask (from) him;' *tá té pucháv léstar,* 'and that I may ask (from) him.'

---

* *Práchos* (aréna), and again, *pracos,* "staub." Pott, ii. 361.

Ass—*khér;* Br., *kher;* Bor., *gel, guel, jeroro*—fem. *kherní;* Bor., *jeni, jerini.*—The Sr. *hara,* from the root *hri,* 'to bring, to bear,' signifies 'bearer,' and secondly 'the ass,' as the Turks call the ass *merkeb,* from the Arabic root *rakaba,* 'to bear.' Thus *hara* signifies 'beast of burden' in general, and, by secondary meaning, 'the ass,' which, through all the East, is the burden-bearer in domestic works. This term is also written *khara:* compare Zend *khara* and Pers. *kher,* 'an ass.' My term *khernj* is 'the female ass.' Those of Borrow are of different provinces, but all of the same origin. *Sigó khér,* 'a swift ass;' *tumari kheréskoro i zén chorghiá,* 'your ass's saddle they have stolen;' *teréla pánj khér,* 'he has (owns) five asses.'

To AWAKE—*jangáva.*—The Sr. root *jágri* is 'to awake, to be awake or watchful.' We shall see in the next Section that the *r* of the Sanskrit, particularly when in composition with other consonants, is frequently dropped, as in this case. *Jangaváva,* the passive form, is 'to be awaked;' *jangavdó,* 'he is awake.' It corresponds to the Turkish *oyanik,* 'awake, a man of talent:' Gr. ἔξυπνος. *Jañganilióm* (pass. aorist), 'I have awaked;' *janganiló,* 'he is awaked.'

AXE—*tovér, tovél.*—This word is pronounced in both ways by many Gypsies, for the liquids are often commutable. It is a pure Persian word, *taber* and *taver,* 'the two-edged axe used in felling wood.' *Toveréskoro,* 'one who uses an axe,' or 'one who makes and sells axes.' The Turkish is *battaji.*

B.

BACK—*dumó.*—This is a frequently used term among all the Gypsies, for the hinder part of the trunk, extending from the neck to the *os sacrum.* The Greeks now call the body κορμίον or κορμί, diminutive of κορμὸς, 'the trunk of a tree.' May not, then, *dumo* be compared with Sr. *druma,* 'a tree,' which, by dropping the liquid *r,* has become *dumó?* To me this origin appears very probable, particularly upon comparing it with *dudúm,* 'a gourd,' in which the same word *druma* appears to exist.

BAD—*górko.*—This is the usual adjective used in opposition to *lachó,* 'good.' *Górko manúsh,* 'a bad man;' *o rasháï maréla e górke chavén,* 'the master beats the bad children;' *gorkipé,* 'badness, wickedness.'

BALD—*pakó.*—The Sr. verb *pach* means 'to mature, by cooking or ripening;' and derivatives from it signify 'maturity, suppuration,' and even 'gray hairs,' as the maturity of age. The Sr. word *páka* has all these significations, and the same term is by the Gypsies referred to baldness, as an attribute of grey hairs and old age. *Pakó isi, ná teréla bál,* 'he is bald, (and) has no hair.'

To BAPTIZE—*boláva.*—This word of the Christian Gypsies, which, like all the rest of this class, is of peculiar interest, seems to belong to the Sr. *bul,* of the 10th class, 'to sink, to dive and emerge again.'

In embracing Christianity, the Gypsies must have been at a loss, at times, to express by appropriate terms the new order of things which they constantly saw before them. They have done, in this matter, what other nations in embracing Christianity had done before them. The Slavonians call the cross *krést"*, undoubtedly from the Greek χριστὸς; and say *krestáyu*, 'I baptize,' analogous with the English "I christen," i. e. 'I baptize, I make one a Christian.' Have not most of the nations who received the blessed tidings of Christianity from the Greeks adopted also Greek terms? But whenever words were found in the idiom of the Gypsies capable of expressing the new idea, they would naturally be adopted by them. We shall see another example in the name of the cross. Βαπτίζω, the transitive of βάπτω, meant originally 'to color by dyeing.' The word to this very day is used for 'dyeing, painting, besmearing the face with rouge,' etc.: it is a neuter and transitive verb. As color was transmitted to cloth by immersing it in water, the word very naturally came to mean 'to immerse in water.' What difficulty then had the Gypsies in giving to this act of Christianity the word which corresponded to the Greek? Those Gypsies unacquainted with the word use *vaptizáva*, 'I baptize,' the Greek βαπτίζω. *Boláva e chavés*, 'I baptize the child;' *bolipé*, 'baptism;' *bolavdó*, 'baptized;' *bibolavdó*, 'not baptized.'

BAREFOOTED—*pirnangó*.—A compound word, *pir, piró*, 'foot,' and *nangó*, 'naked;' literally 'naked-footed.' In another part of the Vocabulary, I treat of the etymology of *piró, pirnó*, the Gypsy terms for 'foot.'

BARLEY—*jov*.—This is the Persian *jav*, 'barley,' which the Gypsies have borrowed directly from the Persians. Sr. *yava*, 'barley.' The Persian form of this term is undoubtedly from the Sanskrit, as the Persian language very generally changes the Sr. *y* into *j*: compare *jugh*, 'yoke,' Sr. *yuga*; *javan*, 'young man,' Sr. *yuvan*.

BASKET—*kóshnika*; Br., *sevlia*; Bor., *cornicha*.—This is a Bulgarian word, from the Slavonic *kosh*' and *kósnitza*, 'a basket.' The origin of Mr. Brown's term is unknown to me.

BATH—*tattó, bágnia*; Bor., *tati*.—Borrow defines this word "fever," Sp. *calentura*. Although it has not the signification of 'bath' in his vocabulary, yet the meaning which he gives may serve to elucidate my own. From the Sr. root *tap*, 'to heat, to burn,' is formed the part. *tapta*, 'hot, burning,' and this, by the customary change of *p* to *t*, becomes *tatta*, just as the Italians pronounce the Latin *aptus* "*atto*." The Arabs, from the word *ḥamma*, 'to heat,' have formed *ḥammâm*, 'bath,' and *ḥumma*, 'fever.' This word, as well as *rat, ratti*, 'blood,' should be written with *tt, tattó*. Some Gypsies use the word *bágnia*, It. *bagno*, a common word in these countries for 'bath.'

BEAN—*bópi*.—A Bulgarian word, *bop*, 'a bean,' but particularly the species called the Egyptian: Gr. κουκκία, Turk. *baḳlá*.—Pl. *bópia*.

BEAR—*richini*.—As numerous Gypsies in Roumelia and the Danubian provinces gain their livelihood by exhibiting bears in the streets and public places, it is natural to suppose that this term would be a common one among them all. To me it appears related to the Sr. *ṛiksha*, 'a bear,' and hence to the Gr. ἄρκτος, Lat. *ursus*. Should this derivation be found to be true, it will be one of the rare examples of the change of *ksh* into *ch*, as I shall have occasion to show in the following Section.

To BEAT—*maráva*.—This verb seems to be of the same root with the verb *meráva*, 'I die.' In order to distinguish it from *meráva*, it is

always pronounced *maráva*, and the aor. *marghióm*. It means also
'to pound, to grind, to bruise.' *O rasháí maréla e chavén*, 'the teacher
beats the children;' *marélula?* 'does he beat her?'

BEAUTIFUL—*sukár*; Br., *shuká*; Bor., *jucal*.—These words are from
the Sr. *sukara*, compounded of the prefix *su*, 'well,' Gr. *εὖ*, and the
adjective *kara*, 'making,' Gr. *ποιός*, from the root *kṛi* (Lat. *creo*), 'to
do, to make.' *Kara*, in Sanskrit as well as in Persian composite
words, indicates action; as *sukara*, 'the well-doer, the generous be-
stower,' and hence 'whoever is beautiful in soul or body.' To Mr.
Brown's word, *shuká*, a final *r* should be added; in Borrow's, the
final *r* is changed to *l*. The fem. *jucali* is the Sr. *sukará*. The Gypsies form all feminine nouns in *i*, as we shall see in speaking of the
nouns (Section V).

BECAUSE—*sostár*.—Appears to be the pronoun *so*, with the ablative
particle *tar* (lit. 'from which'), 'on account of;' precisely as the
Greek *διότι*, composed of the prep. *διά*, and the rel. pron. *ὅ,τι*; also
ὅθεν, rel. pron. and the ablat. *θεν*. *Sostár isás kelipé*, 'because
there was a dance.'

To BEGET—*benáva*.—This term, like its cognate *ben*, 'birth,' I have not
been able to refer to any Sr. root, with any degree of satisfaction.
The term is common to both sexes, in man and animals. *I romní
benéla*, 'the woman begets,' i. e. 'produces, brings forth;' *gurumní
amarí benghiás yék moskáre* (Gr. *μοσχάριον*), 'our cow has brought
forth a calf;' *i chukli benghiás pánj rukoné*, 'the bitch has begotten
(brought forth) five whelps.'

BEHIND—*palál*.—This evidently is the Sr. *para*, 'distant, remote, after.'
Here, as in many other adverbs of location, the term is in the ablative form, a very favorite one with the Gypsies. According to the
formation of other similar adverbs, it would be, in its simple form,
pal: as *avry*, 'out,' *avryál*, 'from the outside,' Gr. *ἔξωθεν; andré, andryál*, and *andrál*, 'from the inner side.' It is often to be heard united
with the comparative particle *po*, as *popalál*, 'still more backwards.'
Lávales palál, 'I take it back;' *palalutnó*, 'the next in order, the
second;' *polaléste*, 'farther back;' *napalál*, 'afterwards;' *kána chinésa
bar, na palalutné ghén*, 'when thou throwest a stone, the afterwards
(i. e. 'the consequences') consider;' *pelióm palál*, 'I fell behind,' i. e.
'I followed him.'

To BELIEVE—*pakiáva*.—This verb I refer to the Sr. root *paksh*, 'to take
a part or side.' *Pakiáva ki aneká isí*, 'I believe that it is so;' *na
pakiáva ki muló*, 'I do not believe that he died.'*

BELLOWS—*pishót;* Br., *pishata*.—Mr. Brown's word is in the plural form.

BELLY—*bor;* Bor., *pos, po*.—This is one of the many terms of the
Gypsy language, the derivation of which is not clear to me. *Terávas
dúk mé poriáti*, 'I had pain in my belly.'

---

* Pott (ii. 346) writes the word *patáv*, and derives it from the Sr. *prati + i*, 'con-
fidere.' The Gypsies here pronounce it as I have written it. I have frequently
heard it. The difference, however, may have been occasioned by the pronunciation
of the consonant *t*, which with the Gypsies is often a soft *k*. A similar commutation is often to be heard among the Greeks, particularly in the island of Lesbos
(Mitelene).

BETWEEN—*maskaré.*—This term comes from the Sr. *madhya,* 'middle, intermediate,' Lat. *medius,* Gr. μέσσος, Slav. *mézdyu,* 'between.' *Maskaré to dúi kér,* 'between the two houses;' *maskaré to dúi drom,* and *maskaré dúi droménde,* 'between two roads;' *maskaré dúi manushénde,* 'between two men;' *maskarál,* 'from between,' Lat. *ex medio, de medio,* Mod. Gr. ἀπὸ τὴν μέσην.

BIRD—*chiriklό;* Bor., *chiriclo.*—The Sr. *chiri,* 'a parrot,' is the only word to which can be referred this Gypsy term. Probably the term had also the more general signification in the Sanskrit, for we have in the present spoken language of the Hindus *chiriya,* for 'birds' in general. The signification of this word among the Gypsies is extremely vague; it is applied to all the feathered tribe. I have heard it used of quails, partridges, pigeons, etc. Never have I been able to ascertain any term for particular species of birds or fishes. The Gypsies call them by their Greek or Turkish names.

BIRTH—*ben.*—See to BEGET.

BITCH—*chukli.*—This is the fem. of *chukél,* 'dog,' by the addition of *i,* the usual affix of Gypsy feminine nouns. The *e* of the final syllable is always rejected: *chukél, chuk(e)li. Amari chukli,* 'our bitch;' *katár kinghián ti chukliá?* 'whence didst thou buy thy bitch?'

To BITE—*dantáva, dantiláva.*—Both these verbs are in use; they have been formed directly from the Sr. noun *danta,* 'tooth' (see TOOTH). The second, *dantiláva,* is a compound verb, formed of *danta* and the verb *láva,* 'I take,' both of which are separately explained in the present vocabulary. Unlike its mother tongue, the Gypsy language is not generally fond of compound words. *Ta o chukél danghiánles,* 'and the dog bit him.'

BITTER—*kerkό.*—This is the Slav. *górkie,* 'bitter,' in general use among the Bulgarians, from whom the Gypsies have received it. It is a common term among all the nations that speak the various dialects of the Slavonic.

BLACK—*kalό* (fem. *kali*);* Br., *calό;* Bor., *calό, callardo, caloro.*— These terms are derived from the Sr. *kála,* 'black, of a dark color.' The second of Borrow is a Spanish form. Compare the Slav. *kalénie,* 'color, dye.' The reader will observe that the Turkish Gypsies have preserved many words of their mother tongue pure from all foreign intermixture. *Isi kali,* 'she is black;' *kalé romá,* 'black men;' *kalό* is used for 'a negro;' *kali,* for 'a negro woman;' *kalό manrό,* 'black bread.'

BLACKSMITH—*mastér;* Br., *masteros.*—*Mastér* is a word very generally used by all classes of people in Constantinople, from the vulgar Italian *maestro,* to designate 'a chief workman,' or artist of any profession: Turk. and Persian *ustad.* Many Gypsies, in place of this term, use their own *shastiréskoro,* 'iron-worker' (see IRON).

BLIND—*korό.*†—Compare the Sr. *giri,* 'a certain disease of the eyes;' *girikána,* 'one blind from the disease *giri.*' This word is used at times by the Gypsies as an imprecation: *o devél te korό kerélman,* 'may God reduce thee to blindness!'

---

* "*Cali,* 'noir et beau.'" Vaillant, p. 179.   † Armenian *goir,* 'blind.'—Tr.

BLIND MAN—*tam-manúsh.*—I give here this second word for 'blind,' as it is applicable only to the human race, whilst the former, *koró,* is used, as in other languages, for inanimate objects. It is a compound word. *Tam* is from the Sr. root *tam,* 'to be senseless, to be dark.' The derivatives of this root signify 'blindness, bodily or mental, gloom, perplexity,' etc.

BLOOD—*ratt;** Bor., *rati, arati.*—From the Sr. root *ranj,* 'to color, to dye' (Pers. *renk*), comes the participle *rakta,* 'colored, dyed, red,' neut. *raktam,* 'blood.' In the above Gypsy terms, the *k* of the Sr. is changed to *t,* for the sake of euphony; like the Italian *prattico* from the Latin *practicus. Dukháva bút e rátt,* 'he likes much to bleed' (lit. 'he likes blood').

To BOIL—*taviáva, tapiáva.*—By the transmutation of the labial *p* into its cognate *v,* this Gypsy verb is easily referred to the Sr. root *tap,* 'to heat, to burn,' and, in the Gypsy language, 'to boil,' as an effect of fire.

BONE—*kókkalo.*—This term is common to all the Gypsies. I have never been able to ascertain any other denomination for bone, even among the Moslem Gypsies. It is the common Greek κόκκαλον, derived from κόκκος, 'the kernel of fruit:' κοκκαλιάζω is 'to become hard,' and is a very common term among the Greeks now.†

BOSOM—*kolín.*—I leave to others to determine whether this word can be referred to Sr. *kola,* signifying, among other things, 'the bosom, the lap, embrace.' The names of parts of the body in the Gypsy language are often extremely difficult and dubious.

BOWEL—*bukó ;* Bor., *porias.*—*Bukó* may be referred to the Sr. *bukka* and *búkka,* both meaning 'the heart,' in the same way as the Greeks called σπλάγχνον every internal organ of the body, and often, to this day, the common people call the stomach and the bowels καρδία. Borrow has the Sr. *puritat,* 'an entrail, a gut,' which seems in fact to furnish the proper etymology of the word used by the Gypsies of Spain.

BOY-CHILD—*chavó ;‡* Br., *schago ;* Bor., *chavo,* pl. *chai.*—

GIRL—*chái ;* Br., *schay ;* Bor., *chavory.*—The Sanskrit has more than one term to which the above words can be referred: *tuch, tuj,* and *toka,* 'progeny, children,' *çáva* or *çávaka,* 'the new born of any animal.' The Gypsy word I have always heard pronounced *chavó.* Some of the Moslem Gypsies reject the *v,* and pronounce *chaó. Mo chavó,* 'my child ;' *dúi chavén teráva,* 'I have two children ;' *rovéla ani khurdó chavó,* 'he cries like a little child ;' *o rashái maréla e górke chavén, e laché chavén na marélalen,* 'the teacher beats the bad children, the good children he does not beat ;' *te chavénghe,* 'to thy children ;' *astarghióm e chavés,* 'I caught the child ;' *e chavéskoro náv só ist?* 'what is the child's name ?' *tá e chavén,* 'and the boys' (acc. case) ; *teréla chavén?* 'has he (or she) children ?' *mi chái,* 'my girl ;' *teréla yék márs, yék chái,* 'he has one boy (and) one girl.'

---

* Armenian *ariune,* 'blood.'—TR.

† This term should always be written with double *κ*—κόκκαλον.

‡ " *Tchai,* 'jeune homme.' " Vuillant, p. 457.

BRAIN—*goti.*—Used by the Gypsies for 'brain' and 'mind.' *Terávales me gotiáte,* 'I keep it in my mind,' i. e. 'I remember it.' It may be referred to Sr. *goda,* 'the brain,' or to *godhi,* 'the forehead.' From this word is formed *gotiavér,* 'having a brain, intelligent.' 'Brain' for 'intelligence' is very common also among the Greeks. *Ἔχει μυελὸν,* 'he is wise,' lit., 'he has brain.' *Mi goti,* 'my mind;' *até alló amaré gotiáte,* 'there came to our mind,' i. e. 'we were reminded;' *té n'avésa me gotiáte,* 'should I not bring to my mind.'

BRAVE—*múrs.*—This term is often used as equivalent to the common Greek *πάλληξ* and *παλληκάριον,* 'a brave, one endowed with courage;' Turk. *yiyit,* Pers. *pehlivan.* The Gypsy term probably originates from the Sr. *mṛi,* 'to die,' and its participle *mṛita,* 'dead, mortal,' Gr. *βροτός, θνητός,* of which we shall speak in elucidating the verb *meráva,* 'to die,' so common in all the Indo-European languages. Compare Slav. *muzz,* 'a man, a male.' The Gypsies frequently use the term for the male sex, whenever they intend to indicate manliness and courage in the person spoken of. It properly signifies a person of courage, but who makes no ostentatious parade of it. It is used also for 'boy:' *teráva dúi chavén, yék chái, yék múrs,* 'I have two children, a girl (and) a boy.'

BREAD—*manró, mandó, marnó, marlý;* Br., *marú;* Bor., *marno. jumeri, tató.*—Cognate with the Sr. *marára,* 'granary or storehouse,' where all kinds of produce, and whatever is used for food in general, are kept. Borrow's *tato* is evidently the Sr. *tapta,* participle of *tap,* 'to heat, to burn,' and consequently signifies that which is heated or cooked, as the Lat. *panis biscoctus,* Fr. *biscuit,* Gr. *ἄρτος δίπυρος,* i. e. 'bread subjected to two fires.' *Manró khandi kháva,* 'a little bread I eat;' *kaló manró,* 'black bread;' *manréskoro,* 'a baker,' or 'one who sells bread.'

To BREAK—*pangáva.*—Sr. *bhañj,* 'to break.' *Panghióla,* 'it broke,' aor. of the mid. voice; *panghiováva,* 'I have been broken.'

BREAST—*chuché, chuchí;* Bor., *chucha.*—From the Sr. *chuchi,* 'breast,' (Gr. *μαστὸς*); *chuchuka,* 'a nipple.' *Chuchi dávales,* 'I give it the breast;' *piéla chuchi,* 'it drinks the breast;' *ná léla chuchi,* 'it does not take the breast;' *chuchia dukéna,* 'the breasts pain.'

BRIDGE—*purt.*—From the Sr. root *par* or *pṛi,* 'to pass over, to go to the other side.' The Greek, from *περῶ, περάω,* has *περάτης,* 'one who passes to the other side,' and *πέρα,* 'on the other side.' Compare Zend *peretus,* 'bridge.'

To BRING—*anáva.*—Perhaps from the Sr. root *ni,* 'to lead,' with the prefix *á,* 'hither, to.' It is extremely common among the Gypsies. Its aorist is *anghióm,* 'I brought;' fut. *kanáv,* 'I shall bring.' *Katár anghián te romniá?* 'whence didst thou bring thy wife?' *so anghián?* 'what didst thou bring?'

BROAD—*bugló.*—This adjective, of which the derivation is unknown to me, means 'broad, wide, expanded:' fem. *bugli.* *Bugló dróm,* 'wide road.' It serves to form the verb *bugliováva,* 'to expand, to stretch, to put out clothes to dry,' probably from the custom of stretching clothes on the ground to dry them. *Bugliarghióm e yismata,* 'I have spread the linen (to dry).' *Bugliováva* means also 'to widen, to scatter;' Gr. *σκορπίζω.*

BROTHER—*pral, plal;** Bor., *plan, plano.*—

SISTER—*pen;* Bor., *plani.*—Except for the first of these forms, one would hardly believe them to be the Sr. *bhrâtṛi,* the correlative of so many Asiatic and European synonymes: in the Zend *brâtar;* Pers. *berader;* Lat. *frater;* Gr. φράτωρ; Goth. *brothar;* Germ. *bruder;* Eng. *brother;* Slav. *brash;* Russ. *brat;* Bulg. *vrat.* The Turkish Gypsies have fortunately preserved the word nearly like its archetype, to which we can thus refer the three forms of Borrow, which are undoubtedly from *bhrâtṛi,* metamorphosed according to the natural ꞏnterchanges of letters. *Plal* approaches the Lithuanian *brolis,* 'brother' (Bopp). *Pen* and *plani* are from the same Sr. original. The Hindus use another word, *svasṛi,* 'sister,' Lat. *soror. Amaré peniá,* 'our sister' (acc. case); *te praléskoro náv?* 'thy brother's name?' *keti pralén terésa?* 'how many brothers hast thou?' *me praléskoro keréste,* 'in my brother's house.'

BUCK—*búzos.*—Related to the Sr. *paçu,* 'an animal in general, a beast, a goat.' A diminutive form of this term is *buznó, buzni,* 'a she-goat.' *Chungali buzni,* 'a good-for-nothing she-goat;' *buznoró,* 'kid;' *kerghiás dúi buznoré,* 'she had (lit. 'begat') two kids.'

BULGARIAN—*dás.*—This appellation is given by the Gypsies to the numerous Bulgarians living among them, or coming from Bulgaria in the summer season to till the lands of the Greek and Turkish landholders. The Bulgarians are found in vast numbers on the lands of Roumelia. They are called Βόυλγαροι by the Greeks, *Bulghár* by the Turks, and *Bulgar* by themselves. To them this appellation *das* is utterly unknown. It is, however, extremely interesting, as being, perhaps, a reminiscence of the words Dacia, Dacian. *Dasháí,* pl. of *dás; dasni,* 'a Bulgarian woman;' *dasoró* (pl. *dasoré*), 'a young Bulgarian;' *dasnióri,* 'a young Bulgarian girl;' *dasikanó,* adj., 'Bulgarian;' *dasikani chip,* 'the Bulgarian language;' *dasikanés,* 'in a Bulgarian manner'—Βουλγαριστί.

To BURN—*tapiáva, tapiováva.*—In speaking of BATH, I have referred to the Sr. verb *tap,* 'to burn, to be hot.' It is only here and in *taviáva,* 'I boil,' that we meet it as a verb, used as *tap* is in Sanskrit.

BUSINESS—*puti, buti.*—This term, in frequent use among all the Gypsies, I have rendered by the term 'business' in English, in preference to any other. It is the Greek δουλεία, 'service, work, business;' the use of which may be illustrated by a few colloquial expressions : thus we frequently say, ἔχω δουλείαν πολλήν, 'I have a great deal of business;' εἰς τίνος δουλείαν εἶσαι? 'in whose service art thou?' The Gypsy word seems to be related to Sr. *bhúti,* primarily 'being, existence,' but ordinarily meaning 'prosperity, success, power:' the Gypsies have made it mean 'work, labor,' as what is necessary to the enjoyment and preservation of one's life, or the acquisition of wealth and pleasure. *Bhukti,* 'eating, possession, fruition,' from *bhuj,* 'to eat,' does not appear to me to have any connection with this Gypsy term. *Siklilián nevé putiá?* 'hast thou learnt (any) new business?' *kapichaváv tút ti pólin* (πόλιν) *yék putiáti,* 'I shall send thee to the city for (one)

---

* "*Prales,* 'frères.'" Vaillant, p. 456.

business;' *teráva bút putiá*, 'I have much business.' *Putí* (pl. *putiá*) is also applied to the implements of work. *Déman me putiá*, 'give me my implements.' *Butiákoro*, 'a day-laborer.'*

To BUY—*kináva.*—This verb I refer to the Sr. root *krt* (pres. *krinámi*), 'to buy, to barter, to exchange.' It is a striking example of the unquestionable relation of the Gypsy and Sanskrit idioms.† The *r* has been lost, as in many other like cases (see Section IV). With *vi* prefixed, *krt* means 'to sell:' so also among the Gypsies, *bikináva* or *biknáva* means 'to sell.' *Kinghióm yék grást*, 'I bought a horse;' *kárin kinghián té chuklés?* 'when didst thou buy thy dog?' *isás léskoro, méya kinghiómles*, 'it was his, and I bought it.'

C.

CABBAGE—*shah ;* Bor., *chaja, resis.*—This may possibly be the Sr. *çákha*, 'plant,' limited by the Gypsies to signify 'cabbage,' in like manner as by the modern Greeks the ancient term λάχανον, 'vegetable.' This conjecture is strengthened by the analogy of Borrow's term *resis*, which we shall have occasion to explain in speaking of VINEYARD : applied in former times to savory substances in general, it has come to be limited exclusively to the vine by the Gypsies of .Turkey, and to the cabbage by those of Spain.

CACARE—*khiáva, khliáva.*—The verb is pronounced in both these ways. Fut. *kamakhliáv*, 'I shall void, *cacabo ;' khlendó* and *khendó*, '*cacatus ;' khlenghióm*, 'I have voided.' The origin of this term is unknown to me.

CANE—*ran.*—Of uncertain etymology.

CARRIAGE—*vordón.*—This term is intimately related to *beró*, 'a sailing vessel,' which we shall note in defining SHIP. Both seem to belong to the Sr. root *bhri*, 'to carry, to bear.' *Vordón* I have heard used at times for 'a pack-horse.'

To be CHEATED—*khokhávniováva.*—Compound verb, from *khokhavnó*, 'a liar, one cheated,' and *aváva. Te dikél sarré o manúsh nána khokhávniovél*, 'were he to see all (i. e. 'every thing'), a man would not be cheated.' For a clear understanding of these compound verbs, the reader must examine the explanation of the component parts of the verb, in their respective places. *Khokhávniovélman*, 'he cheated me.'

CHEESE—*kerál.*—The Sr. *kshíra* is defined 'water, milk,' and from it is derived this Gypsy term. The compound consonant *ksh*, as we shall have occasion to show in the next Section, is constantly changed to the simple *k. Kotór kerál*, 'a little cheese;' *ké o yavér kerásales kerál*, 'and the remainder (i. e. 'milk') we make cheese.'

To CHEW—*chamkeráva.*—This is a compound verb, composed of *cham* —Sr. *cham*, 'to eat, to drink, to take any thing into the mouth as food'—and the Gypsy verb *keráva*, 'I make, I do,' from the Sr. *kri*, 'to make,' which we shall explain in speaking of the verb to MAKE.

CHICKEN—*chavrí.*—This is the usual Turkish *yavrú* or *yavri*, 'the young of any animal;' Gr. νεοσσὸς.

---

* Pott proposes *vritti* as a probable origin of this term.
† The Armenian *kunél*, by change of *r* to *n*, may be from this root.—TR.

CHILD—*rakló;* fem. *raklí,* 'a female child, a daughter.'—This term, though frequently confounded with *chavó,* 'a boy, a child,' means properly 'the little one,' τὸ μικρὸν of the Greeks. *Teréla panjé raklén,* 'she has five children;' *yavré raklénja,* 'with other children.' It is used often for 'the child at the the the breast, the babe;' Gr. μικρὸν.

CHRISTMAS—*khristuné.*—Although I have made particular inquiries after terms of a religious character in the native Gypsy language, I must confess that very few are to be found. I have noted in other parts of the Vocabulary such as are of pure Sr. origin. The rest are from the Greek. Christmas, in modern Greek, is called τὰ χριστόυγεννα (Χριστοῦ γέννησις), i. e. 'Christ's birth,' from which has been formed this Gypsy word, with the accent on the final syllable.

CHURCH—*karghíri;* Bor., *cangrí.*—These two words are of European origin, from the Gr. ἐκκλησία, and κυριακὸς οἶκος; Germ. *kirche,* Eng. *kirk* and *church,* are from the latter. The Latin nations have preferred ἐκκλησία; It. *chiesa,* Fr. *église.**

CLEAN—*shuchó, shuzó.*—The Sr. adjective *çuchi,* from the root *çuch,* 'to be pure or clean,' means 'white, pure,' etc. All the numerous derivatives from this verb have the same idea of cleanliness, physical or mental. By some Gypsies the word is pronounced *shuzó; shuchó,* however, is the more common pronunciation. *Shuchipé,* 'cleanliness,' is formed by the addition of the usual particle *pé. Shuchí romní,* 'a clean woman;' *shuchó chavó,* 'a clean child.'

To CLEANSE—*koshává, goshává.*—The signification of this term is 'to make clean, either by rubbing, washing, or sponging.' The Greeks now use the word σπογγίζω, 'I clean,' from σπόγγος, 'a sponge.' Its etymology is obscure. Aor. *koshlióm,* 'I made clean, I cleansed.'

CLOTHING—*páta;* Bor., *plata.*—This term I derive from the Sr. *paṭa, paṭi, paṭṭa,* etc., all meaning 'cloth, colored cloth, a garment.' The Gypsies of Spain, for euphony's sake, have inserted an *l* in the first syllable. The word, pronounced *patané* by some Gypsies, is by them applied to the bands and various pieces of cloth with which babes are swathed.

COAL—*angár;* Br., *anga;* Bor., *langar.*—This is the unchanged Sr. *angára,* 'coal.' Borrow adds an initial *l* by mistake; or, more probably, it is a fragment of the article *el,* which the Spanish Gypsies have universally adopted. The Gypsy language suffers what many others do, sometimes cutting off from, and sometimes adding to, the most common words: as *Νάξος* (the name of the island), pronounced now *'Αξία;* εἰς τὴν πόλιν ('to the city'), Turk. *Stamboul;* European *Salonica* for *Thessalonica;* Eng. *dropsy* for *hydropsy* (ὕδρωψ). *Angaréskoro,* 'a collier, one who sells coals.'

COCK—*basnó, bashnó;* Bor., *basnó.*—This word, though apparently more changed than many others, I am inclined to refer to the Sr. *pakshin,* 'fowl, bird,' from *paksha,* 'wing, feather.' The interchange of the consonants is natural. *O bashnó kaléskoro isi?* 'the cock, whose is it?' *e basnéskoro,* 'of the cock;' *e basnéngoro,* 'of the cocks.'

---

* The Armenian word for church is *yegeghetzi,* which is ἐκκλησία, transformed to accord with Armenian rules of euphony, and shows us how strangely a word can be modified in passing from one tongue to another.—TR.

Cold—*shil, shilaló;* Bor., *jil, jir, gris.*—These terms are derived from the common Sr. *çtta,* 'cold, frozen.' Borrow's form *gris* is, I think, a mistake; for it seems connected with the Sr. *grishma,* which signifies 'heat, the hot season of the year.' In comparing words of the Gypsy language with the corresponding Sr. adjectives in *ta,* we see that they often change this final syllable to *l;* thus *çatam,* 'hundred,' becomes *shel* and *shevél; sita,* 'grain,' becomes *jil;* and this word *çtta, shil. Shilaló,* 'frigid;' *shil but,* 'very cold;' *shilaló palvál,* 'cold wind.'

To feel cold—*shiláliováva.*—Verb compounded of *shilaló,* 'cold,' and *aváva,* 'to come, to be' (Section V).

Colt—*kurí, furí;* Br., *kuree;* Bor., *saullo.*—May not the first words be related to the Sr. *kuráha,* 'a light bay horse with black legs?'

Comb—*kangli.*—There are two Sr. words to which this term can be referred: *kankata,* 'a comb, an instrument for cleaning the hair,' and *kankála,* 'a skeleton.' I am inclined to give the preference to the latter, as more natural, and more congenial to the commutation of consonants observed in the formation of the Gypsy language.

To comb—*ghantáva.**—This verb seems to have no relation to *kangli,* 'a comb,' but may be connected with Sr. *kanta, kantaka,* 'a thorn, goad,' etc. *Ghantáva mó sheró,* 'I comb my head;' *ghantávaman,* 'I comb myself;' Gr. χτενίζομαι.

To come—*aváva.*—Aor. *avghióm* and *allióm. Ich allióm te dikáv tút,* 'yesterday I came to see thee;' *nashkián t' allián,* 'they left and came;' *sóske allé?* 'why have they come?' *allióm katár ki lén,* 'I came from the river;' *kána kamavés?* 'when wilt thou come?' *but lachés, aváva,* 'very well, I am coming;' *t'avéla tó dát, te penés mánghe,* 'should thy father come, let me know it' (i. e. 'thou shouldst tell it to me').

To conceal—*garáva.*—It is difficult to refer this verb to any known Sr. root, without violating the common rules of Gypsy derivation. *Garáavaman,* 'I hide myself,' κρύπτομαι; *garávtut,* 'hide thyself;' *garaticanó manúsh,* 'a hidden man' (i. e. 'a mysterious person'), μυστικός.

To cook—*pekáva.*—Sr. *pach,* 'to mature by cooking or ripening, to boil, to dress.' Pers. *pukhten,* 'to cook;' *pukhte,* 'cooked, matured;' Slav. *pekú,* 'I cook,' which has changed the Sr. palatal *ch* into the guttural *k,* like the Gypsy. This verb is extremely common, and well known to all the Gypsies. *Pekiló,* 'baked, cooked' (3d pers. aor. pass.); *pekó,* 'cooked;' Sr. *pakva,* 'cooked, matured.'

Cool—*sudró.*—Evidently the Pers. *serd,* 'cold, frigid.' It is often applied to water, to express its freshness. *Sudró pani,* 'cool water;' *sudró tut,* 'cold milk.' It is often confounded with *shilaló,* 'cold.'

To cover—*ucharáva.*—The close coincidence of form between this word and the Sr. *uchcharámi,* 'I arise, go up,' leads me to conjecture their relationship, notwithstanding the difference of meaning. Mid. voice: *ucharávaman,* 'I cover myself;' *ucharávaman e paplomaténja* (Gr. παπλώματα), 'I cover myself with quilts:' part. *uchardó,* 'covered;' *biuchardó,* 'uncovered,' pronounced often *buchardó;* as *bu-*

---

* Pronounced γantáva, with a Gr. γ (γαντάβα).

chardó isi o amáksi (Gr. ἀμάξι), 'the carriage was uncovered.' *Uchar-ghióm* (aor.), 'I have covered.'

Cough—*has;* Bor., *pichiscas.*—

To cough—*hasáva.*—From the Sr. root *kâs,* 'to cough.' The change of the guttural *k* into the aspirate *h* is observable in other Gypsy words, as we shall have occasion frequently to notice in the course of this memoir. Many Gypsies pronounce the noun as though it were written with a Greek χ. Their pronunciation of the aspirate *h* is so feeble at times as to be scarcely heard. Borrow derives his term from Sr. *vikshava,* 'cough.' But *hasáva,* 'I cough much.'

To count—*ghenáva;* Bor., *ginar, jinar.*—The Sr. verb *gaṇ* means 'to count, to reckon up by number, to calculate.' Though applied to calculations of a higher order by the Hindus, it is now by the Gypsies confined solely to counting. Many of them can count no higher than ten in their vernacular tongue. The word is frequently used in the sense of considering or reflecting. *Palalutné ghén,* 'consider the consequences' (lit. 'the afterward things'). So also the Greeks: μέτρα τὰ ὑστερινὰ σου.

Cow—see ox.

CREPITUS VENTRIS—khán.—Of doubtful etymology.

Cross—*tarshúl, trushúl;* Bor., *trijul.*—All the religious terms of the Gypsies are of peculiar interest. Unfortunately for their history, they have few such which are vernacular, and, like the Persians and Turks, have borrowed nearly all from the people among whom they live, and whose religion they have embraced. This, however, is a singular exception. It seems to be related to the Sr. *triçúla,* 'a trident, a three-pointed pike or spear, especially the weapon of Siva.' To many Gypsies this word is entirely unknown, and in its place they use the Greek σταυρὸς: *keráva mo stavrós,* 'I make my cross, I cross myself.'

To cry out—*basháva.*—This Gypsy verb may be referred to Sr. *vâç,* 'to sound, to cry as a bird, to call,' etc. These definitions go to prove that the verb was applied by the Hindus to all those sounds of animals expressed by the Lat. *ululare.* So, too, with the Gypsies, who use it in a very general sense, and apply it not only to quadrupeds, but to birds also. *O basnó bashéla,* 'the cock crows;' *bashéla o chukél,* 'the dog barks.'

Curse—*armán.*—This is an imprecation very much in use among the Gypsies. I will endeavor to explain it by the usages of the natives, both Greeks and Turks. *Arman* and *arma* signify in Sanskrit 'disease of the eyes, and consequent blindness.' The Turks, among their imprecations, frequently make use of the phrases *kiór ol,* 'mayest thou become blind;' *kiór olsún,* 'may he become blind.' The Greeks very often exclaim to one another τύφλα, 'blindness;' νὰ τυφλωθῇς, 'mayest thou become blind.' In a similar manner, as I conceive, this Sr. word in the mouth of the Gypsies became a word of imprecation, having the same signification with the Greek and Turkish terms. They know nothing of the primary Sr. signification of *arman,* and, when asked the meaning of the term, they answer " it is a βλασφημία, 'a curse.'" The phrase *Ma déman armán,* 'do not give me a curse,' is extremely

5

common among them all, and they use it as we use the phrase "do not revile me." *Armán dáva* is 'to curse.' But it is rarely used in any other form than the one given above, precisely as the Greeks never use the term τύφλα save as an imprecation.

To CUT—*chináva;* Bor., *chinelar, achinelar.*—The Gypsies use this word indifferently, either for cutting in the ordinary sense of the word, or for reaping. Borrow also defines the word *chinelar* "to cut, to reap." The Sr. *chhid*, 'to cut, to divide,' inserts an *n* before its final radical, like all verbs of the same conjugation : *chhinna*, from this root, is 'divided, cut.' The Gypsies have rejected the final radical conso- nant, and in its place have preserved the characteristic *n* of the con- jugation. Borrow's addition of an initial *a* to *chinelar* is a pleonasm frequently found in his vocabulary. *Chináva*, and, in the passive form, *chiniováva*, is used frequently in the sense of 'I am tired.' Among the ancient Greeks, the word κόπτω had this signification : ἵππος τὸν ἀναβάτην κόπτει (Xen.), and κόπος, 'pain, labor,' evidently prove it. Compare Mod. Greek ἐκόπην, ἐκόπηκα, 'I am tired;' τὸ ὀδόντι με κόπτει, 'the tooth pains me.' The Turks use the passive, *kesilmek*, 'to be cut' (act. *kesmek*), for 'to be tired or wearied.' So that the Gypsies have imitated the usages of their neighbors. *Chiniováva kána piráva*, 'I get tired when I walk;' *kána shunávales moghi chindó*, 'when I hear him my heart (is) afflicted' (lit. 'cut'): *chinghióm*, aor.

To CUT with a knife, to WHITTLE—*choláva.*—The Sr. root *chhur* we shall have occasion to explain in speaking of *churi*, 'knife,' to which it has doubtless given origin, as well as to this verb *choláva.* It is singular that the liquid *r* should have been retained in the noun, and changed to *l* in the verb.

D.

DAY—*divés, ghivés;* Br., *ghivés;* Bor., *chibes.*—Related to the Sr. *div*,[*] denoting 'heaven, day.' From *divés* comes *disiló*, 'the day breaks.' *Khandí divés*, 'few days;' *diveséskoro*, 'wages for a day's work;' *saró divés*, 'every day;' *ketí divés?* 'how many days?' *Ghivés* is more general among the Moslem Gypsies.

DEAF—*kasukóv;* Bor., *cajuco.*—This is a common word, well known and familiar to all the Gypsies. I am unable to give it any satisfac- tory Sr. derivation, though it seems to be related to that idiom.

DEATH—*moló, meripé;* Bor., *meripen.*—This is evidently from the Sr. root *mri*, 'to die,' which we find in nearly all the European lan- guages, living and dead. *Moló* is the Sr. *mára*, 'death, murder,' by the change of *r* to *l*. The ultimate *pe, pen* is the customary particle forming abstract nouns, numerous examples of which are to be met with in our Vocabulary. For farther elucidation of this term, see to DIE.

DEEP—*khór.*—This term derives itself from the Sr. root *khur*,[†] 'to cut, to scratch, to dig.' *Khor chin ti puv*,. 'deep into the earth.'

To DEPART—*nasháva;* Bor., *najabar, najar.*—This verb I refer to the root *naç*, 'to disappear, to cease to be, to perish.' *Nasghiá t' alliá*,

---

'they left and came;' *kána kanashés?* 'when wilt thou depart?' *but nashéla,* 'it goes swiftly' (of a horse); *nash améndar, oléndar,* 'depart from us, from them;' part. *nastó,* 'departed.'

DEVIL—*bénk;* Br., *benk;* Bor., *bengue, bengui.—Bengó isi,* or *bengósi,* 'he is a devil;' *ja túke bénke,* 'go thou also to the devil,' an imprecation; *bengaló manúsh,* 'a devilish man,' i. e. 'a cunning man.'

To DIE—*meráva.*—We have in other parts of our Vocabulary terms which are connected with this verb, as *moló,* 'dead, death,' *meripé,* 'death,' *merdó,* 'sick' (Bor.), *murtaráva,* 'I murder.' We have occasion, in defining these terms, to speak of the Sr. root *mri,* 'to die,' which is to be found in a great many languages, bearing intimate relation to the Sanskrit. It was naturally to be expected that a word which has retained its place in so many languages, having more or less affinity to the Sanskrit, should also be preserved in the Gypsy. In speaking of *meripé,* 'death,' we have noticed some of the affinities of this verb among the Indo-European languages. The reader may be pleased to see the word running with slight variations through so many languages. The Zend has *mere,* 'to die,' and the transitive *merec,* 'to kill.' Pers. *merden,* 'to die,' *merd,* 'a man,' corresponding to the English use of the word *mortal,* 'one liable to death, a man.' With the Sr. part. *mrita* corresponds the Gr. βροτὸς, and with *amrita,* ἄμβροτος, 'immortal,' and ἀμβροσία, 'the food of immortals.' The Albanians, from the Gr. βροτὸς, have formed their verb βρας, 'to die,' while they have retained the original in a purer form in μόρρἴτ, 'death.' The Lat. *morior* has no need of explanation. The Gr. μαραίνω has even to this day the same signification among the modern Greeks that it had among their fathers : it is applied to the death of plants, and to the wasting of life by long disease, the μαρασμὸς of the ancient Greeks. The European languages, Latin and German, have retained the word, particularly in its transitive form, *to murder.* Slav. *umyráyu,* 'I die,' and *moriú,* 'to kill.'[*] *Mulólar,* 'after dying.'

To DIG—*khatáva.*—The Sr. verbal root *khan* is 'to dig, to delve.' *Khanámi,* 'I dig,' would be in the Gypsy language *khanáva,* instead of *khatáva.* But the Gypsies, as we shall have hereafter occasion to demonstrate, instead of borrowing directly from the original root, have made use of participles as roots, and from thence have formed many of their verbs. We have an example in *dúk,* 'pain,' *dukáva,* 'to be in pain.' So here the part. *kháta,* 'dug, excavated,' has served as the root of *khatáva,* 'I dig.' *Kón khatélalen?* 'who digs (i. e. 'cultivates') them?'

DIRT—*mel.*—

DIRTY—*melaló.*—Compare the Sr. noun *mala,* 'dirt, filth, sediment,' and the same as an adjective, 'dirty, filthy.' The Sr. adjective *malina* may have given origin to the Gypsy adj. *melaló,* by the mutation of *n* to *l.* It appears to me, however, to be a regular Gypsy formation from *mel,* 'dirt,' by the addition of *lo,* which is a common adjec-

---

[*] The Arm. language has *mer-nil.* 'to die;' *mertzoonel,* 'to murder;' *maril,* 'to faint away;' *mah,* 'death;' '*mahganatsou,*' 'mortal;' '*anmah,*' 'immortal.'—TR.

tive termination among the Gypsies. As whiteness is a symbol of purity, so is blackness associated with whatever is filthy and unclean. This word, which has also the signification of 'black' in Sr., is undoubtedly related, then, with the Gr. μέλας, 'black,' and μελάνιον, 'ink.' To the same origin I refer another Gypsy word, *mulanó*, 'dark,' from the Sr. adj. *malina*. Borrow has *mulani*, 'sad.' *Te tikné isi melalé,* 'thy children are dirty.'

To become DIRTY—*melaliováva.*—A compound verb, of the mid. voice, compounded of *melaló*, 'dirty,' and *aváva* (see Section V). *Melalióm,* 'I have been dirtied.'

DOOR—*dar, vudár;* Bor., *burda.*—The derivation of both these terms is very evident. The Sr. *dvára*, 'door, gate, passage,' appears in both ancient and modern languages: Zend *dvara*, Pers. *der*, Gr. θύρα, Goth. *daur*, Eng. *door.**　*Puradvára*, composed of *dvára* and *pura*, 'city,' is the same as our πύλη, 'gate, city-gate.' I refer Borrow's word to this compound, which in the mouth of the Gypsies has lost its last syllable. If this etymology be correct, we may here find the derivation of the Latin *porta*. This term is by some Gypsies pronounced *dal*, by the natural commutation of the liquids. ‹ *Kon déla o vutár?* ‘who knocks at the door?' *bánd o vutár*, 'shut the door;' *dúi dar teréla*, 'it has two doors.'

DOWN, BELOW—*telé, felé;* Bor., *ostelis, osteli.*—This word, common also to the Slavonic (*doly*, 'down'), I refer to the Sr. *tala*, 'deep, a low place, the foundation of any thing.' With it is connected, probably, the Latin *tellus*, 'earth.' The *telé* of the Gypsies is the regular locative case of *tala*—*tale*. The analogy is manifest. In Borrow these forms seem to have an initial euphonic syllable, foreign to the original word.

DREAM—*sunnó.*—Compare Sr. *svapna*, Gr. ὕπνος, Lat. *sopnus, somnus*, 'sleep;' Lat. *sopnium, somnium*, Gr. ἐνύπνιον, 'dream,' lit. 'in sleep' (ἐν ὕπνῳ); Slav. *sónie*, 'dream,' from *son*'', 'sleep.' In the same manner, by the rejection of the radical *p*, has been formed the Gypsy *sunnó*, which, like the Latin *somnium* from *sopnium*, was probably at first *supnó. Me sunnéste*, 'in my dream.'

To DRESS—*uryaváva.*—In order to make intelligible the meaning of this verb, it is well to say that it is used precisely as the Greeks use their στολίζομαι, 'I adorn myself, I put on clean clothes, or fine clothes.' It has also the signification of 'changing clothes,' and often simple 'dressing,' as to dress for a ball or party, etc. To me it seems related to the Sr. adj. *árya*, 'of a good family, apposite, proper:' unless it be rather connected with the root *urnu*, 'to cover, envelop, dress.' *Uryoïpé*, 'raiment;' *uryanghiás tút*, 'thou hast dressed thyself.' Some Gypsies say *uryáva*, 'I dress.'

To DRINK—*piáva;†* Bor., *piyar, tapillar.*—Two Sr. roots exist, intimately related to each other, to which these Gypsy terms can be referred; namely, *pá* and *pí*, 'to drink, to nourish.' Borrow has *pita*,

---

* Armenian *toor.*—Tr.

† "*Napilel*, 'à boire'" (probably *tapilél*). Vaillant, p. 369. "*Tepau, piau, piawe, pi.*" Arndt, p. 391.

'drink,' related to the Sr. *ptta*, Lat. *potum*, Gr. *ποτὸν*. Slav. *piyú*, 'I drink.' *Piliás akhiá mol*, 'he drank that wine;' *án te piás*, 'bring (i. e. 'come'), let us drink;' *khandí mól piáva*, 'a little wine I drink.'

DRUNK, INTOXICATED—*mattó*; Bor., *mato.*—From the Sr. root *mad*, 'to be merry, intoxicated, excited, or mad,' part. *matta*, 'intoxicated.' We find this word in the Latin: Pliny calls the white vine (Brionia alba) *madon*, and Plautus the intoxicated *madulsa*; and although these terms are derived by the lexicographers from *madeo*, still I think they should rather be referred to the Sr. *mad*. Gr. *ματία* and *ματίη*, 'levity, folly,' properly originate from this Sr. root. *Mattó*, coming evidently from the Sr. *matta*, should be written with *tt*. *Mattó ist*, 'he is drunken,' pronounced in an abbreviated form *mattósi*.

To become DRUNK—*máttiováva.*—A compound verb, from *mattó*, 'drunken,' and *aváva*. The form is the usual mid. voice. *Mattilióm* (aor.), 'I became intoxicated;' *mattiovéna*, 'they became intoxicated.'

DRY, EMACIATED—*shukó*; Bor., *juco*, fem. *juqui.*—From the Sr. verbal root *çush*, 'to dry,' is formed the adj. *çushka*, 'dry, slim, emaciated.' Compare Slav. *suhii*, 'dry,' *súshta*, 'dry land,' in distinction from the sea; Lat. *siccus*. *Shukó manró*, 'dry bread,' denoting bread without any other food; *shukó manró na khalióla*, 'bread alone cannot be eaten;' *shukó manúsh*, 'an emaciated man;' *shukí romni*, 'a lean woman.'

To DRY—*shukiaráva*, *shúkiováva.*—Of these two terms, the former is transitive, 'to dry, to expose any thing to the sun or fire to be dried;' the latter is a middle verb, 'to become dry' (Gr. *στεγνόνομαι*), as with other verbs of this formation (Section V). *Shukilióm*, 'I have become dry;' *kashukiovél* (fut.), 'he will be dried.'

DUNG—*goshnó.*—There seems to exist, in the first syllable of this term, the Sr. *go*, 'a cow;' compare modern Greek *βουνιά*, 'the dung of the bovine species,' to which may be referred another Gypsy term, *bunista*, 'dung.' *Goshné*, 'dungs,' corresponds to *κόπρος*, *κόπροι*, *κόπρανον*, *κόπρανα*, 'excrements.'*

DOG—*chukél*; Br., *rikono*; Bor., *chuquel.*—For the explanation of *rikono*, see WHELP. The other two are perhaps from the Sr. *jukuṭa* and *jakuṭa*, 'dog.' *Kon diniás amaré chuklés?* 'who struck our dog?'

DWARFISH, SMALL—*khurdó*; Bor., *chirdó.*—Both these terms are referable to the Sr. *kṛit*, 'to cut off,' whence the Lat. *curtus*,† It. *corto*, Fr. *court*, Germ. *kurz*. Our *κυρτὸς*, which is of the same derivation with the Lat. *curtus*, signifies generally 'humpbacked.' I think also that our *κουρεὺς*, *κουρεῖον*, *κουρίς* are of the same origin. *Khurdó* is applied to a child at the breast, to a young man, etc. *Kaméla te pandrevél khurdó*, 'he wished to be married young' (*pandrevél* — *ὑπανδρεύομαι*); *khurdó chavó*, 'a young child;' *khurdé machorénghe*, 'to the small fish:' *khurdó* is properly 'small in body or mind.'

---

* Pott, under *groñi*, has "Poln. *gnoy*, Walach. *gunoin*, 'mist;' *gréngro gurumniakro grojjo*, 'pferde-, kuhmist.'"

† Armenian *kodrods*, by transposition of *r* and *d.*—TS.

●

E.

EAR—*kann;* Br., *kana;* Bor., *cani.*—The Sr. *karna,* 'ear.'

EARLY—*ráno.*—This is a Slavonic term, *ránv* (adv.), 'early, very early.'
The Gr. ὄρϑριος and ὄρϑρος of the New Testament are always translated by this term. *Ráno ráno* is frequently to be heard in the
mouth of the Gypsies. The Greeks often say in a similar way, πρωΐ
πρωΐ, 'very early.' Turk. *chapúk chapúk,* 'quickly.' *Káde* (κάδε) *ráno,*
'every morning.'

EARTH—*puv, phuv, pfuv.**—This is the Sr. *bhú,* 'the earth.' Many Gypsies pronounce it *bhu,* others *fu.* To the pronunciation of this word
are applicable the observations which I have already made in the
preceding Section (p. 20). *Puvéskero,* 'of the earth;' *chin ti puv,*
'to the ground.'

To EAT—*kháva.*—This is the common Sr. root *khâd,* 'to eat.' *Isi te khás
manró khandí?* 'can (lit. 'is there') I eat a little bread?' *dikáva ka
teрés onghi te khas,* 'I see that thou hast appetite (lit. 'heart') to eat;'
shukó manró ná khalióla, 'dry bread is not to be eaten:' *khalióla* is
the mid. form of *khaliováva.* *Khasói,* 'food,' is applied to whatever
is eaten with bread; Gr. ὄψος, Turk. *katék: arakéla manró, khasói te
khéнa,* 'there is found bread (and) food for thee to eat;' *ta na khávas,*
'and should I not eat;' *khandí khásales,* 'a little we eat (of) it;' *te
khén e chavé gudló tut,* 'that the children may drink (lit. 'eat') sweet
milk.'

EGG—*vanró;* Bor., *anró.*—The Sr. neuter noun *anḍa* means 'an egg,'
also 'a testicle.' It has both these significations among the Gypsies.
In this they have followed not only the usage of their mother tongue,
but that of the Turks and Greeks: cf. Turk. *yumurta,* 'an egg, a testicle;' Gr. ἀυγὸν (anc. ὠόν), 'an egg, a testicle.' The Gypsies of Turkey have added an initial *v* to their noun. This word I have sometimes heard pronounced *vantó.* The pronunciation of the dental consonant in it resembles that of *do* and *ro* in *mindó, minró,* 'mine,' of
which we have already spoken in the former Section (p. 20).

EMACIATED—See DRY.

EMPTY—*chuchó.*—Referable to the Sr. adj. *tuchha,* 'void, empty.' It is
often used by the Gypsies for 'a dull man, an empty mind:' compare
Turk. *bosh,* 'empty.' The Greeks also, borrowing this Turkish term,
say ἄνϑρωπος μπόσικος, 'a good-for-nothing man.'

EXCOMMUNICATION—*kalipé.*—This abstract noun is formed from *kaló,*
'black,' by the addition of the usual particle *pe.* I have noted the
word merely to show its peculiar use among the Gypsies, and because
of its interest as a religious term. Excommunication is frequently
resorted to in order to induce thieves to give up stolen property;
although but rarely in the case of Gypsy delinquents, on account of
their irreligion.

EXTINGUISHER—*vrehtúla.*—This is a Greek term, βρεχτοῦλα. By the
Gypsy blacksmiths it is applied to small pieces of old straw carpet,

---

* "*Bhu, ebhu,* 'terre.'" Vaillant, p. 33; "*pou.*" do., p. 395; "*o bhu,* 'la terre.'"
do., p. 457. "*Pu, bu, pube, epebu.*" Arndt, p. 357.

soaked in water, which is then sprinkled over the charcoal fire, in order to extinguish it. This term is nowhere to be found in the dictionaries of our language, to my knowledge, although it is of a regular formation. It is in use among some of the Greek blacksmiths, but is principally to be heard among the Gypsies.

EYE—*yak;* * Br., *yaka;* Bor., *aquia.*—The final *a* of Mr. Brown's form is the characteristic vowel of the plural. *Yak* is evidently from the Sr. *akshi, aksha,* 'eye,' which is cognate with the words used to denote 'eye' in many of the Indo-European languages. The Latin *oculus* implies an ancient form *ocus,* of which it is a diminutive. The Slavonic has preserved this unchanged, in *oko,* 'eye;' Germ. *auge;* Eng. *eye.* The initial *y* of this term is a euphonic prefix: so, in Greek, we say often *yéma* for αἷμα, 'blood.' *Mono yak,* 'my eye;' *perdilé me yaká,* 'my eyes were full (of tears);' *dikéla man to yaká,* 'he looked me in the eyes;' *bandáva me yaká,* 'I close my eyes.'†

EYE-BROW—*pov.*—This may be referred to the Sr. *bhrû,* 'an eye-brow,' which appears in so many cognate languages, more or less altered: Zend *brvat;* Pers. *ibru;* Slav. *brov;* Gr. ὀφρύς; Eng. *brow,* etc. The rejection of the liquid *r,* when united to other consonants, is extremely common with the Gypsies (see Section IV). *Makavdé pová,* 'painted eye-brows.'

F.

To FALL—*peráva.*—This is the Sr. *pat,* 'to move downwards, to fall, to descend.' Aor. *pelióm,* 'I have fallen.' It is a very common word among all the Gypsies. *O yek pelótar,* 'the one after falling;' *per te devléste,* 'fall on thy back' (lit. 'on thy God'); *piló* and *peló,* 'fallen;' *piló isóm,* 'I am fallen,' 'I fell.' The change of *t* to *r* we have noticed above.

FAT—*parvardó.*—From the Sr. root *vardh,* 'to increase,' with the prefix *pra* or *pari; pravriddha,* 'increased.' *Parvardó mas,* 'fat meat.'

FATHER—*dát;*‡ Br., *dat;* Bor., *bato, batu.*—*Dat* corresponds to the Sr. *táta, tata,* 'father,'§ while *bato, batu* probably come from the Sr. *pitá,* 'father,' which has correlatives in nearly all the ancient and modern European languages, modified according to the spirit of each language: Pers. *beder,* Gr. πατήρ, Lat. *pater,* Germ. *vater,* Eng. *father. Até isí tó dát?* 'is thy father here?' *lákoro dat,* 'her father;' *mró dát, tó dát,* 'my father, thy father.'

FATHER-IN-LAW—*shastró, sastró.*—

MOTHER-IN-LAW—*shasúi, sashúi.*—Both these terms may be easily connected with the well known Sr. words *çvaçura,* 'father-in-law,' and *çvaçru,* 'mother-in-law,' which have passed into the Latin *socerus* and Greek ἑκυρός: compare Germ. *schwäher* and *schwiegervater.*

---

* "*Iak,* 'oeil.'" Vaillant, p. 359. "*Jakch,* 'auge.'" Arndt, p. 374.

† The Armenian *achk* is from the same root, accommodated to the favorite sounds of the language, which indulges freely in transposition of letters and interchange of similar sounds.—TR.

‡ "*Tat,* 'pere.'" Vaillant, p. 481.

§ It is found in many languages, as Eng. *daddy,* Welsh *tad,* Irish *taid,* Russian *tatra,* etc.—TR.

FEAR—*dar;* Bor., *dar, dal.*—

To FEAR, to be AFRAID—*daráva;* Bor., *darabar, daraňar.*—These definitions are all referable to the Sr. verbal root *dṛi, dar,* 'to respect, venerate, dread,' whence comes *dara,* 'fear, terror.'

FEVER—*trésca.*—This is a Bulgarian word for 'fever,' particularly the intermittent autumnal fever, so prevalent in the great valley of the Danube. It is related to the Slavonic *tryasú,* 'I shake, I move.' Both Greeks and Bulgarians, in speaking of intermittent fevers, give them this denomination. Gr. ϑέϱμη and ϑεϱμασία. The Gypsies have followed the usage of their neighbors, and apply this word solely to intermittent fevers. Borrow's term for 'fever' we have already explained (see BATH).

FIG—*khelí.*—

FIG-TREE—*khelín.*—Of doubtful etymology. *Teréla te khelía,* 'it has also figs.'

FILE—*verní.*—Of origin unknown to me: pl. *vernía. Keténghe kinghián oká verní?* 'for how much didst thou buy that file?' *jovénghe,* 'for six' ('pieces of money' understood).*

To FILL—*peráva.*—From the Sanskrit root *par, pṛi,* 'to fill.'

FINGER—*angúst, angrúst;* Br., *wass;* Bor., *angusti.*—See RING. Mr. Brown's *wass* is a mistake for 'hand.'

To FINISH—*resáva.*—This is one of the many Gypsy words whose derivation is to me doubtful. The proper meaning of the word, as used by the Gypsies, is 'to finish business, work, a day's labor:' *resavghióm mi putí,* 'I have finished my business.' It is often used impersonally: as *reséla,* 'it is enough;' *reséla man, tut, les,* 'it is enough for me, thee, him;' *na reséla,* 'it is not enough.' It is used also in the sense of 'arriving, reaching:' *nastí resavghiómles,* 'I could not reach him;' *avdivés resavghióm,* 'today I have arrived;' *kamaresél?* 'will he arrive?'

FIRE—*yak;†* Br., *yak;* Bor., *yaque.*—This word, at first, might seem to be from the Turkish verb *yakmak,* 'to burn,' imp. *yak,* 'burn thou.' But it is my opinion that in the genuine Gypsy language we have no Turkish words. I am not unaware of the general corrupt use of Turkish words among the Gypsies, whether Christian or Moslem, as well as among uneducated Greeks and Armenians. But if the word be Turkish, how did the Gypsies of Spain get it unchanged? They have neither known the Turks, nor had their fathers, in passing through Europe, the slightest intercourse with them. I think, then, that this word *yak* is from the Sr. root *yaksh,* and its derivative and synonym *yaj,* both meaning 'to sacrifice, to offer in worship.'‡ *Tebeshás bashé ti yak,* 'let us sit near the fire;' *murtaráva i yak,* 'I quench (lit. 'I murder') the fire;' *murtár i yak,* 'quench the fire.'

FIRST—*avkós.*—This word, which I translate 'first,' seems to be related to *atiá,* 'here,' with the particle *ka,* expressing presence, time. It

---

* Pott writes the word *yerni,* 'lima, file.'

† "*Iag,* 'feu.'" Vaillant, p. 480. "*Jag, jak, jago,* 'fieber.'" Arndt, p. 357.

‡ See what has been already said respecting this word, in Section II (p. 14).

· may be translated 'this one,' and, in an emphatic tone, 'the first.'
There is some analogy between this Gypsy term and the Slavonic,
which has made its number one *'edyn'*, from the Sr. *ádya*, 'first,
initial.' *Avkós anglé*, 'the foremost.'

FISH—*machó ;* Br., *matchó ;* Bor., *macho.*—This is the Sr. *matsya*, 'fish.'
Machoró, 'a small fish ;' *khurdé machorénghe lon chivéla*, 'to the
small fish he throws salt ;' *machéskoro*, 'a fisherman ;' *londé maché*,
'salted fish.'

FIST—*domúk ;* Br., *domuk.*—A term well known to all the Gypsies.

FLAX—*vus.*—This probably originates from the same root as *bus*, 'straw.'
While the one name was applied to straw, the other was given to
flax. The Sr. has *busha* and *busa*, 'chaff.' It is well to remark that
flax is a very important branch of trade with many Gypsies, in the
neighborhood of populous cities.

FLEA—*pushúm :* pl. *pushumá.*—But *pushumá terávas akhiá ratt*, 'many
fleas I had this night.'

FLOUR—*varó ;* Bor., *roi.*—This term may be referred to the root *bhṛi*,
'to nourish, to cherish, to maintain ;' *bhara*, 'one who cherishes, up-
holds, supports,' etc. *Sóske ná terásas varó*, 'because we had not
flour ;' *déman khandi varó*, 'give me a little flour.'

FLY—*makiá ;* Bor., *macha.*—These terms are referable to the Sr. *makshiká*, 'a fly.' Bopp derives from this term the Latin *musca*, and the
Old German *mucca*, 'a gnat, a mosquito.'

FOOL—*deniló ;* Bor., *dinelo, ninelo.*—The Sr. adjective *dîna* is defined
'poor, distressed, frightened.' By the addition of *lo* the Gypsies
have formed this word, applied now to those who are either extrava-
gant in their speech and actions, or suffering under alienation of mind.
Here in Turkey, it is translated constantly by the Turkish *deli*, 'a
fool,' Gr. λωλός, 'fool, lunatic.' The second word of Borrow has
merely changed the initial *d* into *n*. Borrow, in the etymology of
the word *dinelo*, gives the Pers. *diwanah (divane)*, a word common
also among the Turks. This has no connection with the above mentioned word, being from *div*, Sr. *deva*, 'a god,' by the addition of
the usual Pers. suffix *âne*, meaning 'one in the power of a god or
demon ;' the δαιμόνιος of the Greek, the δαιμονισμένος ('enraged') of
the present Greeks. *Piliás akhiá mol ta deniló*, 'he drank that wine
and (became) a fool,' i. e. 'was intoxicated.' From *deniló* is formed
deniliováva, 'I become a fool :' *méya pilióm ta denilióm*, 'I also drank
and became a fool.'

FOOT—*piró, pindó, pinró, pirnó ;*[*] Br., *peera ;* Bor., *pinro, pindro.*—
The Sr. usually employs the words *pâd* and *pâda*, from the root *pad*,
'to go, to move,' whence our πούς, ποδός, Lat. *pedis.*[†] The above
Gypsy words have no relation to this Sr. root, but appear to come
from the verb *par*, 'to pass, to traverse.' Of the four forms which I
have given, the first appears to me to be most in use among all the
Gypsies. Mr. Brown's *peera* is probably a plural form. *Pindó* is
often pronounced *pinró*, like *mindó, minró*, 'mine' (see p. 20).

---

[*] " *Geroi, pir*, 'fuss.'" Arndt, p. 382.
[†] Armenian *vod.*—TR.

6

Jáva ti Silivrí grastésa, tá ná pindéntza, 'I go to Silivria with a horse (i. e. 'on horseback') and not with the feet' (i. e. 'on foot'); *me piré dukénaman,* 'my feet pain me:' *piripé,* 'gait,' applied particularly to the horse: *pirindós,* 'going on foot;' *pirindós kajés? kamajáv grastésa,* 'art thou going on foot? I shall go with a horse' (i. e. 'on horseback').

FOREIGN—*peryúl.*—This term seems to have originated from the Persian *perghiúl,* 'a stranger, a foreigner.' *Peryulicanó tan,* 'a foreign country' (lit. 'place').

FOREST—*vesh.**—This is the Pers. *bishe,* 'a wood, a forest.' By some Gypsies it is used for 'mountain,' probably on account of the mountains of Roumelia being so thickly wooded.[†]

FORWARDS—*anglé;* Bor., *anglal.*—The Sr. adjective *agra,* 'chief, principal, first,' corresponds with ἄκρος, so often used by the Greek writers: *agre* is its locative case, frequently used as an adverb, signifying 'in front, in the forepart.' By the usual change of *r* into *l,* and by the interposition of a euphonic *n,* it has become *anglé.* Adj. *anglutnó,* 'the first, the one foremost.' *Anglé isás mindi,* 'formerly it was mine (*mea*);' *pó anglé,* 'still more forwards;' *anglál,* 'from the front' (Borrow's form): *anglál to kér,* 'from the front of the house,' or 'from the house in front;' *anglál mánde,* 'in front of me, before me;' *anglál to pashá,* 'before the pasha;' Gr. ἐνώπιον τοῦ πασσᾶ. This ablative form is now mostly used for *anglé. Anglál devléste,* or *anglál to devél,* 'before God, in the presence of God.'

FRIEND—*parnavó.*[‡]—This term is not very common among the Gypsies here. It is related to the Sr. root *pri,* 'to please, to delight, to be pleased or satisfied.' This root has given to the Gothic *frijô,* 'I love,' and *frijonds,* 'loving;' to the Slavonic *priyáte'ie,* 'loved, pleased;' to the Greek φιλῶ, φίλος. The participle *prina,* 'pleased, satisfied,' may have given origin to this Gypsy term, by the addition of the final syllable *vo,* common in forming Gypsy adjectives. *Jáva ti pólin* (πόλιν) *te dikáv me parnavés,* 'I go to the city to see my friend;' *isí mó parnavó,* 'he is my friend;' *po lachés ta terésales parnavó,* 'it is better that thou shouldst have him a friend' (i. e. 'friendly'); *ta te penés sarné parnavénghe t' avén,* 'tell all the friends to come.' From this is formed the abstract *parnavoipé,* 'friendship;' *kér mánghe aká parnavoipé,* 'do me this friendship' (i. e. 'favor').

FROG—*zámpa.*—I do not know the derivation of this word, which, however, appears to me to be of Slavonic origin.

FROM—*katár.*—Ablative part. *tar.* From the rel. pronoun *kón. Katár ti hindovi,* 'from India;' *katár ti pólin* (πόλιν) *aváva,* 'from the city I come;' *katár to sastó,* 'from the right' (i. e. 'side'); *katár ti drák keréna mol,* 'from the grape they make wine.'

---

* "*Vesh*, 'forét.'" Vaillant, p. 457.

† Pott writes the word *weesh, vesz, vash,* more in harmony with *bishe.* I have heard the word pronounced *vest,* though rarely.

‡ "*Tirei, pries'ang pani om,* 'je suis votre ami, votre frère.'" Vaillant, p. 391. This is extremely corrupt. It should probably stand thus: *tiró pries 'som, pral som.*

FULL—*perdó;* Bor., *perdó.*—From the Sr. root *pri,* 'to fill,' is formed the participle *púrta,* 'full, filled, complete.' There is a striking resemblance between the Spanish and Turkish Gypsy words, whenever they can be traced to their proper Sr. root.

To become FULL—*pértiováva.*—A compound verb, of the mid. voice, composed of *perdó,* 'full,' and *aváva,* 'I come.' *Perdilé me yaká,* 'my eyes have become full (of tears);' Greek γεμίζομαι, from γέμω, 'I fill.'

G.

GAIT—*piripé.*—From *piró,* 'a foot,' by the addition of the particle *pe.* It is applied to horses and donkeys, especially to the former, which are valued according to the smoothness of their gait, so much esteemed by the Turks. *Piripé* is mostly applied to that pace of the horse called amble; Pers. *rahvan,* 'easily moving on a road.' *Piripé teréla? teréla,* 'has it a good gait? it has;' *amaré grastéskoro piripé nanái lachó,* 'our horse's gait is not good.'

GARLIC—*sir;* Bor., *sar.*—This word is probably of Persian origin, from *sir,* 'garlic, allium.' The present Hindustani word is *seer,* 'garlic,' as given by Borrow in his vocabulary.

GIRDLE—*kiustik.*—This is a Persian word, *kiustek,* meaning generally 'the fetters put to the feet of horses', as in the stables of the East. *Kiustek,* as it signifies 'something that binds, a tie,' has been applied by the Gypsies to the girdle, as a fastening.

GIRL—See BOY.

To GIVE—*dáva;* Bor., *dinar.*—This is evidently from the Sr. *dá,** 'to give,' which is extremely common in all the Indo-European languages, ancient and modern. This verb is irregular in its conjugation: imp. *dé,* 'give thou;' *déman,* 'give to me:' aor. *dinióm,* 'I gave,' which approaches more nearly to Borrow's form. *Dáva* has also another signification, 'to beat, to strike, to knock,' extremely common among all the Gypsies, taken probably from the colloquial usages of the Greeks. *Kón déla o vutár?* 'who knocks at the door?' instead of *maréla,* 'strikes;' *diniómles ti pak,* 'I struck it on the wing;' *diniás e castésa amaré chuklés,* 'he struck with a stick (i. e. 'wood') our dog;' *o manúsh diniáspes e yek barésa,* 'the man was struck with a stone;' *kon diniás te romnia?* 'who struck thy wife?' *Dinó,* part., 'given, struck, flogged.'

To GO—*jáva.*—This verb I refer to the Sr. *gá,* 'to go, to move.' It is universal among the Gypsies, and used as the Greeks use their ὑπάγω, and the Turks *gitmék.* Aorist, *ghelióm,* 'I went,' pronounced at times *gherghióm: kárin kajés,* or *kamajés?* 'where wilt thou go?' *gelióm tó gáv,* 'I went to the village;' *geló avrí,* 'he went out;' *jéla po górkes,* 'he goes worse;' *jél' avéla,* 'he goes (and) comes,' Gr. ὑπάγει ἔρχεται, Turk. *ghidér ghelir,* meaning to go continually to and fro. At times *jáva* is used in a transitive sense: *gherghióm giv tó vasiáv,* 'I went (i. e. 'I carried') wheat to the mill;' *gelián ti pólin* (πόλιν)? *gelióm,* 'didst thou go to the city? I went;' *jáva te dikáv,* 'I go to see.'

---

* Armenian *dal.*—TR.

To go out—*niglaváva.*—A compound verb, formed of the Sr. root *kram*, 'to go, to walk, to step,' joined to *nir*, 'out.' Aor. *niglistinióm* and *niglistilióm*, 'I went out.' The Sr. *kram* is a favorite word with the Gypsies, and, joined to prepositions, it is frequently to be heard among them. *Niglistinióm avrí*, 'I went out,' Gr. ἐκβαίνω ἔξω; *kamaniglaváv*, 'I shall go out;' imp. *nigláv*, 'go thou out.'

GOD—*devél;*[*] Br., *devél ;* Bor., *debél, ostebel, umdebel.*—These terms have a striking similarity, and are derived from the Sr. *deva*, 'a god,' Lat. *deus*, Gr. θεός. In regard to the first syllables of Borrow's terms, *os-debel* and *um-debel*, I think they are Spanish articles. He says that the *um* of the third word is probably (the *óm*) the ineffable and mysterious name of the Hindu Godhead. Mr. Borrow remarks in his glossary that the word was pronounced by a christian Gypsy *o-del*, *o-dand*, and *o-devel*. The *o* in this case is the Greek article, which the Moslem Gypsies generally reject. In this, the Gypsies have imitated the Greeks, who never pronounce the name of God without the article, ὁ θεός. This term, among the Gypsies, when used as an invocation, admits the pronoun at the end of the word, contrary to the general usages of their language: *devlám*, 'my God;' more usually they say *madél, mo devél. Dúk e devlés*, 'love God :' *devlés* instead of *develés*, a clipped form of the acc. of nouns in *el. Achén devlésa*, 'rest ye with God,' a common form of salutation ; *ja devlésa*, 'go thou with God.' There is a peculiar use of this term which has always appeared to me very curious: *pelióm opré me devléste*, 'I fell upon my back' (lit. 'upon my God'); *per te devléste*, 'fall on thy back;' *per devlikanés*, 'fall on thy back.' *Devlikanó*, adj., 'godly,' Lat. *divinus: devlikanó manúsh*, 'a godly man;' *devlikaní romní*, 'a godly woman.'

GOOD—*lachó ;* Br., *lachó ;* Bor., *lachó, fendó.*—The origin of this word is quite unknown to me. It is extremely common among all the Gypsies, and well known in Roumelia and Wallachia. *Lachó divés*, 'good day, good morning;' *lachó manúsh*, 'a good man ;' *lachí romní*, 'a good woman ;' *laché romnia*, 'good women ;' *lachó mas*, 'good meat ;' *lachó grast*, 'good horse :' *lachés*, adv., 'well ;' *po lachés*, 'better.' The Moslem Gypsies make use of Turk. *dahi*, 'more,' to form the comparative degree (Section V): *dahi lachés*, 'better.'

GOLD—*somnakái, gálpea;* Bor., *sonacai.*—*Gálpea* I cannot explain. The Sr. *kanaka*, 'gold,' to which Borrow refers, appears to me an improbable, not to say an impossible, derivation. The derivation of *somnakái* may be sought in the Sr. word *sánasi*, 'gold.'

GOURD—*dudúm.*[†]—This term is applied to all the species of this plant, common in these countries, and very generally used by all classes of people. The only Sr. word with which I am able to compare it is *dudruma*, 'a green onion.' As to the rejection of the liquid *r*, we have occasion to note numerous examples of it in the course of the Vocabulary.

GRAIN, WHEAT—*giv, iv ;* Bor., *gi, guy, jil.*—These terms, and our σῖτος, 'wheat, corn,' I refer to the Sr. *sitá* and *sitya*, both having the signifi-

---

[*] "*O dél*, 'le dieu.'" Vaillant, p. 457. "*Dewél.*" Arndt, p. 174.
[†] Armenian *tutum*, 'squash, vegetable, marrow.'—TR.

cation of the above. *Sttá* also denotes 'the furrow made by the plow,' as well as 'the goddess of fruits;' *sttya*, 'grain,' and, in general, 'every kind of cereal product,' and 'rice.' The Gypsy forms are made by cutting off the final syllable *ta*, which the Greek has preserved. The Slavonic, which has preserved many archetypal Sanskrit words in their utmost purity, has *zito* and *zeta*, signifying 'all kinds of cereal products.' This term is very frequently pronounced *iv*.

GRAPE—*drak* ; Bor., *dracay, traquias, mollati.*—These are evidently derived from the Sr. *drákshá*, 'grape.' The third word of Borrow I refer to *mol*, 'wine.' Though this term, *molati*, is unknown to the Gypsies near Constantinople, Vaillant has marked it as common among those on the banks of the Danube, writing it *moleti*. The Sr. word is *madhutá*, 'sweetness,' not found, however, in the great dictionary of Wilson. *Draká laché isi*, 'the grapes are good;' *keréla drak*, 'it makes (i. e. 'produces') grape' ('grapes'); *i drak khénala*, 'the grape (grapes), they eat them;' *katár ti drak keréna mol*, 'from the grapes they make wine.'

GRASS—*char* ; Bor., *char.*—

To GRAZE—*charáva.*—The Sr. verb *char*, 'to go, to eat,' is applied also to the grazing of cattle. The Gypsy word *char* is applied principally to hay, and the verb itself to the feeding of animals, by hay or other vegetable substances; it corresponds to the Greek χορτάζειν, which at first was applied to feeding animals with hay (χόρτος), and by degrees came to mean also the taking of food by man; hence our χορταίνω, 'I am satiated.' Borrow defines *char* as 'grass, yerba.'

GREAT—*baró.*—This adjective seems to be related to the Sr. *bhara*, 'much, excessive.' *Mo kér isi baró*, 'my house is great;' *baró man-úsh*, 'a great man.'

GREEK—*balamó* ; Bor., *paillo.*—These two terms, which appear to be related, I am totally unable to explain. It is extremely difficult to give plausible explanations of all the terms which the Gypsies have given to the neighboring nations. Here in Turkey, with the exception of a few names, which I have noted in the Vocabulary as peculiar to them, they use the same terms as the Greeks and Turks. Pl. *balamé*, 'Greeks;' *balamanó gáv*, 'a Greek village;' *balamni*, 'a Greek woman;' pl. *balamnia; balamanés*, adv. form, i. q. Γραικιστί: *bala-manés janés?* 'dost thou know Greek?'

To GRIND—*pisháva.*—From the Sr. verbal root *pish*, 'to grind, to pound, to bruise, to powder,' Lat. *pinsere*. With the Gypsies this word is used merely for grinding corn in mills, or between two large circular stones. *Gív gherghióm to vasiáv, kamapishávles*, 'wheat I have carried to the mill; I shall grind it.'

GUARD—*arakáv* ; Bor., *aracate.*—

To GUARD—*arakáva*; Bor., *aracatear.*—Both these terms can with perfect propriety be referred to the Sr. root *raksh*, 'to guard, to protect.' The initial *a*, so constant in all these forms, may be explained as an inorganic prefix. It may be, however, that the *a* is the remnant of a preposition. The Gypsies have dropped the final sibilant of the Sr. root, a proceeding upon which we shall have occasion to remark in the next Section. This term has often the signification of 'waiting.' *Ta arakavél khandi divés*, 'to wait a few days'—*arakavél* is here in the middle voice; *arakiováva, arakavghióm*, 'I have guarded;' *arakáv*, 'wait thou.'

GYPSY—*róm*.—All the various denominations for this strange race common among foreigners are to the Gypsies themselves totally unknown. It is still more to be wondered at that foreigners should never have adopted the appellation by which they call themselves, and which is common to them wherever they live, whether in Asia or Europe. Before I proceed to the explanation of this term, I will give the various names by which they are known among foreigners in various parts of the world.* The German *zigeuner*, Russian *zigari, zigani*, Persian and Turkish *zengi* and *chingené*, and ἀτσίγγανοι of the Greeks,† seem to come from one and the same original, which Borrow makes to be "*zincali*, the black men of Zend or Ind:" a derivation of no value. Another class of words seem to belong to the term Αἰγύπτιος, 'Egyptian,' they having been formerly supposed to originate from Egypt. This word has been corrupted by us into γύπται, γύφται, a term which we now very frequently apply to dirty and ragged people. The Bulgarians call them *gupti*, the Spaniards *gitanos* (properly *giptanos*), and their haunts in the cities of Spain *gitaneria*. The English *gypsy* is from the same root. The Greeks also have another term, κατζίβελος, more in use in Roumelia. The French call them *Bohémiens*, probably from their having come to France from Bohemia, as they also have been called Germans and Flemish from their coming from those countries. All these terms are known to the Gypsies, but are never used by them; never will a Gypsy call a fellow-countryman ἀτσίγγανον or κατζίβελον; here, as in other parts of the world, they scrupulously avoid all the usual foreign terms. The derivation of the Turkish *chingené* and its correspondents in other languages is still a desideratum, and probably much time will pass before its etymology will be fully explained.

As to the term *rom*, it has a double signification—being used for man in general, and likewise for a man of their own race as distinct from one of other descent; *romni*, in like manner, means 'woman.' *Róm* is also used for 'husband,' and *romni* for 'wife.' *Romanó* (fem. *romani*) is the adjective form. This term, it appears to me, can be referred to the Sr. *ráma*, a name of the god Vishnu, and of three of his incarnations. By the Gypsies it may have been given to their tribe as worshipping in an especial manner this god. *Kárin isi to rom ?* 'where is thy husband?' *chori romni*, 'a poor woman;' *lachi romni*, 'a good woman;' *sávvore o róm*, 'all the men;' *romani chip*, 'the Gypsy language;' *kón diniás amaré romá*, 'who struck our men?' *i romni léskeri isi phurí*, 'his wife is old;' *me praléskoro romni*, 'my

---

* Vaillant (p. 4) gives sixty-eight various denominations of these people, which are mostly varieties of those which I note.

† Alessio da Somavera, who published his "Tesoro della Lingua Greca Volgare" in Paris, 1709, gives the following terms, which are still in use: ἀτζυγχάνα, 'zingana, zingara;' ἀτζυγχαναριὸν, 'bottega di zingano;' ἀτζυγχανίζω, ἀτζυγχανεύω, ἀτζυγχανώνω, 'zinganare;' ἀτζυγχάνιχα, 'da zingano;' ἀτζυγχανόπουλον, 'zingarino;' ἀτζίγχανος, 'zingano, zingaro.'

brother's wife;' *e yavréskoro romní,* 'the wife of the other;' *o dát romniákori,* 'the father of the wife' (i. e. 'father-in-law'); *dikáva e romés,* 'I see the man;' *romanó láv,* 'a Gypsy word:' pl. *romá* 'men;' *romnía* 'women:' *khorakhanó róm,* 'a Moslem Gypsy;' *balamanó róm,* 'a Greek Gypsy.'

The Gypsies themselves call *malkóch* a tribe of their own countrymen, who continually roam from village to village, particularly in Asia, working in brass and iron, and who, on the score of religion,
• are always of the profession of the village where for the time they work. Should a child be born whilst in a Greek village, it is baptized, and in the next circumcised. They travel to Jerusalem, and there become *hadjis,* 'pilgrims.' They are industrious, and are considered by their fellow-countrymen as wealthy. I have never been able to ascertain any other denominations peculiar to their tribes, though I have repeatedly questioned Gypsies from various parts of Turkey.

GYPSY TENT—*katúna.*—This term is applied by the Gypsies in general to the black and dirty tents used by their nomadic fellow-countrymen in their roaming expeditions. They bear no resemblance to the ordinary tents used by Mohammedans in their wars or military expeditions. These Gypsy tents are formed by a pole raised from the ground, of rather more than the height of a man, and supported at its two ends by other poles. Over this horizontal pole is thrown the covering, blacked by the soot and smoke of the fires, and under this frail covering squat the family, with a host of naked and loathsome offspring. So frail and light is this tent, that many of them are placed upon a single horse, and so transported from place to place. *Katúna* has no relation to any of the terms for 'tent' belonging to the countries in which the Gypsies live. I refer it to the Sr. *katin,* 'matted, screened,' from *kata,* 'a mat, a twist of straw or grass,' 'a screen of the same.' Pl. *katunés. Katunénghoro róm,* 'a Gypsy of the tents,' as distinguished from those living in villages and never roaming; *katunéngheri romní,* 'a Gypsy woman of the tents.'

H.

HABITATION—*bashipé;* Bor., *bestipén.*—

To INHABIT—*besháva;* Bor., *bestelar.*—These words are doubtless connected with the Sr. roots *vas,* 'to dwell, to inhabit,' and *viş,* 'to enter, to settle, to sit.' *Bistó som,* 'I am sitting.' *Bashipé* is from this verb, by the change of *i* into *a,* and the addition of the usual particle *pé,* which we have already explained. *Kamabeshés otiá but divés?* 'wilt thou stay there many days?' *beshéla bashé mánde,* 'he resides near me.' Borrow defines *bestipén* as meaning 'wealth, riches.' Let the reader remember that the Latin *possideo,* 'to possess,' and *possessio,* express the idea of 'sitting, residing upon' what is our own, and, in course of time, the property itself. So that we can with perfect propriety translate *bestipen* 'possession.'

HAIL—*kukudí.*—This is a Greek term, κουκκούδιον, diminutive form of κόκκος, 'a grain, any small body.' It is applied by the Greeks to small pustules on the human body, and to the kernels of fruits; Lat.

acinus. In this latter case, the word is written κούχκουτζον and κουκ-
κούιζιον. The Gypsies accent this word on the final syllable, differing much from the universal pronunciation of the Greeks themselves.*

HAIR—*bal ;* Br., *bala ;* Bor., *bal.*—The Sr. *bála,* to which I have referred in speaking of FOOT, is applied by the Gypsies exclusively to the
hair of the head. Compare the Lat. *pilus,* Fr. *poil.†   Pakó isí, ná
teréla bál,* 'he is bald, (and) has no hair :' plur. *balá,* rarely used; Mr.
Brown's word is in the plur. form.   •

HALF—*yekpásh ;* Bor., *pas, pasque, majara.*—My own term for 'half'
is a compound, having the well known Sr. numeral *eka,* 'one,' prefixed
to a word corresponding to Borrow's *pas.* The latter part may be
referred to the Sr. *paksha,* 'a side, a half.' The Gypsies of Turkey,
unlike those of Spain, constantly join it with *yék,* 'one,' like the
English 'one half, a half.' It is found in the terms *yekpasharátti,* ·
'midnight,' *yekpashdivés,* 'noon.' The third term given by Borrow
is related to Sr. *madhya,* 'middle.'

HAMMER—*sivrí ;* Br., *sivree ;* Bor., *casto.*—The etymology of this term
is unknown to me.   *Casto* appears to be from the Sr. *kash,* 'to strike,
to torment,' part. *kashta,* 'the striker, the instrument of striking.'

HAND —*vást ;‡* Br., *domuk ;* Bor., *chova, bas* (plur. *bastes*).—The Sr.
hasta signifies 'hand.' Borrow explains *chova* as derived from *char-
pata,* 'the palm with the fingers open.' This explanation is extremely improbable. *Bas, bastes,* are evidently related to the above Sr.
hasta, and not, as Borrow indicates, to the Persian *bazu,* as that is
from the Sr. *báhu,* 'arm.' Mr. Brown's term, *domuk,* is 'fist.'   *Té
shukiovél mó vást,* 'let my hand become dry' (i. e. 'paralyzed'); *bi-
vasténghoro,* 'without hands' (i. e. 'workmen').

HANDFUL—*burnék.*—This appears to be the Persian *burnuk,* or *burenk,*
'res acquisita, reposita, thesaurus' (Vullers, Lex. Pers.). It is a very
common term among the Gypsies.

HARE—*shoshói.*—Sr. *çaça,* 'a hare, a rabbit.' This is one of the many
words which the Gypsies have inherited directly from their Hindu
ancestors, and has no connection with the names generally given to
this animal by the other Indo-European nations.

HARLOT—*lubní, nublí ;* Br., *lobnee ;* Bor., *lumi, lumiaka.*—The Sr. adjective *lobhiní,* from *lobha,* 'appetite, lust, desire,' signifies 'the de-
sirer, the enamored,' and generally, 'one given to illicit passions.'

To HAVE—*teráva ;* Bor., *terelar.*—Following the analogy of formation
of Gypsy verbs, it is most natural to refer this word to the Sr. verbal
root *trí* or *tar,* 'to pass over, to cross,' also 'to prevail over, to
preserve.' Its signification, however, connects it rather with *dhri,
dhar,* 'to hold, to keep.' *O devél teréla lénke,* 'God has (i. e. 'care')
of them;' from the Greek ἔχει δ'αὐτούς, i. e. φροντίζει; *teráva te penáv*

---

* The Armenian word *gargood* is nearer this Gypsy sound of *kukudí,* and all
these forms probably have a Sanskrit origin. The Greek words introduced into the
Armenian are but slightly changed except in the gutturals.—TR.

† It is a singular coincidence that the Armenian word *hair* is, in orthography and
pronunciation, precisely the English word *hair.*—TR.

‡ "*Wast, wass,* hand." Arndt, p. 382.

túke, 'I have (i. e. 'I intend') to speak to 'thee;' *teráva dúi cha-vén,* 'I have two children;' *teráva yéb grást,* 'I have a horse.'

HEAD—*sheró, shoró ;** Bor., *joro.*—I refer these words to the Sr. *ṣiras,* 'head.' *Mé sheréste,* 'in my head' (i. e. 'mind'); *továva mó shoró,* 'I wash my head;' *gheraló shoró,* 'a scabby head.'

HEALTHY—*shastó ;* Br., *sastó.*—I refer this word to the vulgar Sr. *çasta,* 'fortunate, commendable, excellent,' part. of the verbal root *ças,* 'to bless, to wish good to, to confer a benediction.' It is very natural to pass from this meaning to that of health. To many Gypsies the term is unknown, and in its stead they use the Turkish *sagh,* 'healthy, strong, entire.' *Shastó mardsh,* 'a robust man;' *but shastó,* 'very healthy.' *Shasto* means also 'the right hand,' precisely as the Turks use the above *sagh* for 'the right side:' *katakó shastó teréla vés te rúk,* 'on the right it has a mountain and trees.'

To HEAR—*shunáva;* Bor., *junar.*—From the Sr. root *ṣru,* 'to hear,' present *ṣriṇomi,* which has been changed by the Gypsies into *shunáva,* by throwing out the semivowel *r* of the root. A similar example of the rejection of *r* we shall presently see in *shingh,* 'horn.' Aor. *shun-ghióm,* 'I have heard:' *shunghióm ti pólin (πόλιν) kamajés,* 'I have heard that thou wilt go to the city;' *té ná shunél, só té penén léske,* 'and not to hear what they may say to him;' *na shunél,* 'he does not hear' (i. e. 'he is deaf').

HEART—*oghi, onghi.*—For want of a better derivation, I am inclined to refer this Gypsy term to the Sr. *anga,* 'a limb, member.' *Kaméla m' oghi te lav,* 'my heart desires to take;' *dikáva ká terésa oghi te khás,* 'I see that thou hast heart (i. e. 'appetite') to eat;' *oghéske,* 'for the soul,' i. e. 'alms,' also 'religious austerities for the salvation of the soul.'

HEAT—*tattipé.*—Formed from the adjective *tattó,* 'warm,' Sr. *tapta,* by the addition of the usual particle *pe.* In the place of this word I have frequently heard *tabioipé,* from the same Sr. root *tap,* 'to heat.'

HEAVY—*baró.*—We shall have occasion to notice a similar word, in speaking of STONE. The Sr. *bhára,* 'burden, weight' (Gr. βάρος), has in this term been changed into an adjective by the Gypsies.

HEEL—*kfúr, khúr.*—This belongs to the Sr. *khura,* 'a hoof, a horse's hoof, the foot of a bedstead;' with no other Sr. term can it be so reasonably identified. The pronunciation is very peculiar, nor do the above consonants accurately indicate it.

HEN—*kaïni, kagni, kaïná ;* Br., *kahnee ;* Bor., *cani.*—I derive this term from the Sr. *hansa,* 'goose,' fem. *hansi,* whence our χήν, cutting off the final *s,* Eng. *goose,* Lat. *anser,* cutting off the initial consonant, Germ. *gans* and *hahn,* Slav. *gus'* and *gonsi.* Another Gypsy term, *gustó,* 'goose,' referred to by Borrow, confirms this derivation. A Gypsy woman told me that *kaïná* means 'hen,' and *papina,* 'goose.' But I suspect that the latter is our common *πάπια,* 'a duck.'†

HERE—*até, avatiá.*—The relation of these terms to the Sr. is not perfectly clear. *Até* may be related to *atra,* 'in this place, here,' which,

---

* " *Scheró, tscheró, cheru,* 'kopf.' " Arndt, p. 382.
† Geese in Roumelia are an article of extensive traffic with the Gypsies.

like many other Sr. words, in passing into the Gypsy idiom, has dropped its *r* (Section IV). The second term, also a common one, may have been formed in a manner similar to *divés, avdivés ;* it is more emphatic. Zend. *avadha,* 'here,' from the Sr. *ava,* is probably intimately related to *avatiá. Até isí tó dát?* 'is thy father here?' *na isómas até,* 'I was not here.' *Attár,* 'from here,' ἐδῶθεν, is a corruption of *atiatár,* or *atetár :—tár* is the usual particle forming the ablative cases of Gypsy nouns, the Gr. θεν; see Grammar, Section V.

To HOLD—*astaráva.*—This verb I refer to the Sr. root *stri,* 'to spread, to strew.' The initial *a* of the Gypsy verb is an addition often observed in Gypsy words, and common also to the Turks, who can never pronounce a word beginning with *st* without adding a vowel.* *Astardó,* 'held, seized;' *astardiló,* 'he was taken;' *nastí astarghiómles,* 'I could not seize him;' *kána astarghiánles?* 'where didst thou take it?'

HOLE—*kháv.*—We have already explained the verb *khatáia,* 'to dig.' From the same Sr. root *khan* comes *khani,* 'a mine;' it is applied however to whatever is dug, or excavated. *Kháv* has been formed by the change of the final *n* into *v.*

HONEY—*avghín.*—This appears to be a Persian word, *abgin,* 'a bee,' and *abgin khané,* 'apiarium, alveare' (Vullers, Lex. Pers.). It is singular that the Gypsies should have abandoned the ordinary Sr. *madhu,* 'honey,' and adopted this new and foreign term.

HORN—*shingh ;* Bor., *singe, sungalo.*—Comp. the Sr. *çringa,* 'a horn.' The Gypsies have rejected the liquid *r* in many syllables containing it. The pronunciation of this liquid, in many cases, resembles that of the French at Paris, where the *r* is often a dead letter to a foreign ear, and at times appears like a liquid *l.* Borrow defines *sungalo* 'a he-goat,' evidently analogous to the Sr. *çringina,* 'a ram,' literally 'horned.'

HORSE—*grást ;†* Br., *gras ;* Bor., *gras, gra.*—

MARE—*grastní ;* Br., *grasnee ;* Bor., *grani.*—These terms I derive from the Sr. verbal root *gras,* 'to eat, to feed.' This conjecture of mine may be confirmed by an example from the Greek—φορβάς, 'mare, cow,' from φέρβω, 'to nourish, to feed, to graze.' For the formation of the fem. *grastní* by the suffix *ni,* see Section V. *Lachó grást,* 'a good horse;' *aklé grastésa allián? oklésa,* 'with that horse didst thou come? with that (horse)'; *lachó grást isí,* 'it is a good horse;' *teréla deshé grastén,* 'he has (i. e. 'owns') ten horses.' *Grastéskoro,* 'of the horse,' or 'horseman,' also *grastanó,* ἱππικὸς, *grái* among the Wallachian Gypsies; *grastoró,* 'a small horse.' The reader, in perusing my remarks on the formation of feminine nouns (Section V), will be convinced of the correctness of writing this word with a final *t,* which has been omitted in both Mr. Brown's and Mr. Borrow's terms.

HOUSE—*ker ;‡* Br., *kerr ;* Bor., *quer.*—This term may be related to the Sr. *agára* or *ágára,* 'house, residence.' The change of *gh* to *k* is confirmed by *agosto,* changed to *querosto,* 'the month of August' (Bor.).

---

* See the definition of number six.
† " *Grei,* 'cheval.'" Vaillant, p. 363.
‡ " *Ker,* 'maison.'" Vaillant, p. 363.

Keráva nevó kér, 'I am making a new house;' *ich isómas mé praléskoro keréste*, 'yesterday I was in my brother's house;' *tó tát tó kér isi ?* 'is thy father in the house ?' *baró kér*, 'a large house;' *tapiló o kér*, 'the house was burnt;' *mó kér isi baró*, 'my house is large;' *mokavdó kér*, 'painted house;' *kaléskoro isi o ker ?* 'whose is the house ?' *mé praléskoro kér*, 'the house of my brother;' *isóm tó kér*, 'I am in the house,' or *keréste*, 'in the house.'

How MANY—*kebór.*—*Kebór chavén terésa ?* 'how many children hast thou ?'

How MUCH—*keti.*—Compare Sr. *kati*, 'how many, how much,' a word related to *ka*, the interrogative pronoun. This term has the same uses and significations as the Sr. term. *Keti divés terésa trésca ?* 'how many days hast thou the intermittent fever ?' *keti isánas sávvore ?* 'how many were you all ?' *keti bérsh kerghián tó rashái ?* 'how many years didst thou make with the teacher' (i. e. 'pass in school') ? *keti chavén teréla ?* 'how many children has he' (or 'she') ? *keti bershénghoro isi*, 'how old is he' (i. e. 'of how many years') ? *keti lové dinián ?* 'how much money didst thou give ?' This word is often used in the quantitative case; as *keténghe liliánles ?* 'for how much didst thou take (i. e. 'buy') it ?' *bishénghe*, 'for twenty.'

To be HUNGRY—*bokáliováva.*—Compare the Sr. verb *bhuj*, 'to eat, to enjoy,' *bubhukshu*, 'wishing to eat, hungry.' *Bokaló*, 'hungry:' *bokaló isóm*, 'I am hungry.' The verb is formed from this adjective and the verb *aváva*, and is in constant use in this form. *Te bokaliovéla arakéla manró*, 'and should he be hungry, he finds bread.'

I.

To INCREASE—*bariováva.*—A verb in the mid. voice, from *baró*, 'great,' and *aváva*. *Só keréna te chavén ? bariovávalen*, 'how are thy children ? I am increasing them' (i. e. 'I am rearing them'); *barióna o rúk*, 'the trees grow' (i. e. 'increase').

INFANT, YOUNG—*tiknó.*—This term is used often, like *chavó*, 'a child,' and *rakl*ó, 'a young one.' *Keti tiknén teréla ?* 'how many children has he' (or 'she') ? *tá e tikné isi melalé*, 'and the children are dirty :' here the word is used without reference to a mother or a father. *Penghiás yek tiknés*, 'she begat a young one;' in the same manner a Greek may say ἐγέννησε ἕνα μικρὸν. *Muló o yek tiknó*, 'the one child died;' *achilé o dúi*, 'the two remained.' Fem. *tikni : tiknia terésa ?* 'hast thou female children ?'

To INHABIT—See HABITATION.

INVALID—*naisváli ;* Br., *nashvalli ;* Bor., *merdo.*—The first two terms are composed of the negative *na* and *vali*, the meaning of which we shall examine. The *s* is euphonic. The Sr. *bala* means 'power, strength, an army ;' compare also the Slav. *velii*, and *velikie*, 'strong, powerful.' ♦The etymology of this term is elucidated by the Lat. *debilis*, 'invalid,' formed by the neg. *de* and the word *bala*, 'strength.' Borrow's word, *merdo*, is from the Sr. part. *mṛita*, 'dead, mortal :' among the Gypsies, as with us in the term μαραινόμενος, it means 'emaciated, wasting.' Our ἄῤῥωστος and ἀσθενὴς, and the Slav. *nemozénie*, from the neg. *ne* and *mogú*, 'to be strong,' have the same formation with the Gypsy *naisváli.* Mr. Brown's term should be written with one *l.* To many Gypsies this term is totally unknown, and in its stead they use *namporemé,* a Greek word, composed of the neg. *na* and *ἐμπορῶ,* 'I can, I am able.' *Nampórema,* 'sickness' (δὲν ἐμπορῶ, 'I am unwell'). They have adopted the word from the Greeks, using *ἀνεμπορίαν,* instead of *ἀσθένεια.* Such incongruous combinations of terms from different languages, often remarked even in cultivated European languages, are entirely excusable among the ignorant Gypsies. *Me isómas namporemé,* 'I was sick.'

IRON—*shastír, shastrí ;* Br., *sastir ;* Bor., *sas.*—The Sr. *çastra* signifies 'a weapon made of iron,' and 'iron' itself; it is from the root *ças,* 'to wound, to kill.' *Keréla shastír,* 'he makes (i. e. 'he works') iron'; *shastiréskoro,* 'a worker in iron ;' *to shastír,* 'in iron' (i. e. 'in prison').

ITCH—*ghér ;* Bor., *guel.*—

ITCHY—*gheraló.*—The Sr. noun *gara* is 'poisonous drink, a poison, sickness, disease ;' *garala,* from the same root, is 'venom' in general, and appears to have given origin to *gheraló.* In the word given by Borrow, *guel,* we observe the transmutation of the liquid *r* into *l.* That this general name should have been applied by the Gypsies to a special disease, naturally affords a presumption that the disease was a common one among them, or among the people with whom they had intercourse. Such is the case with the Gypsies, and with the common people of the countries where they have passed, or among whom they have settled. Vermin, scabby heads, loathsome rashes, and the itch, are the usual companions of poverty, filth, and ignorance. It is no wonder, then, that they should have applied the term 'poison' to this particular disease. It is well to remark that the common people of the East, like other people of similar education elsewhere, attribute most of their diseases to internal poisoning, remnants of former medical theories. Borrow defines *garipé,* another similar word, as meaning 'scab.' In this sense *gheraló* is used by some Gypsies, as *mo shoró gheraló,* 'my scabby head.' This is properly a Greek expression—ψώρα, itch; ψωριασμένος, 'one affected with loathsome cutaneous eruptions.' *Ghér,* pronounced *jél,* I have heard applied to the small pox by some Gypsies. It is from the same base as *ghér.*

J.

JEW—*jut.*—This is from the Turks, who call these people *jehud* and *chifut,* by way of contempt. *Yahudí* is also another term in use among the Turks, corresponding to the Greek Ἰουδαῖος. The Greeks now always call them Ἑβραῖοι (pron. Ὀβραῖοι). Pl. *jutné,* 'Jews ;' *jutní,* 'a Jewish woman ;' *jutanó,* 'Jewish ;' *jutoró,* , a young Jew ;' *jutnióri,* 'a young Jewish girl ;' *brakerésa jutanés ?* 'dost thou speak the Jewish language ?'

K.

To KICK—*lahtdáva.*—The Gr. λακτίζω can hardly have given origin to this Gypsy verb, as it has become altogether obsolete among the people, and in its stead we use κλωτζῶ, 'I kick.' Only the educated of our nation make use of λακτίζω. The Persian has *leked zeden,* 'to kick, *calcitrare,*' to which this Gypsy verb can be referred : many Gypsy words are intimately related to the present Persian. I know of no Sr. word to which the Persian can be referred. The verb is a compound one : *dáva,* ' I give,' serves to form also some other verbs.

KING—*tahkár, taakár ;* * Bor., *crallis.*—My word resembles the Pers. *khatkiar,* 'king, ruler,' with transposition of the initial consonants, or more probably with rejection of the initial *kh,* which is pronounced so gently by the Gypsies as often not to be heard at all. Even in pronouncing *tahkár,* the *h* is so gently aspirated as to be virtually omitted, and in fact many Gypsies pronounce the word as I have written it in the second form. The Sr. *chakravat,* 'an emperor,' may bear relation to this term, as perhaps also to the Persian. *Crallis* is the Slav. *kral,* 'a king,' so common among the nations that speak the Slavonic dialects. The absence of a well defined root in all these definitions evidently goes to prove that the Gypsies, in leaving their country, and coming among people under regular regal power, had no appropriate word to express the idea of a king, as he appeared to them in their gradual peregrinations westward. Their word *rájan* we shall meet in ' nobleman.' *Takaréskoro,* ' of the king;' *takarní,* ' queen.'

KISS—*chumí, chám ;* Bor., *chupendi.*—

To KISS—*chumidáva.*—We have here a word easily referable to the Sr. root *chumb,* ' to kiss.' The final *b* has been dropped by the Gypsies, precisely as the Greeks pronounce the Ital. *ampula, ampola,* ' a small flask,' ἄμουλα. *Lióm tutár yek cham,* ' I have taken from thee a kiss' (i. e. ' I have kissed thee'). *Chumidáva* is compounded of *chum* and the verb *dáva,* ' to give.'

KNEE—*kóch.*—Gr. κότζιον and κότζι, generally applied to warts, often to small bones, and at times to bones in general. The Greeks say πονοῦν τὰ κότζιά μου, ' my knees pain me.' By the Gypsies the term has been applied exclusively to the knees. Plur. *kochá,* 'knees.' It is a term well known to all Gypsies, and probably comes from the Slav. *kost',* ' bone.' *Me kochá dukénaman,* ' my knees pain me.'

KNIFE—*churí ;* Bor., *chuló, chori.*—From the Sr. root *chhur,* ' to eat, scindere, secare.' Borrow's first term is formed by a commutation of the liquids, so common in all languages. *Barí churí,* ' a large knife.'

L.

LAME—*pankó, pangó.*—

To LAME—*pangheráva.*—We find in the Sanskrit *pangu,* 'lame, crippled, one who has lost his legs.' *Pangheráva,* ' to lame, to make one lame,' is a compound verb, formed from *pangó* and the verb *keráva,* ' to make.' *K* before *n* is constantly changed to *gh*; the form is properly *pan-keráva.* Of *pangó* united to the verb *aváva* is formed another verb, *panghiováva,* in the middle form, often heard among the Gypsies : ' I have become lame;' χωλαίνομαι. *Panklióm mo pindó,* ' I have lamed my foot.'

---

* This word has a close resemblance to the Armenian word for 'king,' *takavór,* derived from *tak,* ' crown.'—TR.

To LAUGH—*asáva.*—Compare Sr. *has*, 'to laugh.' I shall have occasion to show in the following Section that the Gypsies commute the Sr. gutturals for soft aspirates, and reject these latter in many words. In hearing them pronounce such aspirated words, one doubts whether the word should be written with or without an aspirate. *So asésa?* 'why dost thou laugh?'

LEAF—*patrín;* Bor., *paroji.*—The Sr. *patra* signifies 'a leaf,' and, as in our language, 'any thing light, like a leaf:' it means also 'wing.' From this are probably derived Slav. *peró*, 'wing,' Germ. *feder*, Eng. *feather.** Borrow's form is much changed from the original, and indicates what I have said above, that the Gypsies of Turkey have preserved their language in greater purity than their fellow-tribes in the West. This term is used at times for 'branch.'

To LEARN—*shikliováva.*—A verb in the middle voice, compounded of *shikló,* 'instructed,' and *aváva.* We have the Sr. root *çiksh,* 'to learn, to acquire knowledge;' *çikshá,* 'learning, or the acquisition of knowledge.' I have never heard the verb excepting in this middle form. Like μανθάνω, it is at times neuter, and at times transitive : 'I myself learn, I study,' and 'I make others learn, I instruct.' *Kamáva ta shikliováv katár allé,* 'I wish to learn whence came;' *akaná kaména te shiklión* (for *shikliovéna*), 'now they wish to learn;' *tá ná isánas oté ta shikliovés,* 'and thou wast not there to learn;' *kárin shiklіló* (3rd p. aor.), 'where did he learn' (i. e. 'study')?

LEATHER—*morti;* Bor., *morchas.*†—The Sr. *múrti*, from which originate these two terms, is defined to mean 'matter, substance, solidity, any definite shape or image.' Here, by the Gypsies, the word is often applied to sheepskins before undergoing the operation of tanning, προβέα, προβιά. *Mortiákoro,* 'a worker in leather.'

LIE—*khohaimpé;* Bor., *jojana.*—Connected with the Sr. *kuhaka,* 'deceiver, hypocrite,' *kuhaná,* 'hypocrisy.' *Khohavnó,* 'a liar, one who deceives,' pronounced often *khohanó.* I have no doubt that *khohaimpé* is formed from *khohanó, khohanipé* having been corrupted into *khohaimpé;* since all the abstract nouns ending in *pe* are formed from adjectives or participles. From this adj. *khohavnó* is formed *khohávniováva,* 'to be cheated, to be deceived.' *Chachipanés o manúsh kayék far nána khohávniovél,* 'in truth man would never be deceived.'

LIGHT—*lokó.*—From the Sr. *laghu,* 'light;' Gr. ἐλαχὺς.

LINEN—*yísmata.*—Used always in the plural form. It designates that part of dress which can be subjected to washing; Eng. *linen,* It. *biancheria,* Gr. ἀσπρόρουχα, 'white garments.' *Tovdé yísmata,* 'washed clothes.'

LIP—*vúst;* Br., *ushta.*—This is the Sr. *oshṭha,* 'lip.' We shall explain the term *múi,* 'mouth,' in its proper place. Respecting the addition of *v* at the beginning of words, the reader will see in Section IV.

LITTLE—*khandi.*—The Sanskrit word *khaṇḍa* signifies 'a part, a portion, a fragment.' That the Gypsy term means properly 'a portion

---

* Armenian *pedúr.*—TR.   † Armenian *mórte.*—TR.

or part,' there is no doubt, and the transmutation of the word 'portion, fragment' into an adverb, 'little,' is corroborated by both the
Greek and Turkish languages. Κόμμα, from κόπτω, and its diminutive κομμάτιον, are universally used by the Greeks of the present day
in the sense of 'little;' as δός με κομμάτιον, 'give me a little.' The
Turks say *bir parchá su ver,* 'give me a little water' (lit. 'give me a
piece of water'). *Khandisi,* often to be heard, is *khandi-isi,* 'a little
(it) is,' used for 'it is not enough.' *Khandi* is used also as an adjective, Lat. *parvus,* Gr. ὀλίγος. *Déman khandi pani,* 'give me a little
water;' *chikhandi,* 'in a little while,' Gr. ἐντὸς ὀλίγου (καιροῦ understood); *khandi varó,* 'a little flour;' *khandi piásales, khandi khásales,
o yavér kerásales kerál,* 'a little we drink, a little we eat, (and) the
rest we make (into) cheese;' *khandi achiló te meráv,* 'I came near
dying' (i. e. 'little was wanting'); *khandi divés,* 'few days.'

To LIVE—*jivává.*—This is undoubtedly related to the Sr. root *jtv,* 'to
live,' which is to be traced in some of the Indo-European languages,
and particularly in the Slavonic (*zývu,* 'I live'), which has preserved
so many of the Sr. roots in their utmost purity. It is used also in
the sense of 'inhabit,' similar to the usage of the word in other languages: ἔζησα ἐν Εὑρώπη, 'I lived in Europe, j'ai vécu en Europe.'

To LOSE—*nashavává;* Bor., *najabar.*—There seems to be an intimate
connection between this Gypsy verb and *nasháva,* 'to depart.' Both
have their origin from the Sr. root *naç,* 'to destroy, to annihilate, to
lose.' Borrow's *najipen,* 'loss, perdition,' is from the same.

LOUSE—*juv.*—We have seen, in speaking of BARLEY, the transmutation
of the Sr. *y* into *j* : *yava,* Gypsy *jov,* 'barley.' We might with perfect reason seek the origin of this term in a Sr. word having a similar
initial consonant, viz. *yůka,* 'a louse.' Plur. *juvá,* 'lice.'

M.

To MAKE—*kerává;* Bor., *querar, querelar.*—This is the well known Sr.
root *kṛi* or *kar,* 'to make, to do,' which can easily be traced through
the Persian, Greek, Latin, and other cognate European languages:
comp. Pers. *kerden* (Sr. inf. *kartum*), 'to make, to do;' Gr. κραίνω, whose
ancient signification was 'to do, to accomplish;' Lat. *creo,* 'to create.'
The Gypsies of Spain, like those here in Turkey, have preserved the
pure sound of the initial radical consonant. Some Gypsies here pronounce the word as though written *gherává.* The signification which
I have given above is the most general, both in the Danubian provinces and in Turkey. The word has, however, another, contracted
from the colloquial usages of the Turks, who employ their verb *yap-
mak,* 'to make, to do,' in the sense also of 'building:' *yapý yapárym,*
'I am building.' The Greeks also, in imitation of the Turks, frequently join to their verb κάμνω, 'I do,' the Turkish *yapý,* saying
ιαπί κάμνω, 'I am making a building.' Though the Sr. verb has an
extraordinary latitude of meaning, and though it may reasonably be
applied to any verb expressive of action, still I am inclined to think
that many of its definitions among the Gypsies of Turkey should be
elucidated and explained by the colloquial usages of the Greeks and
Turks, with whom they are constantly associated. Gypsies in Turkey

never hear any other language, Turkish or Greek, but the most vulgar and corrupted, for they are debarred from polite society, which they themselves also avoid. *Keráva nevó kér,* 'I am making a new house;' *lachés kamakerén,* 'they will do well,' pronounced by others *kamkerén,* or *kakerén* (see Section V); *so keréna te chavé?* 'what are doing thy children' (i. e. 'how are thy children')? *só te keráv?* 'what can I do?' *τι νὰ κάμω; so kerghián?* 'what hadst thou done?' *ker túya yavréske,* 'do thou also to others;' *tu kerghiánles?* 'didst thou do it?' *so kerés?* 'how art thou?' a usual salutation: Gr. *τι κάμνεις?*

MAN—*manúsh ;** Br., *manush ;* Bor., *manu, manus, maru, marupé.*— From the Sr. *manusha* and *manushya,* 'man, a human being,' *manushi,* 'woman, the companion of man:' among the Gypsies, *romni* is now in general use in the latter sense. It comes from the root *man,* 'to think, reason, examine.' In Borrow's third form the *n* is changed to *r;* in his fourth appears the terminal *pe,* elsewhere *pen: marupe,* 'mankind,' *ἀνθρωπότης. Amaré manushénghere,* 'of our men;' *shastó manúsh,* 'a robust man;' *isámas peninda manúsh,* 'we were fifty men;' *sarré o manúsh,* 'all the men,' and 'all men;' *manushénghe,* 'to the men.'

MARE.—See HORSE.

MARKET-PLACE—*fóros ;* Bor., *foros, foro.*—This term reminds us of the Latin *forum,* which signified anciently 'the market-place,' and was afterwards given to certain cities, as the Turks call many towns from the market fairs held there. Among us the term *φόρος,* 'a duty, impost,' comes from the Sr. *bhára,* 'a weight, burden.' Borrow defines his two words 'city,' Sp. *ciudad.* The Sr. *pura* and *puri* both mean 'city,' preserved in the names of many Indian cities, as Hastinapoor, Singapoor, etc. By a customary change of *p* to *f* comes the present Gypsy term, which the Gypsies here sometimes use for 'city,' but more often for 'market-place.'

MARRIAGE—*biáv, piáv.*—This is of Sanskrit origin, though it has a Persian form, like some other words, as *deryáv,* 'sea,' *vasiáv,* 'mill.' The Sr. root *vah,* 'to carry, to bear' (L. *veho,* Gr. *ὀχέω*), means also 'to marry, *ducere uxorem.*' When joined with the preposition *vi* it has constantly the signification of 'marrying,' as in *viváha,* 'marriage,' *viváhita,* 'married.' Very probably these words have given origin to *biáv.* It is a common term, and, united to *keráva,* 'to make,' it means 'to marry, to celebrate a marriage.' *Kamakerés biáv?* 'wilt thou make marriage' (i. e. 'art thou to be married')? *te praléskoro biavesti,* 'at the marriage of thy brother;' *tumaró biáv isi?* 'is it thy marriage;' *kána kamovél o biáv?* 'when will the marriage be?'

MEAT—*mas ;* Bor., *maas, mang.*—The origin of these terms is clear. I refer them to *ámisha,* 'meat, food, anything eaten with bread;' compare Slav. *mast,* signifying 'fat,' which the Bulgarians have changed to *méso,* understanding by it 'meat;' Goth. *mats,* Eng. *meat,†* Albanian *mishe, misht. Κρέας* and Lat. *caro* are connected with another Sr. word, *kravya,* denoting for the most part 'the flesh of

---

* *"Manusch, rom, gadshe,* 'mensch.'" Arndt, p. 375.
† Armenian *mis.*—TR.

wild animals.' Besides the above *ámisha*, there is another term, *mánsa*, 'flesh, food,' from which originates Lat. *mensa*, signifying sometimes 'the table,' and sometimes 'the food upon the table.' To this I refer the Eng. *mess, mess-mate. So keréna? mas biknéna,* 'what are they doing? they sell meat;' *maséskoro,* 'a butcher;' *londé masá,* 'salted meat;' *avdivés mas khása,* 'to-day we eat meat' (not a day of fasting).

MILK—*tut, sut;* Br., *sout;* Bor., *chuti.*—This word Mr. Brown designates as Turkish *sud,* 'milk.' But the comparison of the three terms gives a better explanation of their etymology. In the definition of BREAST, we have spoken of the Sr. root *chush,* 'to suck.' Derived from that root, the present terms signify properly 'what is sucked from the breasts.' I may add that there is no known Turkish word in the vocabulary of Borrow. *Gudló tut,* 'sweet milk; *sudró tut,* 'cold milk.'

MILL—*vasiáv.*—A Persian word, which, like many others derived from that language, has been preserved almost unaltered: *asya,* 'a mill-stone,' anciently, and more properly, *asyab,* or *asyav,* to which the Gypsies have only added an initial *v.* All the Persian dictionaries of an older date write the word *asyab,* and such was probably the pronunciation of the Persians when the Gypsies passed through their country. *Ghiv gherghióm to vasiáv,* 'I have carried grain to the mill.'

MISERABLE—*chungaló.*—This adjective, applied to persons in distress as an expression of commiseration, corresponds to the Turk. *zavál* and the Gr. κακόμοιρος. It is extremely common among the Gypsies. Fem. *chungali.* Though apparently of Hindu origin, I have not been able to refer it to any Sr. word. *Chungali rakli,* 'the miserable daughter.'

MONEY—*lové.*—This term is mostly used by the Gypsies in the plural number: *lové,* 'money' in general. They make use, like the natives, of *pará,* and *ghrush,* the Turk. piastre. *Me lové liné,* 'my money they have taken;' *keti lovén dinián?* 'how much money hadst thou given?' *linián te lovén?* 'hadst thou taken thy money?' *keti lovén teréla?* 'how much money has he?' or, 'how much is he worth?'

MONTH—*chon, masék;* Bor., *chono.*—We shall speak of *chon* in speaking of MOON. The Gypsies, like many other nations, use the same word for 'moon' and 'month.' Compare Gr. μήνη, anc. 'the moon, the half moon;' μήν, 'month;' Lat. *mensis. Chon* is used by the Moslem Gypsies, imitating their coreligionists the Turks, who say *ay,* 'moon, month.' *Masék,* the second term, is from the Sr. *másika,* 'monthly, relating or belonging to a month;' it is in very common use among the Christian Gypsies. Compare Slav. *miesiach,* 'a month.' In this word appears plainly the tendency of the Gypsies to make use of adjective forms, instead of substantive. Similar examples we see in MOUSE, WELL, etc. *Keti masekéngoro isi?* 'of how many months is she' (i. e. 'pregnant')? *yek masekéstar nápalal,* 'after a month.'

8

Moon—*chon;** Br., *chon;* Bor., *chimutra, astra.*—The derivation of these words is a little obscure, as the difference between the two first and Borrow's is considerable. Mine and Mr. Brown's are derived from the Sr. *chandra,* 'moon.' The second word of Borrow, *astra,* is a name given to the moon precisely as we often call the moon ἄστρον τῆς νυκτὸς, 'star of night.'

Mother—*dái, dé;* Br., *dy;* Bor., *day, chinday.*—*Dy,* pronounced *dái,* is a child's pet term for its mother, as Borrow testifies in his vocabulary, under the word *day,* remarking that this word, sometimes applied by children to their mother, signifies 'nurse.' *Dais* is used by the Christian inhabitants of these countries, sometimes for 'father,' mostly however for 'uncle' and 'benefactor.' The derivation of this word is very obscure, and that it has any relation to the common Sr. *mâṭri,* 'mother,' does not appear to me probable. It is pronounced *dái* and *tái. Mi dái,* 'my mother;' *me daiákori lové,* 'my mother's money;' *ti tái isí keréste,* 'thy mother is in the house.'

Mother-in-law—See Father-in-law.

To mount—*ukliáva.*—This verb may be referred to the Sr. root *kram,* 'to go, to walk, to step,' with the preposition *ut,* 'up.' *Oklistó,* 'mounted:' this term is applied to a young man who has been presented to his future bride, and has gone to her house. The Greeks have the same term, ἀνεβασμένος, 'gone up,' i. e., to the house of the bride.

Mouse—*mishákos, mushó.*—Derived evidently from the Sr. *músha, múshaka, múshikâ,* 'mouse, rat,' from the root *mûsh,* 'to steal.' We find this word in many languages: Gr. μῦς, μυῖσκος; Lat. *mus, muris;* Slav. *mish';* Germ. *maus;* Eng. *mouse.†* *Ker mushó,* 'house-rat:' here the term approaches nearer to the Sr. *músha.*

Mouth—*múi.*—Compare the Sr. *mukha,* 'mouth.' The final guttural *kh* has been dropped, as in *nái,* 'nail,' from *nakha.* From this term *múi,* by the addition of *al,* is formed the adverb *muyál* or *muiyál,* 'on the face, in front, from the front.' *Pelióm muyál,* 'I fell on the face.'

Much—*but;‡* Br., *bout;* Bor., *bus, baribu.*—This may possibly be referred to the Sr. *puru,* 'much.' The common and most usual words in a language are frequently most metamorphosed. *But* is used as an adjective and an adverb. *But manushé,* 'many men;' *but chavé,* 'many children;' *but romnía,* 'many women;' *but lové,* 'much money;' *but dukélaman,* 'it pains me much;' *but nashéla,* 'it goes well;' *but lachés,* 'very well;' *but vuchés,* 'very high.' At times it is heard as *butló,* 'much.'

Mucus of the nose—*lim.*—This word is extremely common among the Gypsies. I refer it to the Sr. *lip,* 'to anoint, to smear,' whence *limpa,* 'smearing, anointing.'

Mud—*chik, chiká;* Bor., *chique.*—The only Sr. word to which I am able to refer this term is *chikila,* 'mud, mire,' from the root *chik,* 'to obstruct.' Borrow defines *chique* as 'earth, ground,' a natural transi-

---

* " *O-tchanda,* 'la lune.'" Vaillant, p. 457. " *Tschon, schon, tschemut, mrascha,* 'mond.'" Arndt, p. 366.
† Armenian *moog.*—Tr. ‡ " *But,* 'longtemps.'" Vaillant, p. 363.

tion of meaning of the word. *Isi ko drom but chiká,* ' there is in the road much mud.'

TO MURDER—*murdaráva.*—We have often had occasion to refer to the Sr. root *mṛi,* ' to die,' whence comes this transitive, precisely as the Germ. *morden,* Eng. *murder,* Fr. *meurtre.* *Murdaráva tut,* ' I murder thee,' a common expression in the mouth of a person intending to strike another ; *murdarghiómles,* ' I have murdered him ;' aor. *nápalal murdarghiáles,* ' afterwards he murdered him.' This verb is used also of the killing of animals. When applied to fire, it signifies ' to quench :' *murdaráva i yak,* ' I quench the fire ;' *murdár i yák,* ' quench the fire.'

MUSKET—*pudinó ;* Bor., *púsca.*—Both these terms are Slavonic, from the verb *pushtáyu,* ' to send, to throw out, *emittere.*' I have spoken to many Gypsies about the word *púsca,* which they constantly avoid, as foreign to their idiom. *Púsca* is known only to the Bulgarians, who use it in common with the Russians. *Mo pudinó isi inglís,* ' my musket (gun) is English.'

N.

NAIL, FINGER-NAIL—*nái ;* Bor., *ungla.*—Borrow's word is from the Latin *ungula,*[*] ' hoof,' from the common *unguis,* ' nail.' The Spanish is *uña.* My own term is from the Sr. *nakha,* ' nail.' Borrow has in his vocabulary another term, *turra,* ' nail,' unknown to me.

NAKED—*nangó.*—This is easily referable to the Sr. *nagna,* ' naked.'

NAME—*nav ;*[†] Bor., *nao.*—There is hardly an Indo-European word that is so general in its occurrence. Compare Zend *náman,*[‡] Pers. *nam,* Lat. *nomen,* Gr. ὄνομα, Goth. *namu,* Slav. *nma,* Bulg. *ime.* The final syllable of *náman* has been changed into a simple *v* by the Gypsies of Turkey, whilst those of Spain have changed the whole syllable into *o.* This change of *m* into *v* we shall have occasion to observe in other words. *É chavéskoro nav,* ' the child's name ;' *e pashéskoro náv,* ' the pasha's name.'

NAVEL—*pol.*—The usual term among the Hindus for ' navel' is *nábhi* or *nábhtla.* It has given birth to Pers. *naf,* Germ. *nabel,* Eng. *navel.* As to this Gypsy word, I am unable to give any satisfactory account of it, unless we suppose that the first syllable *ná* has been thrown off by the Gypsies from the second term *nábhtla.*

NEAR—*bashé, pashé ;* Bor., *sumpacel.*—Concerning the etymology of this term I can form no probable conjecture. *Bashé to len,* ' near the river ;' *bashé túte,* ' near thee ; *kaléste bashé dulevésa* (Gr. δουλεύω) ? ' near whom workest thou ?' *bashé to bahtzé* (Turk. *baghche*), ' near the garden ;' *bashé mánde, tuménde, lénde,* ' near us, you, them ;' *bashál,* ' from near.' *Sumpacel,* Borrow's word, is a phrase common among the Gypsies, formed of *sun,* imperative of *sunáva,* ' to hear,' and *bashál.* It is an order to ' go and be attentive,' lit. ' hear from near.' I have frequently heard it. Pott has fallen into the same error as Borrow, in considering it a simple term. *Ja ta sun pashál,* ' go and hear from near.'

---

* Armenian *ungunk.*—TR.   † " *Nam,* ' nom.'"   Vaillant, p. 180.
‡ Arm. *anun.*—TR.

NEEDLE—See to SEW.

NEGATION—*na, nanái, nasti, ma* ; Br., *nee* ; Bor., *na, nanái, nasti, ne.*—
There are few words in all the range of the Gypsy language so clear
and well defined as these terms. *Na* is the Sr. *na*, a particle of negation. *Na*, in Gypsy colloquial usage, is employed principally with
verbs : as *na janáva*, 'I do not know ;' *na kamáva*, 'I do not wish ;'
na isámas oté, 'I was not here ;' *na pakiáva*, 'I do not believe ;' *na
dikliómles*, 'I did not see him ; *nái, isi tindó*, 'no, it is thine.' They
never say *nanái dikliómles*, or *nanái janáva*. In the subjunctive, *na*
is inserted between *te* and the verb ; as *te na dikáv*, 'that I may not
see ;' *te na jav*, 'that I may not go ;' *te na khél*, 'that he may not
eat.' It is to be observed in adjectives : as *naisvali*, 'invalid ;' *naisukár*, 'not handsome ;' *namporemé*, 'sick.' *Nanái* is properly used
to express negation joined to the third person of the auxiliary verb
isóm, 'I am,' which is always understood : it means properly 'it is
not.' It has evidently taken the place of the following *nasti*, which
by the Gypsies is applied to other usages. *Nanái* is a reduplication
of *na*. *Nanái mindó*, 'it is not mine ;' *nanái lachó*, 'it is not good ;'
nanái but phuró, 'he is not very old ;' *ta na kamniovél nanái lachés*,
'not to perspire is not well ;' *nanái palvál*, 'there is no wind ;' *nanái
khohaimpé*, 'it is not a lie.' *Nasti* is evidently the Sr. *nâsti*, 'it is
not,' from *na* and *asti*, the 3d pers. sing. of the verb *as*, 'to be,' Gr.
ἐστι. The Persian has a similar phrase, *nist*, composed of the neg.
ne and *est*, 'is.' So also the Slav. *niest*, 'non est,' used in this form.
Nâsti is defined by Wilson 'non-existence, not so, it is not.' The
Gypsies, however, have given this definition to *nanái*, and have re-
served *nasti* to express impossibility or difficulty. Having lost all
traces of its proper signification, it is now applied by them to all
persons indistinctly, and to all numbers, whilst the similar phrase in
Persian retains its proper signification. *Nasti astarghiómles*, 'I could
not seize him ;' *nasti kerávales*, 'I cannot do it ;' *amén nasti kerásales*,
'we cannot do it ;' *nasti sováva*, 'I cannot sleep ;' *nasti piráva*, 'I
cannot walk'—and in a similar manner with all the persons and tenses
of a verb. It is never used except with verbs, and the inflection of
the verb itself shows the person speaking. *Ma* is a particle which,
like the Gr. μὴ, is always prefixed to the imperative. It is the Sr. *má*,
a prohibitive and negative particle, chiefly prefixed to verbs in the
imp. mood : as *má kuru*, 'do not do.' With the Gypsies, though
heard sometimes alone, as the modern Gr. μὴ, 'don't,' it supposes a
verb which by the speaker is not uttered. *Ma ker túya*, 'do thou not
also ;' *ma déman armán*, 'do not curse me ;' *ma küsh*, 'do not revile ;'
ma vrakér, 'do not talk ;' *ma ja*, 'do not go ;' *ma dik*, 'do not look ;'
ma sun, 'do not hear ;' *ma kha*, 'do not eat ;' *ma le*, 'do not take' ;
ma pi, 'do not drink.' With the exception of this negative particle,
there is a striking similarity between mine and Borrow's terms.

NEW—*nevó* ; Bor., *nebo, nebel, ternoró.*—With the exception of *ternoró*,
all these words are from the Sr. adj. *nava*, with which correspond the
Gr. νέος, Lat. *novus*, Slav. *nov'ie*, 'new, young,' and many other similar
words in the present spoken languages of Europe. *Nebel* of Borrow
has been formed from the primitive Sr. in a way similar to the Lat.

novellus from *novus.* *Ternoró* will be explained under YOUNG MAN. *Nevó ker,* 'new house;' *nevó gav,* 'new village;' *nevé yismata,* 'new clothes.'

NIGHT—*rat, ratti, aratti;* Br., *rakilo;* Bor., *rachi.*—The Gr. νὺξ, Lat. *nox,* Slav. *nosht,* correspond with Sr. *nakta,* 'night.' These terms have left no traces in the Gypsy language, which has preserved the more usual Sr. *rátri,* 'night.' By the assimilation of *r* to *t,* so common in modern languages, it has become *rat,* 'night,' and *ratti,* 'in the night-time,' Lat. *nocte.* Mr. Brown's *rakilo* is the 3d pers. aor. passive, 'it is getting dark.' *Ratti* seems to be a remnant of a locative case. This term is sometimes pronounced with an initial *a, aratti.* This initial *a* is less common here than among the Gypsies of Spain. *Yek rat,* 'one night;' *yekpasharát,* 'midnight;' *saró rat,* 'every night.'

No ONE—*kayék jenó.*—This term, extremely common among the Gypsies, is composed of two words, the relation of which to the Sanskrit is extremely evident. The latter word is never used alone. *Kayék* seems to be the Sr. *ekâika,* 'singly, one by one,' from *eka,* 'one,' repeated. Like the Gr. κανείς, from κὰν εἶς, 'no one,' so likewise this word among the Gypsies is at times affirmative, and at times negative. Negat.—*kayék jenó na janéla man,* 'no one knows me;' *nasti dulavéna* (Gr. δουλεύω, 'to work') *kayék jenó,* 'no one can work.' Affirm. —*te kamniovél kayék jenó lachés isi,* 'for one to perspire is a good thing.' *Kayék* alone signifies 'no one,' Fr. *aucun, personne: kayéke,* 'to no one;' *kayéke manushe,* 'to no man,' Gr. εἰς κανένα ἄνθρωπον; *kapenáv túke yek lav, ta na penésles kayéske,* 'I will tell thee a word, but thou shouldst not tell it to any one.' This term, in receiving the particle *ke,* is pronounced *kayékske* and *kayékke;* the latter is the proper mode. *Kayék* is joined to other terms: as *kayék far,* 'sometimes, never;' *po kayék far,* 'oftentimes.' *Jenó* is evidently the Sr. *jana,* 'man,' individually or collectively, 'mankind,' from the root *jan,* 'to be born;' compare Pers. *jins,* Lat. *genus,* Gr. γένος, etc. I have never heard it used except in connection with *kayék.*

NOBLEMAN—*rái.*—The peculiar circumstances in which the Gypsies are placed in these countries have made all foreign words of this category of little use to them. The common terms among them for persons ennobled, either by wealth, education, or political authority, are pure Turkish. Even the lowest order of the Greeks rarely use any but the Turkish terms, as *agha, efendi, pasha,* and the like. Εὐγενὴς, εὐπατρίδης, etc., are totally unknown to them. I once asked an illiterate Bulgarian, what 'famous' meant in their language. He gave me the word *chorbadji,* i. e. 'the magistrate of a small rural district.' The Gypsies, however, have retained the word *rái,* referable to the Sr. *rájan,* 'a king, a monarch, a prince.' It is applied particularly to those persons of their clan who are set over them by the local Turkish authorities, as collectors of the capitation-tax and other duties due to the government. It is also given to the head men of their corporations. Those foreign to their tribe are called by their usual Turkish titles. This term is not known to all. The wife of the *rái* is called *ráni,* Sr. *rájñi,* so common to this day for the wives of the

Rajas and other native rulers of Hindustan. *E rayéskoro chavó,* 'the child of the *Rái ;*' *dikáva e rayés,* 'I see the nobleman.'

NOSE—*nak ;* Br., *nak ;* Bor., *naqui, pavi.*—The first three of these words are derived from the Sr. *nas,* 'nose,' *násiká,* 'nostril.' Some Gypsies use the word *rutuní* for 'nose;' it is the Gr. ῥωϑώνιον, dim. of ῥώϑων, 'nostril.' To a great many of them *nak* is unknown. The *pavi* of Borrow is unknown to me.

To NOURISH—*parvaráva.*—This is the verb of which the word *parvardó,* given above for FAT, is properly a participle. Perhaps a more plausible etymology than is there proposed for it may be found in the Sr. root *bhṛi,* 'to bear, sustain, nourish,' with the prefix *pari* or *pra.*

Now—*akaná, okaná ;* Bor., *ocana, acana.*—This term, common and well known to all the Gypsies, both in Spain and Turkey, I compare with the Sr. *akshna,* 'time;' the Sr. *ksh* being constantly changed by the Gypsies to *k.* There is another cognate Sr. term, *kshaṇa,* 'a moment.' By the prefixion of an *a,* as in *avdivés,* 'this day, to-day,' the word would signify 'this moment,' resembling the Gr. τ'ωρα, 'this hour, now.'

NUMBERS.—

ONE—*yek ;* Br., *yak ;* Bor., *icque, iesque, ies.*—From the Sr. *eka,* 'one.' The Pers. has the same form, in *yek,* 'one.' In the Greek, the word *eka* is to be found in ἐκάτερος, a comparative form of *eka,* Sr. *ekatara* —ἔκαστος, ἐκάστοτε.

TWO—*dúi ;*[*] Br., *duy ;* Bor., *dui.*—From Sr. *dvi,* 'two,' with which correspond the synonymous arithmetical terms of Europe, as Pers. *du,* Gr. δύω, Lat. *duo.*

THREE—*tri, trin ;* Br. *triu ;* Bor., *trin.*—From the Sr. *tri,* 'three.' *Trin* is the Sr. neuter *trîṇi.* Both these terms are used. The Pali has *tiṇṇi,* 'three' (Essai sur le Pali, p. 92).

FOUR—*ishtár ;* Br., *ushtár ;* Bor., *estar.*—The Sr. *chatur* is here changed more than the preceding terms.

FIVE—*panch ;* Br., *pandji ;* Bor., *panche.*—Sr. *pancha,* 'five.' This Gypsy word is nearer the original than the corresponding term of any other language, and in Spain and Turkey it has been preserved almost unchanged.

SIX—*shov ;* Br., *sho ;* Bor., *job.*—Sr. *shash,* 'six.' The Greek has laid aside the initial *sh,* the Latin has preserved it: ἕξ, *sex,* 'six.' Slav. *shesht.*[†]

SEVEN—*eftá ;* Br., *efta ;* Bor., *efta.*—From the Sr. *sapta,* 'seven.' Here also the Greek has laid aside the initial *s* of the Sr. At first sight one would think this word to be our ἑπτά, commonly pronounced ἐφτά. So too the Persian *heft.* The *eftá* of the Gypsies presents the natural change of *p* into *f,* to euphonize with *t,* a change daily heard among us, as vulgar rather than classical, but regular among the Persians. The ancient Greeks made a similar change, saying ἕβδομος, ἑβδομήκοντα, instead of ἕπτομος, ἑπτομήκοντα (Bopp). Compare Zend *haptan,* 'seven,' changing the initial *s* to *h,* whence the Pers. *heft,* as above.

_____

[*] "*Dúi,* 'deux'" Vaillant, p. 379.
[†] The Armenian has *vets,* and, in combination, *vesh :* as *veshdasan,* 'sixteen.'—TR.

ᴇɪɢʜᴛ—*ohtó* ; Br., *ohtó* ; Bor., *ostor, ottolojo.*—Sr. *ashṭa,* 'eight.' Compare Zend *ashtan,* Pers. *hesht,* Gr. ὀϰτὼ, Lat. *octo,* Germ. *acht.*

ɴɪɴᴇ—*iniya ;* Br., *iniya ;* Bor., *eñia.*—Sr. *nava,* 'nine.' In Greek we have prefixed the vowel *e* for the sake of euphony, and the Gypsies *i.*

ᴛᴇɴ—*desh ;* Br., *desh ;* Bor., *deque.*—Sr. *daça.* The Gypsies of Turkey have preserved the original word better than those of Spain, who approach nearer the languages of Europe; Gr. δέϰα, Lat. *decem,*[*] Slav. *desyat.*

ᴇʟᴇᴠᴇɴ—*desh-i-yek ;* Bor., *esden-y-yesque.*

ᴛᴡᴇʟᴠᴇ—*desh-i-dúi ;* Bor., *esden-y-duis.*

ᴛʜɪʀᴛᴇᴇɴ—*desh-i-tri ;* Bor., *esden-y-trin.*

ꜰᴏᴜʀᴛᴇᴇɴ—*desh-i-ishtar ;* Bor., *esden-y-ostar.*

ꜰɪꜰᴛᴇᴇɴ—*desh-i-panch ;* Bor., *esden-y-panche.*

ꜱɪxᴛᴇᴇɴ—*desh-i-shov ;* Bor., *esden-y-jobe.*

ꜱᴇᴠᴇɴᴛᴇᴇɴ—*desh-i-eftá ;* Bor., *esden-y-estar.*

ᴇɪɢʜᴛᴇᴇɴ—*desh-i-ohtó ;* Bor., *esden-y-ostor.*

ɴɪɴᴇᴛᴇᴇɴ—*desh-i-inia ;* Bor., *esden-y-esñe.*

Mr. Brown has omitted the above numbers.

ᴛᴡᴇɴᴛʏ—*bish ;* Br., *bish ;* Bor., *bis.*—The form of this number, from the Sr. *vinçati,* resembles the Pers. *bist,* which preserves the final consonant *t.*

ᴛʜɪʀᴛʏ—*tránda ;* Br., *otrenta ;* Bor., *trianda.*

ꜰᴏʀᴛʏ—*saránda ;* Br., *saranda ;* Bor., *estardi.*

ꜰɪꜰᴛʏ—*peninda ;* Br., *paninda ;* Bor., *pancherdi.*

ꜱɪxᴛʏ—*shovardéri ;* Br., *showur ;* Bor., *joberdi.*

ꜱᴇᴠᴇɴᴛʏ—*eftavardéri ;* Br., *eftawardesh ;* Bor., *esterdi.*

ᴇɪɢʜᴛʏ—*ohtovardéri ;* Br., *ohtowardesh ;* Bor., *ostordi.*

ɴɪɴᴇᴛʏ—*iniyavardéri ;* Br., *iniyavardesh ;* Bor., *esnerdi.*

In Mr. Brown's term for 'sixty,' *showar,* the final *desh* has been omitted by mistake.

The first three terms of Mr. Brown and myself, and the first of Borrow, are the common forms of our Modern Greek numbers, used by the common people,[†] which the Gypsies in passing through or residing here have adopted, while they have rejected the others. The remainder are formed regularly from the numerals with the addition of *desh,* 'ten.' In my glossary the *sh* of *desh* is changed into *ri ;* in Borrow's the final *desh* is changed into *di.*

ʜᴜɴᴅʀᴇᴅ—*shil, shel ;* Br., *shevel ;* Bor., *gres.*—The first two are related to the Sr. *çata,* 'hundred ;' the origin of *gres* is unknown to me.

ᴛᴡᴏ ʜᴜɴᴅʀᴇᴅ—*du shél.*

ᴛʜʀᴇᴇ ʜᴜɴᴅʀᴇᴅ—*tri shél.*

ᴛʜᴏᴜꜱᴀɴᴅ—*mília ;* Bor., *milan.*—From the Lat. *mille.* This is foreign to the Sr. *sahasra,* 'thousand.'[‡]

I have not given the Sr. numerals, as the reader can easily obtain them from the ordinary Sr. grammars.

---

[*] Armenian *désa,* and in composition *dasán ;* as *medasan, megdasan.*—Tʀ.

[†] For those unacquainted with the Modern Greek, it may be well to say that these numerals have been modified as follows : τριάϰοντα we call τριάντα ; τισσαράϰοντα, σαράντα ; πεντήϰοντα, πενῆντα ; ἰξήϰοντα, ἰξῆντα, etc.

[‡] Armenian *hasar* or *hazar,* of Sr. origin.—Tʀ.

The Gypsy numerals, when joined to nouns in the accusative case, receive a final *e*; *deshé grastén teráva*, 'I have ten horses;' *shelé bakré teréla*, 'a hundred sheep he has (owns).'

Nut—*akhór, akór.*—

Nut-tree—*akhorín, akorín.*—The Pers. *kerdu* has relation with the Gr. *κάρυον* and *καρύδιον*, 'a nut.' The Sr. term to which it may most probably be referred is *akota*, 'the betel-nut-tree' (Areca faufel, or catechu). It is here used for the fruit of the great walnut tree (Corylus avellana), so common in every part of Turkey.

O.

Old—*phuró, phurú, puró, furó*; Br., *pooree*; Bor., *puró.*—This is a pure Sr. word, *pura*, 'former, more ancient.' By the addition of *pe* is formed *puripé*, 'old age.' *O phuró kaméla ta dikéna to phuripé,* 'the old man desires that they should see (i. e. 'nurse') him in his old age.' Fem. *purí: i romní léskeri isí puri*, 'his wife is old.'

Old, ancient—*puranó.*—From the Sr. adj. *purána*, 'old, ancient.' Among the Gypsies it has also the signification of 'old in age,' like the preceding *purú*. It is frequently to be heard, and is often interchanged with the preceding term.

To grow old—*phuriováva.*—A compound verb, from *phuró*, 'old,' and *aváva*: lit. 'to become old;' Gr. *γηράσκω*, Lat. *senesco. Te phurióla te dikénales e chavé*, 'when he becomes old, the children should nurse (lit. 'see') him.'

Opposite—*mamúi.*—A compound word, from the poss. pronoun *ma, mo*, 'my,' and *múi*, 'mouth.' Similar expressions are common in many languages: compare Pers. *ru-be-ru*, 'opposite,' lit. 'face to face;' Fr. *en face;* It. *in faccia. Kon isí mamúi mánde?* 'who is opposite me?' *mamúi to gáv*, 'opposite the village.' *Mamuyál*, 'from the opposite side,' is formed like other similar adverbs, by the addition of *al: mamuyál aváva*, 'I come from the opposite side;' *pelióm mamuyál*, 'I fell on my face.'

Onion—*purúm.*—A very common word among all the Gypsies: plur. *purumá.*

Other—*yavér*; Bor., *aver, avél.*—This term can be referred to the Sr. *apara*, 'other.' The *p* has been changed to *v*, and the semivowel prefixed to the initial *a*, as in many other Gypsy words. *Ma ker túya yavréske*, 'do not thou also to others:' *yavréske*, a clipped form of *yaveréske; e yavréskero romní*, 'and the other's wife;' *te penás améya e yavréske t' avéna*, 'that we also may communicate (lit. 'say') it to others, in order that they may come;' *diklióm e yavrés*, 'I saw the other (one).'

Oven—*bov.*—This term is applied to the furnace, to lime-kilns, and to the oven for baking bread. Its origin is not clear. *E bovéskero na pekéla mo manró*, 'the baker does not bake my bread;' *e bovéskero na délaman manró*, 'the baker does not give me bread.'

Over the water—*perdál, predál.*—This is used precisely as the Greeks use *πέρα* and *πέραν*, 'in another place, between which and the speaker there is a sheet of water.' *Perdál* is in the ablative form of adverbs. It is not solely confined to this signification. *Jáva perdál*, 'I go on the other side.' It supposes another term *perd*, which may be referred to the Sr. *paradeça*, 'a foreign country,' from which has been elegantly formed the Gr. παϱάδεισος, Pers. *ferdus*, and all the cognate terms of the European languages. *Perdál tan*, 'a place on the farther side.'

Out—*avrí*; Bor., *abri*.—Probably derived from the Sr. *bahis* and *bahir*, 'out, outside.' By transposition of letters it becomes *avrí*. *Dikáva avrí prágmata* (πϱάγματα), 'I see strange things;' *avriál*, 'from the outside, out of:' *avriál to ker nastótar*, 'after they departed out of the house;' *avrutnó*, 'a foreigner,' Gr. ἐξωτεϱικὸς: *avrutnó manúsh*, 'a foreigner, a stranger, a man not of the Gypsy race.'

Ox—*gurúv, guri*; Br., *ghuree*; Bor., *gorbi*.—

Cow—*guruvni, gurumni*; Br., *ghurumnee*.—The Sr. *go* or *gáu* signifies 'the ox kind in general;' this is preserved in the Gr. γά-λαϰ(τος), Lat. *lac, lactis*, anciently denoting 'the milk of the cow.' We have also in Sanskrit *gaura, gaurí*, signifying 'a buffalo.' This Gypsy term has suffered alterations for which it is difficult now to account. The feminine is pronounced as I have written it. It is regularly formed, by the addition of *ni*, the common termination of feminine nouns. *Kapucháv léstar te kaméla te kinél gurumni*, 'I shall ask him if he wishes to buy a cow;' *i gurumni isi mindí*, 'the cow is mine;' *parvardí gurumni*, 'fat cow.'

P.

Pain—*duk*;* Bor., *duquipen, duga, dua*.—

To be in pain—*dukáva*.—These terms are from the Sr. *duḥkha*, 'pain, sorrow, affliction.' The first term given by Borrow is formed by the addition to the noun of the suffix *pen*: he defines it 'grief.' *Duk teráva*, 'I have pain;' *dukélaman*, 'it pains me;' *dukéna lákari chuchía*, 'her breasts pain.' This verb at times means 'to be in love:' hence *dukhaipé*, 'love;' *dukhaní*, 'a mistress;' *dukéla m'oghí*, 'my heart loves;' *duk e devlés te oghésa*, 'love God with thy heart.'

To paint—*makáva*.—Possibly from the Sr. *maksh*, 'to fill, to mix, to combine.' This term is applied by the Gypsies to the painting of houses, the smearing of women's faces with rouge or other colors—a practice extremely common among the young women—the painting of the eyebrows and eyelashes with black, and the like. *Makavdó*, part., 'painted, besmeared:' *mo ker isi makavdó*, 'my house is painted;' *makavdé pová*, 'painted eyebrows;' *bimakavdó*, 'not painted.'

Pantaloon—*dimí, dimísh*: plur. *dimnía* and *dimía*.—*Dimía isi buglé*, 'the pantaloons are large;' *dimialó*, 'wearing pantaloons, *braccatus*;' *bidimnialó*, 'without pantaloons.'

Paper—*lir, lil*; Bor., *li*.—The Sr. *likh* means generally 'to write, to draw;' *likha*, 'one who writes,' or 'what is written,' and hence, 'what is written upon,' as paper, iron or stone tablets, etc. The Gypsies of

---

* Armenian *dukhrootiane*, root *dukhr*. The Armenian language loves to increase the guttural sound, and often changes *h*, and even *k*, into the strongly aspirated guttural *kh*; and, what is more singular, it generally changes the liquid *l* of foreign languages into the deep guttural *ghad* or *gh*; e. g. λάζαϱος, *ghazaros*.—Tr.

Turkey have corrupted the word by adding an *r*, and changing it at times to *l*. In Spain they have cut off the final syllable, or, more properly, it is changed to an *i*, and blended with the foregoing one: compare Sr. *mukha*, Gypsy *mui*. Compare Slav. *list*, 'leaf, page.' This term is also used in the sense of 'epistle:' *picharáva lil*, 'I send a letter.'

PARTNER—*amál.*—A Persian word, *hemal*, 'companion,' Mod. Greek σύντροφος. Though used as 'companion' is in English, it is more generally applied to those who work together, as partners in business. *Tovghióm man amál*, 'I have taken a partner.'

To PASS—*nakáva.*—Evidently related to the Sr. *naksh*, 'to approach, to arrive at.'

PASSOVER—*patranki;* Bor., *pachandra, ciria.*—This is undoubtedly a corruption of the Gr. πάσχα or πασχαλία, 'Easter.' The word cannot be Bulgarian, as this people have retained unchanged the Gr. term *páskha*. The second word given by Borrow, *ciria*, may have originated from the Greek κύριος or κυριακὴ, 'Sunday,' 'the Lord's day.' The Greeks very frequently call Easter λαμπρά, 'glorious, resplendent.'

PEAR—*ambról.*—

PEAR-TREE—*ambrolin.*—This is a Persian word, from *emrud*, and *enbrut*, 'a pear,' from which comes the Turkish *armud*, 'a pear.' Names of trees terminate in *in*. The reader will see a few other examples in this Vocabulary.

PERSPIRATION—*kamlioipé, kamnioipé.*—This appears to me to be of pure Sr. origin. I have noted both forms of the word, since they are equally common. *Kamlióm*, 'I have perspired,' supposes a present *kamáva*, which, however, I have never heard: for it is used *kamló isom*, 'I am perspiring,' from *kamlo*, 'perspiring, in perspiration,' and *kámniováva, kamlióváva*, from the same and *aváva*.

PIASTRE—*astaló.*—We have met with another word in the Vocabulary, *lové*, 'money,' in use among the Gypsies. This is frequently used for 'piastres' in the plural, as is the Turk. *ghrush* in the singular. I know of no clue to the etymology of the term, unless it can be referred to Pers. *astar*, 'pondus quoddam indefinitum et varians, quum hic decem, illic sex drachmarum cum semisse ponderi aequet. Vox e Gr. στατὴρ corrupta esse videtur' (Vullers, Lex. Pers.). It does not resemble any of the terms used by the natives here. Plur. *astalé: keti astalé terésa te désman*, 'how many piastres hast thou to give me' (i. e. 'owest thou')? *yek astaló*, 'one piastre;' *eftá astalé*, 'seven piastres.'

To PIERCE—*chinkeráva, chingheráva.*—This word signifies 'to perforate, to cut through, to pierce with a sharp sword.' It is a compound verb, made up of *chin* and *keráva*, 'to do.' *Chin* I refer to Sr. *chhid*, 'to divide, to cut, to split.' Aor. *chingherghióm*,- 'I have pierced, I have wounded.'

PIT—*gúva, khar.*—The first of these terms can be referred to the Sr. *gupti*, from *gup*, 'to hide,' meaning 'hiding, a hole in the ground, a cavern.' As to the other word, *khar*, I leave to others to say whether it can be referred to *khan*, 'to dig,' a verb which has given sundry words to the present Gypsy language (see WELL). *Bashé to bahtzés* (Turk. *baghché*, 'garden') *isi yek khar*, 'near the garden is a pit.'

PITY—*bezéh.*—This is a Persian word, *beze*, 'crimen, peccatum, injuria, violentia' (Vullers, Lex. Pers.). It is used by the Gypsies as the Greeks use their κρίμα, 'pity, commiseration.' *Bezéh chorénghe,* 'pity to the poor;' Gr. κρίμα·εἰς τοὺς πτωχούς: i. e. 'the poor are to be pitied.' The plural, *bezéha,* is very rarely to be heard.

PLACE—*tan.*—From the root *sthâ,* 'to stand,' Gr. ἵστημι, Lat. *sto, sisto,* comes the noun *sthâna,* which is so frequent in the Persian language, as *stan:* compare *gulistan,* 'a place of roses;' *hindistan,* 'the place of the Hindus,' etc. It is natural that a term so common in so many languages should have left traces of its existence in the Gypsy language. Among the Gypsies it has precisely the same signification as among the Hindus. *Kamojáv me tanéste,* 'I shall go to my (native) place;' *so penéna to tan?* 'what do they call thy place?' In this sense *tan* is more generally used than *gáv,* 'village.' *Peryulikanó tan,* 'a foreign place (land).'

PLATE—*charó.*—I refer this term to *charu,* from the root *char,* 'to eat,' signifying 'an oblation of rice, barley, and pulse, boiled with butter and milk for presentation to the gods or manes; and the vessel in which such an oblation is prepared.' The word *charó* is now used for plates of wood, metal, or clay, in which the Gypsies eat, but more commonly an ordinary plate of red clay, in which poor people take their food. Plur. *charé: aklé tanéste keréna charé,* 'in that place they make plates;' *khor charé,* 'deep plates;' *charéskoro,* 'a plate-maker.'

To PLAY (on instruments of music)—*kelâva, ghelâva.*—This I refer to the Sr. *kal,* 'to sound, to throw or cast:' *kalatâ,* from this root, is 'melody, music.' The consonant *k* is often changed to *gh.*

PLUM—*kilâv.*—

PLUM-TREE—*kilavin.*—The origin of these terms is to me unknown. Plur. *kilavá,* 'plums.'

POMEGRANATE—*daráv.*—

POMEGRANATE-TREE—*daravin ;* Bor., *meligrana.*—This word appears to be connected with the Sr. *dârava,* 'wooden, made of wood,' Lat. *ligneus,* from the word *dâru,* 'wood, timber.' Borrow's *meligrana* is connected with the Ital. *melagranata* and the Spanish *granada.*

POOR—*choró.*—Connected with the Sr. *chivara,* 'the tattered dress of a Bauddha mendicant, or of any mendicant.' Bopp defines it "*vestis pannosa.*" It may be connected also with another Sr. term, *chira,* 'a rag, an old and torn cloth.' *So kamakerén e choré?* 'what will the poor do?' *choripé,* 'poverty:' *but chitáva choripé,* 'I suffer (lit. 'I draw') much poverty;' *me choriákeri,* 'of me the poor (woman).' The word is applied to a poor man and to professional beggars by the Gypsies here in Turkey. Fem. *chorì;* dim. *chororó,* 'a beggar boy.' *Choró* I have heard used for 'an orphan.'

To PRAISE—*asharáva.*—This transitive verb I refer to the Sr. root *arch,* 'to worship, to honor or treat with respect, to praise.' Pass. *asharávaman,* 'I praise myself,' ἐπαινοῦμαι ; *asharghiómman,* 'I have praised myself;' so *asharéstut,* 'why dost thou boast' (lit. 'praise thyself')? *ashardó,* 'praised:' *ashardó isóm,* 'I am praised.'

PREGNANT—*kamni;* Br., *kamnee;* Bor., *cambri.*—Related to the Sr. *garbhini,* 'a pregnant woman,' from *garbha,* 'an embryo, a child.' *Teréla chavén? na, isi kamni,* 'has she children? no, she is pregnant.'

PRIEST—*rashái;* Bor., *erojay, arajay.*—Borrow defines these terms "friar, frayle" (Span.). By the Gypsies of Turkey the name is given to the ordinary priests in the churches, and is an equivalent of the παππᾶς of their coreligionists the Greeks. They often also apply the term to the διδάσκαλος of the Greeks, following in this respect the usages of the Christian inhabitants of Turkey, among whom, till a few years ago, the priest was always the teacher (διδάσκαλος) of the village, and was called indiscriminately by the inhabitants both "priest" and "teacher," παππᾶς and διδάσκαλος. I am not aware of any word among the Gypsies for the order of monks as distinct from this denomination of *rashái.* *Rashani,* 'the wife of the *rashái.*' As priests are frequently married in the villages, the term of course is given to the priest's wife; Gr. παππαδία.

No Sanskrit term can have given origin to this word but *rishi,* 'a saint, a sanctified personage,' and I accept it, on account of the similarity of sound, and of the idea of sanctity attached to the term both by Hindus and Gypsies.

PROP—*pikaló.*—A long stick, used in loading pack-horses; it supports the weight of one side before the other is loaded.

PUDENDUM VIRILE—*kar.*—I know of no satisfactory derivation of this term, which however appears to me of Hindu origin.

PUDENDUM MULIEBRE—*minch.*—This term does not appear connected with the Sr. *madana.* It appears to be related to terms such as *mingo,* ὀμίχω, μίγνυμι; this latter often implying carnal connection. Compare Sr. *miçr,* 'to mix, to mingle,' *mih,* 'to sprinkle, *effundere, praesertim mingere.*' It is proper here to remark that in all languages such terms have usually been difficult of derivation, owing to the indelicacy of the subject, and because they have been altered and distorted according to the unchecked inclination of the most vulgar of the people.

Q.

QUICK, QUICKLY—*sigó;* Bor., *singo.**—This term may be referred to the Sr. *sanga,* 'meeting, encountering, joining, uniting,' if it does not rather come from *çtghra,* 'swift, quick.' It is used at times for 'often.' *Dikésales sigó,* 'dost thou see him often?' *sigó ker,* 'a quick ass;' *sigó sigó,* 'very quickly.'

R.

It RAINS—*déla.*—This term is the 3d pers. sing. of the pres. tense. It is difficult to find a Gypsy who can give the first person of the verb. According to the formation of the Gypsy verb, which I shall explain in Section V, *déla* is the 3d pers. sing. pres., *désa,* 2d pers., *dáva,* 1st pers., 'I rain.' *Dáva* I refer to the Sr. *und* or *ud,* 'to wet, to moisten, to be or become wet.' From this verb comes *uda,* 'water;' compare

---

* "*Sigo,* 'vite.'" Vaillant, p. 357.

the Gr. ὕδος, ὕδωρ, and Slav. *voda*, 'water.' The Latin *unda* has preserved the *n* of the root. The Gypsies have cut off the initial syllable of the Sr. root. *Kamáva te del*, 'I wish it would rain;' *but déla avdivés*, 'it rains much today.'

RAIN—*brishindó, burshín; Bor., brijindel.*—Comp. Sr. *prish*, 'to sprinkle, to pour out water;' also *vrish*, 'to sprinkle, to pour out, to rain.' In the Gypsy, *b* has taken the place of the Sr. initial. Borrow explains *brijindel* by the Sr. *purana* (*púraṇa*), which, though meaning sometimes 'rain,' is generally used for 'perfection, a work well wrought out,' etc. *But brishindó*, 'much rain.' *Burshín* is less frequently used.

RAISIN—*porík, porikín.*—The same confusion exists among the Gypsies as to the signification of this word as among the Greeks, from whom undoubtedly the Gypsies have borrowed it. Ὀπώρα, in ancient Greek, designated that time of the year in which fruit ripened, from July to November; ὀπωρικός, 'autumnal' and 'matured;' ὀπωρικὸν and 'πωρικὸν we now call the fruits themselves, applying the term particularly to esculent fruits growing on trees, and these trees, formerly called ξύλα κάρπιμα, we now call ξυλοκαρπία, in order to distinguish them from trees giving no fruit. Πωρικὸν is a very vague term, and the Gypsies very rarely can agree to what fruit or particular tree the word *porikín* should be applied. I have heard it applied to plums, to plum-trees themselves, and very often to raisins and figs. *Porikín* is similar in formation to *kilavín*, 'plum-tree,' and *ambrolín*, 'pear-tree.'

RED—*loló; Bor., lolo, lole.*—Compare Sr. *lohita*, 'red, reddish, blood.' The Gypsies have preserved the first syllable, which they have doubled. Borrow defines the word in his vocabulary 'tomato,' the well known vegetable called by us τομάτα. The rejection of whole syllables is common in many languages.

To REJOICE—*losháxiováva.*—A verb in the middle voice, composed of *loshanó*, 'rejoicing,' χαιρόμενος, and *aváva*. It is a very common verb among the Gypsies. I refer it to Sr. *lush*, 'to adorn, to decorate.' This verb I have never heard excepting in the middle form. *Loshanoipé*, 'joy.'

To REST—*acháva.*—This I refer to the Sr. root *ach*, 'to go to or towards, to worship.' *Ach devlésa*, 'rest thou with God,' addressed to persons departing; *achardó isí*, 'he has remained.'

To REVILE—*kusháva.*—This may be connected with the Sr. *kuça*, 'wicked, depraved, mad, inebriate,'[*] resembling the Gr. κακός, which has given origin to κακίζω, 'to revile one as a bad man.' *Ma kush*, 'do not revile.'

RICH—*baravaló.*—This may be referred to Sr. *prabala*, 'strong, powerful.' *Isí kilavdó, ta but baravaló*, 'he is fat, and very rich.'

To RIDICULE—*prasáva.*—This is a compound term, composed of the prep. *pra* and *has*, which we have defined: see to LAUGH. It is rare in the Gypsy language to meet with verbs' united to prepositions. Even in modern Greek there has always been a tendency among the

---

[*] Armenian *kesh*, 'bad, wicked.'—TA.

more uncultivated of the people to strike off all those prepositions which vary the primary signification of the verb. The same remark is also applicable to the Bulgarians, as regards their mother Slavonic.

RING, FINGER-RING—*angrusti, angustri.*—The form is Persian, though it has been borrowed from the Sr. *anguri* or *anguli,* 'a finger, a toe;' *angushta,* 'the thumb:' Pers. *engiusht,* 'finger;' *engiushter* and *engiushteri,* 'finger-ring.'⁕

RIPE—*mulanó.*—

To RIPEN, to become RIPE—*mulanokeráva.*—Of doubtful etymology.

RIVER—*len;* Bor., *len.*⁕—This is one of many Gypsy words whose derivation, at first sight, is not so palpable as that of many others. But it may plausibly be referred to the Sr. root *lt* or *rt,* 'to dissolve, to flow.' *Bashé to len,* 'near the river;' *sigó len,* 'a swift river.'

ROAD—*drom;* Bor., *dron, drun.*—Some light may be thrown on the derivation of this word by the Gr. δρέμω; δρόμος, 'a road.' This Gr. term has its origin from the Sr. *dram,* 'to go, to move;' and probably the same Sr. root has given origin to these Gypsy words. *Bugló drom,* 'a wide road.'

ROD—*rubli.*—Applied to represent the common Gr. ῥαβδίον, dim. of ῥάβδος, 'a rod,' and denoting something larger and stouter than the *ran,* 'switch, cane.' Of its origin I know nothing.

ROOT—*korin.*—A Bulgarian word, very common among the Gypsies: Bulg. *kóren,* 'root;' Slav. *kóren',* 'root.' *E rukéskero korini,* 'the root of the tree.' This term is by some Gypsies used for the 'bark,' corresponding to the Slav. *korá,* 'bark;' Gr. φλοιός.

ROPE—*sheló.*—Compare Sr. *çulla,* 'a cord, a rope, a string,' and its cognate *çulva,* of the same signification.

RUSSIAN—*moskovís.*—The ordinary term used by the Turks, *moskov,* 'a Russian;' Gr. μόσκοβος. The Greeks also often call them ῥώσσους.

S.

SACK—*kisé.*—Probably the Turkish *kiesé,* 'sack, bag.'

SADDLE—*zen.*—A Persian word, *zen,* 'a saddle,' often written *zen-i-asp,* 'saddle of the horse.' This term, as used by the Gypsies, is properly 'a saddle upon which a person can ride;' for 'a pack-saddle,' they have adopted the Turkish *semer,* as have the Greeks, σαμάρι. *Chorghiá tumaré kheréskoro i zén,* 'they have stolen your ass's saddle.'

SALT—*lon;* Bor., *lon.*—These two identical words I refer to the Sr. *lavana,* 'salt, mineral and marine.' Hence, as with us, it signifies 'salted, well seasoned or flavored, any fluid containing salt.'

To SALT—*londaráva.*—From the above *lon.* It is a transitive verb. *Londarghióm,* 'I have salted.'

To be SATED—*chaliováva.*—A compound verb, formed of *chal* and *aváva. Chal* appears to me to be the verb *char,* 'to go, to graze,' which I have had occasion to explain in speaking of to GRAZE. As *char* by the Gypsies is used for 'grass,' and for 'the grazing of animals,' it came very naturally to correspond, in course of time, to the χορτάζω and χορταίνω of the Greeks. United to the usual *aváva,* like

---

⁕ " *Lom,* 'ruisseau.'" Vaillant, p. 364.

most of the middle verbs of the Gypsy idiom, it has become *chario-váva*, and, by the commutation of the liquids, *chaliováva*. These words literally mean ' I have grazed.' *Ta kháva khandí chaliováva*, ' and though I eat little, I am sated ;' *chaliovéla*, ' he is satiated.'

To SAY—*benáva, penáva ;* Bor., *penar.*—There are two Sr. verbal roots to which this verb may be referred : *bhan*, ' to say, to speak,' and *pan*, ' to praise :' the former of them is much the more likely to be the origi- nal of the Gypsy term. The 3d pers. of the present, *benéna*, is used frequently as an impersonal : ' it is said, they say ;' Gr. λέγουν, λέγεται. *Benéna ki o takár kamuló*, 'they say that the king has died ;' *so kaméva te penés mánghe ?* ' what dost thou wish to say to me ?' *na penéna chachipés*, ' they do not speak the truth ;' *na penghiómles*, ' I did not say it ;' *ma pén*, ' do not say' (i. e. ' speak'); *penghióm yav- réske t' avén*, ' I told the others to come.' This term is generally pronounced *benáva*, very rarely *penáva.*

To SCRATCH—*khanjováva, khandiováva.*—This verb can be referred to the Sr. *kandú*, ' itching, scratching.' It is in the middle voice, and means ' I scratch myself.' The neuter is *khanjáva*, ' I scratch.' By some Gypsies the word is pronounced *khandiováva*, approaching nearer to the Sr. form. The change of *k* into *kh* is common.

SCYTHE—*fárkia.*—This term appears to belong to the Wallachians, from whom the Gypsies have borrowed it. As the language spoken in Wallachia and Moldavia is a corrupted Latin, springing from the language of the Roman legions settled in those parts by the Roman emperors, *falx*, ' a sickle,' may have given origin to this term, with commutation of the liquids. Compare also Pers. *evrak*, ' falx foenaria.' The Latin origin appears to me the more probable. Some Gypsies, instead of this word, use *kosa*, the Bulgarian word for ' scythe.'

SEA—*deryáv, mára ;* Br., *daráv ;* Bor., *loria.*—This is a Persian term, *derya* and *deryah*, very usual also among the Turks. It signifies ' a sea,' and at times ' a river,' or ' any great collection of water.' By the change of *d* into *l* has been formed Borrow's word. My second term, *mára*, I have repeatedly heard from Moslem Gypsies. It is the Sr. *vári*, ' water,' Slav. *móre*, Lat. *mare*. Though *derya* is usual among the Turks, it is never to be heard except in a high flown style, very rarely in conversation ; and certainly it can never have come to the ears of the rude Gypsy, who hears only the usual term of the people, *deniz*, ' sea.' *Mára* may have been learned from the Slavonic nations, and the Bulgarians particularly, who still make use of it : *móre*, ' sea.'

SECRETLY—*choryál.*—Formed from *chor*, ' a thief, a robber,' and in the ablative form, like many other adverbs. Secresy and robbery are always intimately united : compare κλεψίνοος, κλεψίφρων, Mod. Gr. κλεφτάτα, ' secretly ;' Fr. *furtivement. Choryál diniómles*, ' I struck him secretly.'

To SEE—*dikáva, dikháva ;* Bor., *dicar, diar.*—I know of no Sr. verb to which this term may be so reasonably referred as to *drís*, ' to see, to behold,' Gr. δέρκομαι. We have had occasion to notice in many in- stances the omission of an *r*, and the conversion of the Sr. sibilant *s* into the guttural *k*. The second form of Borrow, *diar*, resembles the pronunciation of many Turkish Gypsies, who give the word as though written *dikháva*, and *diháva, diáva.* In fact, the aspirate *h* is so gentle as to be scarcely heard. This pronunciation of the guttural *k*, or rather its mutation into a soft aspirate, cannot be attributed to any local usage of the Gypsies, acquired from the natives, as it is prevalent only in the Asiatic provinces of Turkey, in the west of Asia Minor. *Dikiniló,* 'he appeared;' *dikióla,* 'it appears;' *dúi manushé diklióm,* 'two men I saw;' *te na dikáv,* 'that I may not see;' *dikliómla yek divés,* 'I saw her one day;' *dikáva léskere chavén,* 'I see his children.'

To SELL—see to BUY.

SERPENT—*sapp.*—The Sr. *sarpa,* 'a snake, a serpent,' from the root *srip,* 'to glide, to creep.'* The Gypsies have assimilated the *r* to the following *p*, as in many other like cases (see Section IV). The term is extremely common in all the cognate dialects of the Sr.: compare Lat. *serpens,* It. *serpe,* Fr. *serpent,* Gr. ἕρπης and ἕρπω, by the aspiration of the initial *s*, so common among the Greeks. Ὄφις is probably derived from Sr. *ahi,* 'a snake,' by the commutation of the aspirates (Bopp).

To SEW—*siváva.*—

NEEDLE—*súv ;* Bor., *jutia.*—Both these terms have a common origin, from the Sr. root *syû, siv,* 'to sew,' Lat. *suere,* Slav. *shiyu.* Compare also Sr. *súchi,* 'needle,' from a cognate root *súch,* 'to sew.'

To SHAVE—*muntáva ;* Bor., *palabear.*—The origin of this word is very clear; it comes from the Sr. root *mund,* 'to grind, to cut the hair, to shave.' Its derivatives have all a similar meaning: as *mundaka,* 'a barber;' *mundana,* 'the act of shaving.' Borrow's term, *palabear,* is derived from *palyula* in his vocabulary. This is the Sr. *palyul,* 'to eat, to purify.' But the word appears to me of Spanish origin.

SHEEP—*bakró, bakrichó ;* Br., *bakroo ;* Bor., *bracuñi, bacria.*—I have placed here Borrow's second term, although he defines it 'a goat:' it appears to be a word of the same origin. The Hindus call the goat *bukka.* Compare also Germ. *bock,* Eng. *buck,* Fr. *bouc. Bakri,* 'ewe;' *bakrichó,* 'lamb,' dim. form, instead of *bakroró. Allé bakré,* 'sheep have come ;' *teréla shelé bakré,* ' he has (owns) a hundred sheep.'

SHIP—*beró ;* Br., *ghamee ;* Bor., *bero, berdo.*—*Beró* seems to be naturally related to the root *bhri,* 'to uphold, to support, to cherish.' Borrow's *berdó* I refer to another cognate word, *bhartri,* 'a supporter, a holder.' This derivation is corroborated by *vordón* or *bordón,* 'a carriage,' which is referable to the same word. Mr. Brown's *ghamee* is the Turk. *gemí,* 'a vessel, a ship.' *Beréskoro,* 'a seaman,' ναύτης, Turk. *gemichi.*

SHOE—*triák.*—I have nothing satisfactory to propose for the derivation of this singular term, which does not resemble any of the words usually applied by the people of these countries to shoes. The Mod. Gr. παπούτζια is from the Pers. *papush* and *pabuj,* 'shoes;' τζαρούχια is from the Turk. *charuk,* 'shoes formed of a piece of thick leather, fastened to the foot by strong thongs of the same material,' worn by farmers and shepherds. Plur. *triaká* and *triakhá : lákoro pral keréla triakhá,* 'her brother makes shoes.'

---

* Armenian *zeral,* 'to creep.'—TR.

ʃʜᴏᴏᴛ (of a vine)—*vicha.*—This is a Bulgarian word, coming from Slav. *vich*', 'a twig, a switch.' It is not a very common word. The Greeks also say βιτζα, but more commonly βέργα·, from the Italian *verga*, Lat. *virga. É manukléri vicha*, 'the shoot of the stump.'

Sʜᴏᴜʟᴅᴇʀ—*vikó, pikó.*—Of origin unknown to me.

To sʜᴜᴛ—*bandáva.*—This is the well known Sr. root *bandh*, 'to bind, to tie,' which corresponds with many terms in the cognate languages: Pers. *bend*, 'a bond,' *bend kerden*, 'to bind;' Germ. *binden, band ;* Fr. *bande ;* Eng. *band, to bind, bondage, bonds*, etc. Among the Gypsies this verb has the signification also of 'tying,' as both are intimately related : thus, *band o vutár*, 'shut the door;' *bandéla pi kori*, 'he ties his neck' (i. e. 'his neckkerchief'); *bandáva mi kori*, 'I tie my neck-kerchief;' *bandloipé*, 'band:' *bandloipé me móste*, 'a band to my mouth.' Aor. *bandlióm*, 'I have shut, or tied:' *bandlióm mo grast*, 'I have tied my horse.'

Sɪᴇᴠᴇ—*résheto.*—A common word, borrowed from the Bulgarians, who pronounce it *riséto.*

To sɪɢʜ—*acharáva.*—This word I have not been able to refer to any corresponding Sr. term. It means 'to groan, to lament, to sigh deeply.' Aor. *acharghióm* and *akiarghióm. Saró divés acharéla*, 'all day (long) he sighs.'

Sɪʟᴠᴇʀ—*rup ;* Bor., *paquilli, plubi, pomi.*—This term is evidently from the Sr. *rûpya*, 'worked silver, silver and gold.' Our common word ἀσήμιον, used now for ἄργυρο;, 'silver,' which some regard as derived from σῆμα, 'a stamp, a sign,' is cognate with the Pers. *sim*, 'silver,' and 'silver coin.' The reader must not confound *rup* with the common Turk. *rub*, derived from the Arabic *rub*', 'fourth.' The three forms of Borrow I do not know how to explain. The second, how-ever, may be the Sp. *plomo*, 'lead,' which Borrow may have written by mistake. I do not agree with him as to its derivation from *rupi.* The Sr. word has given name to the common Hindu coin of the pres-ent day, commonly written "rupee." *Rupovanó*, 'made of silver, *argenteus.*' No doubt, also, the Russian *ruble* has an intimate con-nection with this Sr. term.

Sɪᴍɪʟᴀʀ, ʟɪᴋᴇ—*sar.*—*manúsh sar char*, 'man (is) like grass;' *sar luludí* (Gr. λουλόνδιον, 'flower') *e puviákeri*, 'like the flower of the earth;' *sar tut*, 'like thee;' *sar lubní*, 'like a strumpet.'

Sᴏɴɢ—*ghilí.*—

To sɪɴɢ—*ghiliáva, ghiliováva ;* Bor., *guillabar.*—The Sr. root *ġṛt* is 'to sound, to speak, to sing :' from it comes *gir*, 'a song.' *Ghiliáva* is derived from this root, by the commutation of *r* for *l*, in accordance with all the Gypsy verbs derived from Sr. verbal roots ending in *ṛi* or *ṛt.* Borrow's term corresponds with the one used in Turkey. He has another in his vocabulary, *labelar*, ' cantar, hablar,' which he re-fers to the Sr. *lap*, 'to speak, to utter.' It appears to me to be con-nected rather with the Sp. *hablar*, 'to speak.' *Ghiliováva* is in the middle voice, formed from *ghiló*, 'song,' and the usual *aváva.*

These terms are extremely common among all the Gypsies of Tur-key, and particularly among their women, who gain their livelihood by roaming in the streets, and singing every kind of lascivious and erotic song. *Ghilimpé,* 'an instrument of music;' *i ghiliá e devléskero,* 'the songs of God.'

SISTER—See BROTHER.

SLEEP—*lindr.*—This is evidently the Sr. *nidrá,* 'sleep, sleepiness, sloth.' From this noun is formed an adj. *lindraló,* 'sleepy;' *bilindraló,* 'sleepless:' *na isóm lindraló,* 'I am not sleepy.' Here we see the commutation of the liquids *n* and *l,* so common among the Gypsies and Greeks.

To SLEEP—*sováva;** Bor., *sobelar, sornar.*—Comp. the Sr. *svap,* 'to sleep,' *svapna,* 'sleep,' with which correspond Gr. ὕπνος, Lat. *sopnus, somnus.* The final radical of the Sr. root has been changed into the kindred *v. Sottisóm,* 'I am asleep' (for *sottó isóm*). *Sottó,* 'asleep,' is the Sr. part. *supta,* 'sleeping, asleep:' *sottó 'si i likhnari* (Gr. λυχνάριον), 'the lamp is quenched' (lit. 'asleep'). This phrase I have heard from Gypsies residing near Constantinople. · It is taken from the Greeks, who call λυχνάριον ἀκοίμητον the lamp that is kept burning night and day before the household images. *Na sováva,* 'I am not sleeping.'

SLIM—*sannó.*—Compare the Sr. part. *sanna,* 'shrunk, diminished,' from the verbal root *sad,* 'to wane, to perish gradually.' *Léskeri i romni isi sanní,* 'his wife is slim.'

SLOWLY—*parés.*—This seems to originate from the Sr. *para,* whose definitions are exceedingly numerous and varied. I have often heard it used in this sense. As it is an adverb, it supposes an adj. *paró,* 'slow.' *Parés parés,* 'slowly;' *parés ker,* 'work slowly.'

To SNEEZE—*chiktáva.*—This, like many other similar verbs, is a compound, made up of *chik,* 'a sneeze,' and *dáva,* 'I give.' Compare Sr. *chhikkâ, chhikkana,* 'sneezing.' The verb *dáva,* 'I give,' is frequently joined to nouns. Some of these are never used in their simple form, and are extremely rare, even in the mouth of other Gypsies. An example of the usage of the simple and compound verb we have in *tapáva,* 'to strike,' which is also frequently used in the compound form, *tap dáva,* 'I give a stroke, I strike.' Aor. *chiktinióm,* from *dinióm,* aor. of *dáva.*

SNOW—*iv, biv;* Bor., *bifi, give.*—From the Sr. *hima,* 'snow,' is derived our χιὼν, χεῖμα, Lat. *hiems,* Slav. *zima,* 'winter.' *Iv* is a regular formation; *h* is dropped, and *m* changed to *v* (see Section IV).

SOIL—*poshik.*—This is one of many terms which, in want of a better definition, I refer conjecturally to the root *push,* 'to cherish or nurture, to rear or bring up.' This definition might have been given to the soil, as the ultimate source of nutrition.

SON-IN-LAW—*jamutró.*—The Sr. possesses two cognate terms, with which this word closely coincides: *yâmâtṛi* and *jâmâtṛi,* 'a daughter's husband.'

To SPEAK—*vrakeráva.*—A compound verb, *vra* and *keráva,* 'to make.' *Bhran, bran,* and *vran,* are cognate Sr. verbs, signifying 'to sound;' but I prefer as the origin of this Gypsy verb the root *brû,* 'to speak, to say,' which is to be met with in many European languages. The

---

* "*Sovko,* 'il dort.'" Vaillant, p. 363. "*Passjuval,* 'schlafen.'" Arndt, p. 391.

word is a very common one among all the Gypsies, particularly when they wish to impose silence. *Ma vrakér,* 'do not speak' (i. e. 'be silent'), Gr. σιώπα; *na vrakeráva,* 'I do not talk;' *ta i romnía ka dukéna but ta vrakeréna,* 'and the women that love to talk much.'*

To spin—*katáva.*—This Gypsy verb cannot easily be referred to a satisfactory Sr. original. But compare Sr. *kṛit,* 'to cut,' also 'to spin,' and its derivative *kartana,* 'cutting, spinning.'

To spit—*chungárva.*—I know of no Sr. root to which this Gypsy word may with propriety be referred. It means 'to spit upon, to revile.' Among the common people in these countries, spitting upon one another is an act of contempt and reviling. *Chungartinióm,* aor. pass., 'I was spit upon,' i. e. 'I was insulted;' *chungér,* 'spittle, phlegm,' and whatever else is ejected from the mouth.

Sponsor—*kirvó.*—This is a term common to all the Gypsies, who certainly cannot have brought it from India. The Greek ἀνάδοχος, 'godfather, sponsor,' designates one who undertakes to execute something, a guarantee. May it not then be allowable to refer this term to the Sr. *kurvat,* 'doing, acting, an agent,' from *kṛi,* 'to make, to do?' *Kirví,* 'god-mother;' *mo kirvó isi but baravaló,* 'my godfather is very rich.'

Spoon—*róyi, rói.*—The origin of this term is unknown to me.

Stake—*kiló.*—Compare Sr. *kíla,* 'a stake, a pin, a bolt,' etc. This term by the Gypsies is used for poles set up around a field, upon which is formed the fence; also, for the poles set up around the threshing floors; and again, for poles stuck deep into the ground, to which horses are fastened while grazing. *Bandlióm mo grastés to kiló,* 'I have tied my horse to the stake.' Compare Slav. *kol',* 'stake, pike.'

To stand—*terghiováva, tertiováva.*—This is a verb in the middle voice, in common use among the Gypsies. Aor. *tertinilióm,* and by some pronounced *terghinilióm.* Like the Greek στέχομαι, it is always used in the passive voice. *Terghiováva* supposes *teráva* as the active voice, which we have referred above (see to HAVE) to the Sr. *dhṛi,* 'to have, to hold, to keep.' *Atiá terghiováva,* 'here I stand;' ἐδῶ στέχομαι.

Star—*chergheni;†* Br., *tcherhinee;* Bor., *cherdillas, trebene.*—Compare Sr. *tárâ,* 'star, planet, constellation,' probably from the Vedic *stârâ,* by throwing off the initial *s.* From this is our ἀστὴρ and ἄστρον, Lat. *aster, astrum.‡ Cherdillas,* and *cherdino,* found in another place in Borrow's glossary, I conjecture to be of Spanish origin.

To steal—*choráva, choláva.§*—

Thief—*chor;* Bor., *chor, choro.*—These terms, so similar to each other, are referable to the Sr. root *chur,* 'to steal, to rob.' According to Bopp, this root gives origin to the Lat. *fur* and Gr. φώρ. From it

---

* Pott writes the word "*Rakkeraf,* 'sprechen, reden.'" Nearly all the authors on the Gypsies write the word in a similar manner. The word is pronounced by the Gypsies here as I have written it, and I have heard it very often with the initial *v* strongly marked.

† "*Tcheacren,* 'astres.'" Vaillant, p. 457. "*Tschergeny, zerhene,* 'stern.'" Arndt, p. 366.

‡ The Armenian *asdegh* is evidently of the same origin, as that language often changes *r* and *l* to the guttural *gh.*—Tr.

§ "*Tchordel,* 'tu voles'" (write *tchorêl,* 'il vole'). Vaillant, p. 369.

comes *chaura*, 'a thief, a robber, a pilferer,' whence the above *chor* and *choro*. At times, instead of *chor*, the Gypsies use *chornó* and *churnó*, 'a thief.' *Chordicanó*, 'stolen;' *kon chorghiáles?* 'who stole it?' *astarghióm e chorés*, 'I have taken the thief.'

STEEL—*abchín.*—This term, ordinarily meaning 'steel,' is very often applied to the steel and flint used generally in Turkey for striking fire, and which people always carry with them for lighting their tobacco-pipes. It is difficult to refer it to any known Sr. term. I bring to the memory of the reader the Pers. *abgine*, 'vitrum, crystallum,' a name given to substances similar to the flint, and so, perhaps, in course of time to the steel itself, which constituted a necessary accompaniment of these instruments. In this manner the word may have come to be applied to steel in general.*

To STEP—*ukiaváva, uktiaváva.*—This verb is derived from the Sr. *kram*, 'to go, to walk, to step,' with some preposition prefixed. It is used also for 'stamping, trampling,' etc.

It STINKS—*kándela.*—Of doubtful etymology. *Kandíniko*, 'stinking.'

STONE—*bar ;* Bor., *bar.*—Compare Sr. *bhára*, 'weight, burden.' It is possible that the Gypsies gave this name to 'stone,' as being preëminently heavy. It is very well known to all of them. *Diniáles yek baré barésa*, 'he struck him with a large stone;' *ov isás ta chivghiás o bar*, 'it was he who threw the stone;' *baréskoro*, 'a stone-cutter, a worker in stones.'

STRAW—*bus.*—Referable to the Sr. *busa*, 'chaff.' Compare FLAX.

To STRIKE—*tapáva, tap-dáva.*—*Tap* is not a very usual word among the Gypsies, and when used, it is mostly joined to *dáva*, 'I give:' *tap dáva*, 'I give a blow, I strike.' *Tap déla*, 'it beats' (i. e., the pulse). Both *tap* and *tapáva* seem to be related to the Sr. *tup*, 'to injure, to hurt, to kill,' which has passed into Greek, as τύπτω. It may be well to remark that *tap*, 'to heat, to torment,' may possibly have given origin to this verb.

STRONG—*zoraló.*—This is a word of Persian origin, very common among the Gypsies, from *zor*, 'strength, vigor.' It is very usual with the Turks also, who have formed from it adjectives of their own: *zorlu*, 'strong,' instead of the Pers. *zormend* or *zordar*, 'having strength.' *Bizoraló*, 'weak;' *but zoraló isóm*, 'I am very strong.'†

STUMP of a vine—*manukló, manikló.*—Applied to the vine in vineyards, before the plant has shot out the sprouts upon which the grapes are produced. It is like the trunk of a tree. *E manukliéri vícha keréla drak*, 'the shoots of the stump make (i. e. 'produce') grapes.'

SUMMER—*nilái.*—Of doubtful etymology.

SUN—*kam ;*‡ Br., *cam ;* Bor., *cam, can.*—The similarity of these words makes their common derivation plain. The usual name of the sun

---

* All the derivations of Pott are as unsatisfactory as mine. They may serve as a guide to others.

† Armenian *zoravor*, 'strong;' *zoranal*, 'to grow strong;' *zorutiune*, 'strength.'—TR.

‡ "*O-cham*, 'le soleil.'" Vaillant, p. 457. "*Kam, cham, okam*, ' sonne.'" Arndt, p. 356.

among the Hindus was *sûrya*, from the root *sur*, 'to shine.' The above *kam, can* seems related to the Sr. root *kan*, 'to shine;' compare Lat. *candeo*, whence also *candela, candidus*, 'white;' like our σελήνη, 'moon,' from σελάω, 'to shine,' and Mod. Gr. φεγγάριον, 'moon,' from φέγγω, 'to shine.'*

SUNDAY—*kurkó ;* Bor., *culco, curque.*—See CHURCH.

SWEET—*gudló ;* Br., *goodlu ;* Bor., *busni.*—Concerning these terms I have nothing satisfactory to propose. *Gudló tut,* 'sweet milk.'

SWINE—*baló, balichó ;* Br., *baleetcho ;* Bor., *balicho.*—Compare the Sr. adjective *balin*, 'strong, powerful,' and, as substantive, among other meanings, 'swine.' *Balichó* is a diminutive form, probably from the language of the Turks, as the word, according to the general formation of the Gypsy diminutives, would be *baloró. Parvardó baló,* 'a fat pig.'

SWORD—*hanló ;* Bor., *estuché.*—Neither of these words appears to me to have any clear relation to Sr. roots. In want of anything better, I propose for *hanló* (at times *khanló*), the common Sr. *han*, 'to hurt or kill.' The final syllable *lo* is the regular adjective form of many Gypsy nouns. Borrow's *estuché* may be related to the Italian *stocco*, ' a small sword.' We have seen another Italian word in Borrow's vocabulary, viz. *meligrana.*

T.

TAIL—*pori.*—I know of no Sr. word to which this term can be traced.

To TAKE, to GET—*láva ;* Bor., *lillar.*—Undoubtedly related to the Sr. *lâ*, 'to take, to obtain.' This verb I formerly considered as referable to Sr. *labh*, 'to take, to seize,' from which originates the Gr. λαβαίνω, λαμβάνω; but its indicative present should in that case be *laváva*, and its aorist *lavghióm. Kamalél yek grast,* 'he will take (i. e. ' buy') a horse;' *liniómles panjénghe,* 'I bought it for five' (i. e. 'pieces of money'). Borrow's form *lillar* does not appear to be connected with *láva.*

TALL—*vuchó, uchó ;* Br., *utchó ;* Bor., *saste.*—This word is the Sr. *uchcha*, 'high, tall.' Probably Borrow's *saste*, 'high, tall,' is related to the Sr. *çasta*, 'fortunate, excellent, great.' This term is by nearly all the Gypsies pronounced *vuchó : uchó* is in use only among a few of the Moslems. *Vuchó manúsh,* ' a tall man ;' *vuchó ruk,* 'a tall tree ; adv. *vuchés*, 'highly :' *po vuchés*, 'more highly.'

TEAR—*úsfa.*—The Sr. *vâshpa*, written also *vâspa*, 'vapor, tear,' by dropping its initial consonant, and converting the *p* of the last syllable into its cognate *f*, has formed the present *asfa.*

TENT—*sahriz ;* Br., *serka.*—Words of origin unknown to me.

TESTICLE—*peló.*—I have inserted another word in the Vocabulary, used for 'testicle' (see EGG). *Peló* (pl. *pelé*) may be referred to the Sr. *pela*, 'a testicle.'

THIEF—See to STEAL.

---

* Armenian *loosin*, 'moon,' from *loosnil*, ' to shine.'—TR.

THIRST—*trush, trust.*—

To THIRST—*taráva.*—These terms have a common origin, from the Sr˙ *trish,* 'to thirst.' From this root have originated the Germ. *durst,* Eng. *thirst.* As thirst implies the idea of want of water and dryness, it is consequently natural to suppose that from the same Sr. root have sprung the Gr. τέρσομαι and τερσαίνω, 'to dry.' The Sr. semi-vowel *r* is rarely lost in the European languages; it is, in fact, the most constant of all the Sr. consonants. *Trushaló,* 'thirsty:' *trushalo 'sóm,* 'I am thirsty.'

To become THIRSTY.—*trusháliováva.*—A verb in the middle form, composed of the above *trushaló,* 'thirsty,' and *aváva.* The Gypsies are extremely fond of these compound verbs, and neglect the simple, as in this case. The same is true of the Greeks. The Moslem Gypsies make use of *teráva,* and, though they understand *trushaliováva,* will not employ it.

THIS—*avaká, avká.*—There is a great confusion in the use of this demonstrative pronoun. Even among the Gypsies themselves, one hears the word continually varied, without any apparent reason: *avaká,* 'this;' *avakhá* (or *akhá*) *isí minró,* 'this is mine;' *avaklía* (or *aklá*) *resá,* 'these vineyards;' *akhiá mol,* 'this wine;' *okhiá romní,* 'this woman;' *oklé manushénghere,* 'of these men.' Both masculine and neuter have the same termination. *Avakhá manúsh,* 'this man;' *avakhá chavó,* 'this child.' It is difficult to say to which of the Sr. pronouns this term should be referred.

THREAD—*tav.*—This word appears to be of pure Sr. origin. The root *tap,* 'to heat, to vex, to torment,' we have noticed in this Vocabulary, as the parent stock of many words among the Gypsies here in Turkey. It appears also in the Pers. *tabiden* and *tuften,* 'to burn, to vex, to torment.' To this verb properly belongs *tab,* 'curvatura funis, comae' (Vullers), and *risman taften,* 'to weave,' *charkh risman-i-tav,* 'an instrument for weaving.' All these terms imply the idea of tormenting, as is the case with any filament when it is twisted into thread, or rather tormented into this new form. In Greek, κλωστή, from κλώθω, 'to twist, to weave,' is used now very generally for νῆμα, 'thread.' So too in Latin, *torquere,* 'to twist, to torment,' gave origin to *torques,* 'a chain worn round the neck.' From στρέφω, 'to turn, to whirl,' came the στρόφος of the ancient Greek physicians, by which they indicated violent shooting pains in the bowels, the *tormina* of the Romans. In this way I conceive that the Gypsy word *tav* was either borrowed from the Persians, or formed directly from the Sr. root from which the Persians have taken their own *tabiden.* The Persians have also *tav,* 'thread,' and *tabdi,* 'torquens funem,' which the Turkish translator (Vullers s. v.) explains by *ip ve iplik bukiji,* 'a weaver of thread or rope.'

THROAT—*kurló.*—A very indefinite word: it signifies 'the back of the mouth,' and frequently 'the neck,' particularly its front part. To me it appears to be the Bulgarian *gurló,* 'throat, pharynx.' *T' astàrghiovél mo chip me kurléste,* 'may my tongue be bound (lit. 'held') in my throat.'

To THROW—*chiváva, chitáva.*—Compare Sr. *kship,* 'to throw or cast,' part. *kshipta,* 'thrown, despatched,' which seems to have given origin to this Gypsy verb, which retains the same signification as the Sr. original. By the usual change of the consonants, this participle becomes *kshitto* or *chitto*, and hence the verb *chitára*. Aor. *chivghióm* : *chivghióm yek bar*, 'I threw a stone;' *kána chivésa bar*, 'when thou throwest (a) stone;' *chivdiló o bar*, 'the stone was thrown;' *chivghián bar, dik nápalal*, 'thou hast thrown (a) stone, look behind'—a common proverb, 'consider the consequences of thy actions.'

TILL—*chin.*—This term is common to all the Gypsies, wherever they are to be found. *Ketí dur isí* (pronounced *dúrsi*) *chin ti Silivrí?* 'how far is it to Silivria?' *chin ti puv*, 'to the ground;' Gr. ἕως εἰς τὴν γῆν; *chin vuchés*, 'on high.'

TIME, TIMES—*far, var.*—Corresponds to the Gr. φορά, as πολλὰς φορὰς, ὀλίγας φορὰς, used now in the place of πολλάκις, ὀλιγάκις. The word is pronounced indifferently *far* and *var*, and in this the Gypsies imitate their neighbors the Greeks, who say φορὰ and βολὰ. *Yek far*, 'one time, once;' *kayék far*, 'sometimes' and 'never;' like the Gr. καμμίαν φορὰν, which has both these significations. This term is the Pers. *bar*, which has often the meaning of the Lat. *vicis*, Turk. *defa'*, 'turn:' compare Pers. *yek bar*, 'one time, once.' Vullers derives it from Sr. *bhára*, from the root *bhrí*, Gr. φέρω, whence φορά. But compare Sr. *vára*, 'a turn, a successive time.' *Ke yavér far diniás man*, 'and at other times he struck me;' *po kayék far*, 'at times, sometimes;' *duvár, trivár, panjvár*, 'twice, thrice, five times.'

To be TIRED—*chiniováva.*—See to CUT.

TOBACCO-PIPE—*chukní.*—This is a common term for the long tobacco-pipes, used in the Levant by all the inhabitants indiscriminately. *An i chukní*, 'bring the tobacco-pipe.' The usual term among the Turks is *chibuk*, Gr. τζιμπούκιον.

TODAY—*avdivés, apdivés;*[*] Bor., *achibes.*—We have in this term the Sr. *divá*,[†] which I have had occasion to mention in explaining the term *divés*, 'day, morning.' The initial *a, av* may be the Sr. dem. pron. *sa*, which has rejected, like many Greek words, the Sr. *s* at its beginning. The formation of this adverb may be explained by the Gr. σ-ήμερον, τ-ήμερον, 'this day;' τῆτες, τ-ἔτος, 'this year;' τ-ὥρα, 'this hour, now.' *Avdivés aváva*, 'today I am coming.'

TOGETHER—*eketané.*—This appears to me a pure Sr. term, coming from *eka*, 'one.' Compare Lat. *una*, 'together, in company;' Pers. *yekser*, 'together, at the same time.' Here is an example of a purer preservation of this Sr. numeral than we have in the term *yek*, 'one.' The Gypsies always pronounce it as I have written it. *Achái chor eketané*, 'and other thieves together;' *eketané améntza*, 'together with us;' *eketané e chavéntza*, 'together with the children.'[‡]

TOMB—*mermóri, mnemóri.*—Of modern Greek origin. Μνημόριον and μνημούριον are diminutive forms of μνῆμα, 'a tomb.' The ancients

---

[*] "*Abdés, odés*, 'aujourd'hui.'" Vaillant, p. 456.

[†] Armenian *div*, 'day.'—TR.

[‡] Pott writes the word *kettené, kétáne, keteny, catané, catanar, catañar*, 'to assemble.' In speaking of its etymology he says: "der Ursprung höchst zweifelhaft." It is certainly clearer, as pronounced in these countries. Similar comparisons may serve to illustrate many other passages.

also had their diminutive, μνημάτιον. In the use of terms of this class, the Gypsies have always adopted those of the new faith which they have embraced. The Moslem Gypsies say *mezár*, 'a tomb,' from Turk. *mezar*.

TOMORROW—*takhiára.*—I have nothing to propose for this term. *Po tukhiára*, 'day after tomorrow;' *takhiára aváma*, 'tomorrow I am coming;' *takhiára kamovés otiá?* 'tomorrow wilt thou be there?' *tukhiára kamajél*, 'tomorrow he will go.'

TONGS—*ksillábi, ksillávi.*—I have noted this word, which is of the purest Greek, though nowadays no Greek understands it, and it could not have been lately borrowed from the Greeks, since they make no use of it, nor is it to be found in any of the modern Greek glossaries. Πυράγρα was anciently the name of the instrument by which heated or burning substances were seized, also λαβίς, from λαβαίνω, λαμβάνω. Λαβίδα we now call the long-handled and extremely shallow spoon used in administering the communion. Λαβή and λαβίς, with συν— συλλαβή and συλλαβίς, or ξυλλαβή and ξυλλαβίς,—is an instrument for seizing anything. These latter terms are not in use now among the common people, but the existence of such a Greek term in the language of the Gypsies certainly proves the employment of it among the Greeks at the period of their irruption into these countries. It may be well to remark that the proper term for tongs, πυράγρα, is nearly forgotten, and that the Greeks now use the Turkish *mashá*, 'tongs.' The term *ksillábi* is peculiar to the Gypsy blacksmiths. In other cases they use the Turkish *mashá*. The presence of the compound consonant *ks* amply proves the word to be foreign, as this consonant never occurs in pure Gypsy words.

TONGUE—*chip;* Bor., *chipe, chipi.*—From the Sr. *jihvâ*, 'tongue,' *j* being changed to *ch*, as is common in many languages. *Romaní chip*, 'the Gypsy language;' *me chipéste*, 'on my tongue.' *Chip*, 'tongue,' as in many other idioms, is used both for 'tongue' and 'language.'

TOOTH—*dánt;* Br., *danda;* Bor., *dani.*—From the Sr. *dat* or *danta*, 'tooth.'

TREE—*ruk.*—This Gypsy word bears no relation to the Sr. *dru*, with which are connected the synonymous terms in so many other Indo-European languages, but may be referred to the root *ruh*, 'to grow from seed, to grow as a tree,' by the changing of the aspirate, *h*, into a guttural, *k*. From this root come *ruhvan*, 'a tree,' precisely as the Greeks applied the term φυτὸς to trees and plants in general, and *rúksha*, 'a tree in general.'[*] Plur. *ruká : opré to ruká*, 'upon the trees;' *vuchó ruk*, 'a high tree.'

TROUGH (wooden)—*kopána.*—A Bulgarian word, *kopánka*, from the Slav. *kopáin*, 'I dig,' precisely as the corresponding Gr. term, σκάφη, comes from σκάπτω, 'I dig.'

TRUTH—*chachipé;* Bor., *chachipe.*—We have the following derivation by Borrow: "This word, which the English Gypsies pronounce

---

[*] In their Essai sur le Pali, Burnouf and Lassen compare the Pali *roukkha*, 'a tree,' to the Sr. *vrikcha*, 'a tree.' Both the Pali and Gypsy appear to me to be from the above *rúksha*. The same form, *roukko*, 'a tree,' is found in the Prakrit. Ibid., p. 159.

tsatsipé, seems to be a compound of the Sr. *sat,* which signifies 'true,' and the word of Sanskrit origin *chipé,* 'a tongue.' *Chachipé* therefore is literally 'a true tongue.'" This is one of Borrow's random derivations. He has said elsewhere in his vocabulary that *pen* is a particle frequently used in the Gypsy language in the formation of nouns: e. g. *chungalipen,* 'ugliness,' from *chungaló,* 'ugly.' Here, however, the final *pe* or *pen* is this very particle, common to the Gypsies of Spain with those here in Turkey, as we have already seen in the course of this memoir. The rest of the word is probably the Sr. *satya,* 'true, sincere, honest.' From *chachipé* is formed the adj. *chachipanó,* 'true,' and the adv. *chachipanés,* 'truly :' *chachipé isí,* 'it is true,' lit. 'it is a truth,' like the Gr. ἀλήθεια εἶναι, for ἀληθὲς εἶναι.

Turk—*khorakhái.*—The Turks, who call themselves *osmanly* and *othmanly,* as descendants from the house of Othman, would be surprised to hear such a name applied to them. Their language, however, they call *turk.* The Greeks always call them τούρκους. Borrow defines the Gypsy term, written by him *corajay,* as follows: "'The Moors, *los moros,*' probably derived from the word *kurrek,* a term of execration and contempt too frequently employed by the common Moors in their discourse." The similarity of the two terms, as employed here and in Spain, amply proves the necessity of looking for another origin than that which has been advanced by Borrow. *Khorakhái* is both singular and plural. *Khorakhanó,* 'Turkish ;' *khorakhani, khorakhni,* 'a Turkish woman ;' *khorakhnía,* 'Turkish women ;' *khorakhanó gav,* 'a Turkish village ;' *khorakhaní chip,* 'the Turkish language ;' *khorakhanés janésa ?* 'dost thou know Turkish ?' *khorakhniori,* 'a young Turkish woman ;' *khorakhané rom,* 'Turkish Gypsies,' i. e. 'Gypsies of the Mohammedan religion.'

U.

Ugly, not beautiful—*nasukár ;* Bor., *chungaló.*—For *chungaló* see miserable. My own term is from *sukár,* 'beautiful,' with the negative particle *na.* See negation and beautiful.

Unfortunate—*bahtaló.*—This originates from a Persian term, *bakht,*[*] 'fortune, luck,' to which the Gypsies have given the form of their vernacular idiom, precisely as we have observed in other words borrowed by them. So the Greeks have made, from the Turkish *zavál,* ζαβάλικος, ζάβαλης, and ζαβάλισσα, 'miserable.' Though *bahtaló,* from *bakht,* 'good fortune,' would properly indicate prosperity and happiness, still it is given to men and animals as a term of affection and hearty commiseration. *O bahtalá peló ti puv,* 'the unfortunate (i. e. 'bird') fell to the ground.'

Up—*opré ;* Bor., *aupré, opre.*—From the Sr. *upari,* 'above, up, up above :' compare Gr. ὑπὲρ, Lat. *super,* Germ. *ober,* Eng. *over.*[†] *Opretár tut (tar,* abl. particle), 'from the rest of the milk ;' *besghióm opré to amáksi* (Gr. ἀμάξι), 'I sat upon the carriage ;' *opré to ruká,* 'upon the trees ;' *opré to bar,* 'upon the stone ;' *opré ti púv,* 'upon the ground

---

[*] Armenian *pakht* or *paht,* 'fortune ;' *pakhtávor,* 'fortunate.'—Tr.

[†] Armenian *veri, ver, verd.*—Tr.

11

(earth);' *oprál* and *opryál*, 'from above:' *oprál pelióm*, 'I fell from on high.'

URINE—*mutér.*—

To void URINE—*mutráva* ; Bor., *mutrar, muclar.*—These terms bear the stamp of undisputed descent from the Sr. *mútra*, 'urine.' Borrow's *muclar* is probably a corruption of the original *mutrar*, although I have not met elsewhere the change of *trar* into *clar.*

V.

VILLAGE—*gav* ; Bor., *gao.*—Compare Sr. *grâma*, 'village,' which has lost the liquid *r*, and changed the final *m* into *v*, a change which we have already observed elsewhere (see NAME), and shall have occasion fully to prove, in speaking of the commutation of the consonants. The Gypsy word is often applied to denote 'one's native town' or 'home,' πατρίς, just as the Greeks use χωρίον, and the Turks *kióy*, for their native place. *Mo gav*, 'my village,' is to be understood as 'my native town;' *ghelióm to gav*, 'I went to the village;' *gavudnó*, 'a villager:' *mo gavudnó*, 'one of my village;' *túya kamovés to gáv?* 'wilt thou also be in the village?' *te gavéskoro manushé isi but górke*, 'of thy village the men are very bad.'

VINEGAR—*shut* ; Br., *shutt* ; Bor., *juter, juti.*—Compare Sr. *çata*, 'sour, astringent.' It is worthy of remark, that this term by some Gypsies is pronounced *shutkó*, and applied to 'vinegar,' although it properly means 'sour.' From this noun, by the addition of *lo*, has been formed *shutló*, 'sour:' *shutló mol*, 'sour wine:' it is pronounced also *shudló: shudló tut*, 'sour milk,' the Turkish *yaghurt.*

VINEYARD—*res, rez* ; Bor., *eresia.*—Compare Sr. *ras*, 'gustare, amare;' the noun *rasa* has also the definition of 'grape,' though its general signification is 'taste of any kind.' Persian *bagh rez*, 'a vineyard.' By the Gypsies this term is applied particularly to the vine. *Keréna resá*, 'they make (i. e. 'plant') vineyards;' *kaléskoro isi e resá?* 'whose are the vineyards?'

VOMITING—*chartimpé, chattimpé.*—

To VOMIT—*chartáva, chattáva.*—Compare Sr. *chhard*, 'to vomit, to be sick.' The Gypsies, in pronouncing *chartáva*, give such a slight sound to the *r* that it is scarcely heard, or even, at times, is not heard at all. Many Gypsies contend that it contains no *r*, and pronounce always *chattáva. Chartimpé* is the Sr. *chhardi*, 'vomiting,' by the addition of the common *pe* or *pen*, which we have already noticed.

W.

To WALK—*piráva* ; Bor., *pirar.*—Compare *piro*, 'foot,' which I have referred above to the Sr. *prt* or *par*, to pass.' But *pirél*, 'he walks fast;' *kapiráv*, 'I shall walk.'

WALLACHIAN—*vlákhia.*—The Greek βλάχος, a denomination given to the inhabitants of Wallachia and Moldavia. *Vlakhína*, 'a Wallachian woman.'

WARM—*tattó.*—This word I have explained in speaking of BATH. I notice it here merely to add that the Gypsies use it in this sense also, apart from its signification of 'bath.'

To WASH—*továva.*—This verb may be referred to the Sr. verbal root *dháv*, 'to cleanse, to be clean or pure.' Aor. *tovióm* and *tovghióm: tovióm mo shoró keraló*, 'I have washed my scabby head;' *toávaman* (mid. voice), 'I wash myself,' used for the Gr. νίπτομαι, λούομαι, πλύνομαι: *so kerés?* *toávaman*, 'what art thou doing? I am washing myself;' *továva me yismata*, 'I wash my linen;' *tovdó*, 'washed:' *tovdé yismata*, 'washed linen.'

WATER—*pani, pai;*[*] Br., *pagnee;* Bor., *pani.*—The Sr. adj. *pántya*, from *pá*, 'to drink,' signifies 'anything fit to drink, potable,' and consequently 'water.' Water is also termed *páya*, from the same root *pá*. *Déman khandí pani*, 'give me a little water;' *sudró pani*, 'cool water.'

To WATER—*panidáva.*—A compound verb, from the above and *dáva*, 'I give.' The verb has been formed in imitation of the Greeks and Turks: the former often say δίδω νεϱὸν, instead of ποτίζω; the Turks, *su veririm*, for *ichirmek.*

To WEEP—*rováva;* Bor., *orobar.*—Both these words I am inclined to refer to the Sr. verbal root *ru*, 'to cry, to make a noise, to yell, to shriek.' Compare *viráva*, 'sound, noise;' *virávin*, 'shouting, weeping, crying.' Weeping with howling and yelling, amongst barbarous people, is an ordinary phenomenon, on all occasions where the exhibition of sorrow is necessary or official. The initial *o* in Borrow is euphonic. *O rakló rovéla*, 'the child cries;' *saró divés rovéla*, 'all day he cries.'

WEIGHT—*vária.*—This term, usual among the Gypsy blacksmiths, is applied to the hammer which beats the heated iron. It is from the Gr. βάϱος, 'weight,' from which comes βαϱῶ, 'to strike.'

WELL—*khanínk, khaínk;* Bor., *putar.*—These words differ so much from each other that they cannot be referred to the same origin. My own are from the Sr. *khan*, 'to dig, to delve,' whence the Gr. χαίνω. From this archetypal root *khan* probably comes the Lat. *canalis*, and also *cuniculus*, denoting 'the hare' and 'a mine' (Bopp). Compare from the same root the Sr. adj. *khanaka*, 'whatever pertains to digging, and to making canals and wells,' whence the present *khanínk* and *khaínk*, denoting 'whatever is dug,' and consequently 'a well.' The use of an adjective for a substantive is extremely common. Borrow's *putar* I regard as Spanish, or rather as from the Lat. *puteus*, and not, as he explains it, as from *pátála.*

WELL—*lachó.*—An adverb, from *lachó*, 'good.' *Lachés isi*, 'it is well;' *po lachés*, 'better:' *po lachés isóm*, 'I am better;' *nanái but luchés*, 'it is not very well;' *po lachés te jas*, 'it is better for thee to go.'

WHAT—*so.*—This term, the neuter of the interrogative pronoun *kon*, is used precisely as the Eng. 'what.' The following phrases will explain it: *so terésa?* 'what hast thou?' (i. e. 'what is the matter with thee')? *so kamésa?* 'what dost thou wish?'

WHEEL—*asán.*—Compare Sr. *ara*, 'the spoke or radius of a wheel.' The change of *r* into *s* is extremely common, not only in Sr., but in many other languages.

---

[*] "*Pany, panio,* 'wasser.'" Arndt, p. 357.

WHELP—*rukonó*.—This term is used for the young of dogs; Gr. σκύμ. νος, Mod. Gr. σκυλάκιον. It seems to me to be related to the Sr. *ruh*, 'to grow, to be produced or become manifest, to be born.' *I chuklí penghiás panj rukoné*, 'the bitch has produced five whelps.'

WHEN—*kánna*.—Compare Sr. *kadá*, 'when.' *Kánna kanashés?* 'when wilt thou go?' *kánna kamuló?* 'when will he die?' *kánna kinghiánles?* 'when didst thou buy it?' *kánna kamabiél?* 'when will she be delivered' (i. e., 'of a child')?

WHENCE—*katár*.—Intimately related to the pron. *kon* and *ka*, 'who' and 'which.' The final *tar* is the ablative particle (see Section V). *Katár alló amaré manúsh?* 'whence came our men?' *katár avésa?* 'whence comest thou?' *katár anghián te romniá?* 'whence didst thou bring thy wife?' *katár allián?* 'whence hast thou come?'

WHERE—*kárin*.—Also related to the interrogative pron. *kon*, 'who.' *Kúrin kamajés?* 'where wilt thou go?' *kárin isí to rom?* 'where is thy husband?' *kárin jésa?* 'where art thou going?' It is used at times as the Italians use their *ove*: *takhiára kamováv ti pólin* (Gr. πόλιν) *kárin ta isí to dat*, 'tomorrow I shall go to the city, where also thy father is.'

WHITE—*parnó*; Bor., *parno, parne*.—The origin of this term, so common among all the Gypsies, is extremely obscure. Borrow defines *parno* "*blanco*, Sr. *pandu*." This term, *pándu*, well known in the history of India as the name of the founder of the Pandava race, means also 'white, yellow, jaundice.' I see no relation between the Sr. and Gypsy terms. *Parnó manró*, 'white bread; *o yék kaló, o yék parnó*, 'the one black, the other white.'

WHO—*kon*.—This is evidently the Sr. *ka*, neut. *kim*, which, with slight variations, is found in most of the Indo-European languages. *Kon diniás e chukél?* 'who struck the dog?' *kaléskoro isí o ker?* 'whose is the house?' *kaléste bashé?* 'near whom?' *ta kalés?* 'and whom?' These examples show that the oblique cases of this pronoun are extremely irregular, and are far from resembling the declination of the Sr. *kim*. To *kon* is related the relative *ka* and *ke*, which is extremely common with the Gypsies, and used as the Italians use their *che*, and the Mod. Gr. their ποῦ, relative pronouns that have lost both gender and number. A few illustrations will give the reader a clear idea of this pronoun: *ki ov ka isí*, 'and he who is;' *ta i romnía ka dukhéna*, 'and the women that love;' *sávore ka kamél*, 'all that he desired;' *oká gorkipé ka na kamésa te kerén túke*, 'whatever evil that thou dost not desire they should do to thee;' *lachó o manúsh ka kamadél tut*, 'happy (good) the man who will give thee.'

WHY—*sóske*.—Related to *so*, 'what,' the neuter of the interr. pron., with the particle *ke*, of which we shall speak in treating of the cases (Section V). *Sóske allián?* 'why did they come?' *sóske puchésa?* 'why dost thou ask?' *sóske isánas otiá?* 'why were ye there?'

WIDOW—*pivli*.—This appears to be a corrupted form of the Sr. *vidhavá*, 'a widow.' It is found more or less altered in many cognate dialects: compare Pers. *beva*, 'widow,' Lat. *vidua*, Germ. *wittwe*, Eng. *widow*.

WIFE—*romní*; Br., *milomnee*; Bor., *romi*.—For the explanation of these terms, see GYPSY. Mr. Brown's *milomnee* should be written *mi romní,* 'my wife.' So gentle is the pronunciation of the liquids, that whoever is not somewhat conversant with the idiom easily falls into such mistakes.

WIFE'S BROTHER—*saló.*—

WIFE'S SISTER—*salí.*—This term may be referred to the Sr. *çálin,* 'belonging to a house, domestic,' from *çála,* 'a house.' We have in Eng. *domestic,* and Fr. *domestique,* 'a servant,' while the term *domesticus* is properly 'any one belonging to a house.' The Gypsies, who are in the habit of living together in such numbers, must naturally have been inclined to give such names to members of a family.

WIND—*palvál.*—This is used for the Gr. ἄνεμος, which at present is mostly applied to mean 'a strong wind, a gale.' It is difficult to give any satisfactory etymology of it, although it appears to be of Hindu origin. *Teréla palvál,* 'it has (i. e. 'there is') wind;' *palvál but,* 'strong wind.' The word is often used for 'the atmosphere, air:' *ti palvál vuchés,* 'high in the air.'

WINE—*mol;** Br., *mol;* Bor., *mol.*—The similarity of these terms makes their etymology plain. Borrow says the word *mol* is "a pure Persian word." It is true the Persian word for wine is *mol,* but the Persians and Gypsies both derive it from the Sr. *madhu,* Gr. μέθυ and μέλι, 'an intoxicating drink,' Lat. *mel,* Lithuan. *madus,* Slav. *med,* and Bulg. *met. Kamésa te mol?* 'dost thou wish wine also?' *shudló mol,* 'sour wine.'

WING—*pak.*—Compare Sr. *paksha,* 'a wing.' The Gypsies give this denomination indifferently either to the wing or to feathers, like the Gr. πτερὸν, 'feather, wing.' Plur. *paká. Te sas charés* (Turk. *charé*) *te terél pak o manúsh,* 'if it were possible that man should have wings;' *ta diniómles ti pak,* 'and I struck it on the wing.'

WINTER—*vent.*—I have spoken of the term *iv,* 'snow,' elsewhere, as from the *hima* of the Hindus. The Sr. adj. *himavant* is 'cold, freezing, chilly, frosty.' As in the word *iv,* 'snow,' the initial aspirate was dropped, so in this word the vowel also, and the word thus mutilated is now in use among all the Gypsies.

To WISH—*kamáva;* Bor., *camelar.*—This verb is the Sr. *kam,* 'to desire, to love;' *káma* is the Cupid of the Latins, the ἔρως of the Greeks. This verb among the Gypsies is used whenever they intend to express desire, wish, or love, in perfect accordance with the definitions generally given to the Sr. root. Borrow defines *camelar* 'to love, Sp. *amar.*' I have placed it with my own word, as it is evidently the same verb, proceeding from the same original. In treating of the derivation of the tenses, I shall have occasion to speak of this verb, as an auxiliary forming the future. It is there that its signification becomes extremely clear. *So kamésa?* 'what dost thou wish?' *akaná kaména te shiklovén,* 'now they wish to learn;' *kamáva te desman,* 'I wish thee to give me;' *kamávales: so kamakerés les?* 'I wish him' (i. e. 'I have need of him'): 'what art thou to do with him?' *avdivés kamáva te jav to réz,* 'today I wish to go to the vineyard;' *ka na kamésa te kerén túke,* 'which thou dost not wish that they should do to thee.'

---

* "*Moleti,* 'vin.'" Vaillant, p. 369.

WITHIN—*andré ;* Bor., *andre, enre.*—This is evidently from the Sr. *antar,* 'in, within, between.' In compound words its signification is 'internal, interior.' *But andré ti puv,* 'deep into the earth' (lit. 'much within'); *jáva andré,* 'I go in, I enter;' *andrál,* 'from within,' ἔσωθεν: *andrál akata ti pólin* (Gr. *πόλιν*), 'from within the city;' Mod. Gr. *ἀπὸ μέσα ἀπὸ τὴν πόλιν.*

WITHOUT—*bi.*—This negative particle is extremely common, and corresponds to the Sr. *vi,* a preposition signifying separation or disjunction. The Slavonic is extremely fond of this particle, to which it has added a *z,* forming *bez ;* as *glas',* 'voice, echo,' *bezglásn'iy,* 'without a voice, mute;' *bog,* 'God;' *bezbózn'iy,* 'atheist, ἄθεος.' It exists in the Persian *bi,* 'without,' generally corresponding to the Lat. *sine,* and denoting absence or want: as, *bi ab,* 'without water;' *bi edeb,* 'without civility, uncultivated.' We have noticed it among the Gypsy verbs: see to SELL, *biknáva.* It is used with adjectives: as *uchardó,* 'covered,' *buchardó (bi-uchardó),* 'uncovered;' *namporemé,* 'sick,' *binamporemé,* 'healthy;' *bimakavdó,* 'not painted;' *bizoraló,* 'not strong;' *bilindraló,* 'not sleeping;' *bibahtaló,* 'not fortunate.' When *bi* is united to nouns and pronouns, these are constantly in the genitive case of both numbers: as *bi sheréskoro,* 'without a head' (i. e. 'a fool'); *bi lovéskoro,* 'without salt;' *bi maséskoro,* 'without meat;' *bi lovénghoro,* 'without money;' *bi gotiákoro,* 'without mind;' *bi balaménghoro,* 'without Greeks;' *bi khorakhénghoro,* 'without Turks;' *bi vasténghoro,* 'without hands' (i. e. 'workmen'). With pronouns: *bi mángoro,* 'without me;' *bi oléskoro,* 'without him;' *bi lákeri, aménghoro, tuménghoro,* 'without her, us, you.'

WOLF—*ruv ;* Bor., *orioz, aruje, luey.*—The first two terms seem to be related to the Sr. verbal root *ru,* which I have noticed in speaking of the verb to WEEP. This verb, among the Hindus, gives origin to two names of animals, in imitation of their sounds: *ruru,* 'a sort of deer,' and *ruvathu,* 'sound, noise, a cock.' I see no difficulty in supposing that the Gypsies may have applied it to the wolf, an animal remarkable for howling, which is one of the most common significations of the verb *ru.* The third form of Borrow, *luey,* seems to be of Spanish origin: compare *lobo,* 'a wolf.'

WOMAN—*romní ;* Br., *rumenee.*—See GYPSY.

WOOD—*kasht, kash ;* Bor., *casian.*—Related to the Sr. *káshṭa,* 'wood.' Borrow's *casian* may correspond to the adj. *káshṭin,* 'woody.' *Kast* is used for 'a stick;' *diniásman kastésa,* 'he struck me with a stick.' This word is sometimes pronounced without the final *t,* as *kash,* and most of the Greek Gypsies pronounce it *kas.*

WOOL—*posóm.*—In want of a better derivation, I propose for this word the Sr. verbal root *push,* 'to cherish, to nurture.'

WORD—*lav.*—Compare Sr. *lap,* 'to speak, to utter;' *lapana,* 'the mouth, talking.' I have not observed in the Gypsy language any other traces of this Sr. verb, which has given to the Indo-European languages so many terms. As the Hindus have denominated the mouth *lapana,* as the instrument of talking, so also have the Persians their *leb,* the Romans *labium, labrum,* and the Greeks *λάλος* and *λαλέω,* by the change of *p* to *l.* *Lav,* plur. *lavá,* is well known to all the Gypsies. *Kapenáv túke yek lav,* 'I will tell thee a word;' *lav romané,* 'Gypsy words.'

WORM—*kermó;* Bor., *cremen.*—Compare Sr. *krimi,* written also *krimi* and *krami,* 'worm, insect.' It has also the signification of the Gr. *ἕλμινς,* which is applied exclusively to intestinal worms. By some Gypsies the word is pronounced *ghermó.*

To WRITE—*grafáva.*—I have noted this word merely to show the manner in which the Gypsies have introduced Gr. words into their idiom, by giving them a Gypsy form. *Grafáva* (Gr. *γράφω*), 'I write;' aor. *grafghióm* (*ἔγραψα*), 'I have written.' It would be useless to note the numerous instances of such words which the Gypsies have borrowed from the Greeks. Their origin is generally very evident. Some are distorted, because borrowed from terms which the Greeks themselves have corrupted: so *dialezáva,* 'I select,' from *διαλέγω,* pronounced by us often *διαλέζω.* They have adopted another form of verbs similar to those in use among the people with whom they intermingle: thus *kholiteráva,* 'I am angry,' lit. 'I have bile,' from the Gr. *χολή* and their own verb *teráva,* 'to have;' also *kholiázava,* 'I am angry,' Gr. *χολιάζομαι,* 'to be angry:' hence *kholiniakoro,* 'angry.' *Kholiteráva* is common among them.

Y.

YEAR—*bersh;* Bor., *berji.*—Both these words are from Sr. *varsha,* 'rain, the rainy season, year,' from the root *vrish,* 'to be wet, to moisten.' The term was first applied to the rains, then to the season in which the rains were prevalent, and in course of time to the year itself. This use of 'rainy season' for 'year' is corroborated by the usage of the Anglo-Saxons and other northern nations, who reckoned by winters instead of years. Both, of course, were struck by circumstances peculiar to their own climate. *Keti bershénghoro isi?* 'of how many years (i. e. 'how old') is he?' *keti bersh kerghián to rashái?* 'how many years was he (lit. 'did he make') with the teacher (priest)?'

YESTERDAY—*yich;* Bor., *callicaste.*—I leave to philologists to determine whether this term bears any relation to the Sr. *hyas,* 'yesterday.' *Yich penghiás mánghe,* 'yesterday was said to me;' *yichavér,* 'day before yesterday,' composed of *yich* and *avér, yavér,* 'other,' which latter term I have explained in its proper place: *yichavér o kurkó,* 'day before yesterday, (which was) Sunday;' *poyichavér,* with the comparative part. *po,* 'two days before yesterday,' Gr. *ἀντιπροχθές.*

YET, STILL—*achái.*—*Achái but kamadikés,* 'yet more thou wilt see;' *achái chor eketané,* 'and other thieves together;' *achái palál,* 'still more backwards:' for this phrase another, *po polaléste,* is frequently used; *achái lav romané,* 'still more Gypsy words.'

YOUNG—*ternó, yernó;* Br., *yernee;* Bor., *dernó.*—This is the Sr. *taruna,* 'young.' It is often pronounced *yernó,* or rather, the pronunciation of *t* so much resembles that of *y* that to all purposes it can be written with this semivowel. The Sr. *yuvan,* 'young,' which is found in many Indo-European languages, I have not been able to detect in the Gypsy idiom. A diminutive form of *ternó* is *ternoró,* 'a youngster.' *Ternó* is principally used in opposition to *phuró* or *puró,* 'old.'

SECTION IV.

COMPARATIVE PHONOLOGY OF THE GYPSY LANGUAGE.

1. VOWELS.

These are five : *a, e, i, o, u.* The union of many vowels is rarely to be met with in the Gypsy language. Of diphthongs there are almost none. In verbs of the middle voice occurs the combination *io,* resulting from the blending of *o* and *a*: as *mattó-aváva, mattiováva.* So also in the formation of abstract nouns: *parnavó, parnavoipé,* 'friendship;' *bandló, bandloipé,* 'band.' The reader cannot but have observed the rarity of other combinations of a like character in the Vocabulary. Terms such as *nái,* 'nail,' *múi,* 'mouth,' are not diphthongs: the vowel of the final syllable has merely dropped its aspirate. The distinction of the vowels into long and short is difficult to be determined. So, too, in modern Greek, where in most cases such distinctions are of no practical value: *o* and *ω* have a similar sound ; only the accent seems at times to occasion a prolongation of the sound of a vowel. It is for this reason that I have noted with accuracy all the accents upon the Gypsy vowels.

A.—This vowel, which represents the Sr. *a* and *á,* seems to have but one simple sound.

A is retained unaltered in many words: as Sr. *manusha,* '.man,'[*] G. *manúsh;* Sr. *angâra,* 'coal,' G. *angár;* Sr. *nakha,* 'nail,' G. *nái.*

It is frequently changed to *e*: as Sr. *daçan,* 'ten,' G. *désh;* Sr. *rasa,* 'taste,' G. *rés,* 'grape;' Sr. *nava,* 'new,' G. *nevó;* Sr. *hara,* 'ass,' G. *kher;* Sr. *tala,* 'ground,' G. *tele,* 'down;' Sr. *taru-na,* 'young,' G. *ternó.*

The Gypsies of Spain are fond of adding an initial *a* to words beginning with *r*: as *eresia* (Turk. Gyp. *rés*), 'vineyard;' *ara-shai* (T. G. *rashái*), 'priest;' *orobar* (T. G. *rováva*), 'to weep,' etc. Here in Turkey, I have noted this initial *a* in *arakáva,* 'to guard,' and in *aratti,* 'tonight.' Both, however, may justly be referred to Sr. words which have this initial *a* as an actual component member.

The final *a* of the Sr. adjectives and participles is invariably changed to *o,* and strongly accented: as Sr. *kâla,* 'black,' G. *kaló;* Sr. *uchcha,* 'high,' G. *uchó;* Sr. *matta,* 'glad,' G. *mattó,* 'drunk;' Sr. *tapta,* 'burning,' G. *tattó,* 'warm;' Sr. *sanna,* 'slim,' G. *sannó;* Sr. *kritta,* 'cut,' G. *khurdó,* 'small;' Sr. *çushka,* 'dry,' G. *shukó;* Sr. *pûrta,* 'full,' G. *perdó;* Sr. *purâna,* 'old,' G. *pura-nó;* Sr. *mrita,* 'mortal,' G. *merdó,* 'sick.'

---

[*] When both Sanskrit and Gypsy terms have the same signification, I have noted only that of the Sanskrit. In other cases I write both.

Also in other words it is changed to *o:* as Sr. *shash,* 'six,' G. *shov;* Sr. *çaça,* 'rabbit,' G. *shoshói.*

E.—*E* is more constant: as Sr. *deva,* 'God,' G. *devél;* Sr. *eka,* 'one,' G. *yek.*

I.—*I* and *ni* are the most usual terminations of Gypsy feminine nouns: *chukél,* 'dog,' *chuk(e)li,* 'bitch;' *devél,* 'God,' *dev(e)li,* 'goddess;' *grast,* 'horse,' *grastni,* 'mare;' *rom,* 'Gypsy,' *romni,* 'Gypsy woman;' *kher,* 'ass,' *kherni,* 'she-ass;' *manúsh,* 'man,' *manushni,* 'woman;' *gurúv,* 'ox,' *guruvni,* 'cow;'[*] *plal,* 'brother,' *plani,* sister.[†]

In numerous Gypsy words the *i* and *î* of the Sanskrit remain unchanged: as Sr. *dvi,* 'two,' G. *dúi;* Sr. *tri,* 'three,' G. *tri;* Sr. *rátri,* 'night,' G. *aratti,* 'tonight;' Sr. *gili,* 'sound,' G. *ghili,* 'song;' Sr. *chhuri,* 'knife,' G. *churi;* Sr. *pániya,* 'potable,' G. *pani,* 'water.'

The Sr. vowel *r,* or *ri,* undergoes many changes, which are of much importance in the study of the Gypsy language, and in the explanation and philosophical analysis of the verbs, and also extremely interesting. *Ri* is changed to *ri* in Sr. *riksha,* 'bear,' G. *richini:*—to *ro* in Sr. *jámátri,* 'son-in-law,' G. *jamutró:*—to *ru* in Sr. *triçúla,* 'trident,' G. *trushúl, turshúl.*

In the verbal roots, *ri* or *rî* is changed to *ar* or *er* in Sr. *dri,* 'to be afraid,' G. *daráva;* Sr. *mri,* 'to die,' G. *meráva;* Sr. *kri,* 'to make,' G. *keráva;* Sr. *pri,* 'to fill,' G. *peráva:*—to *il* in Sr. *gri,* 'to sound,' G. *ghiliáva.*

O.—No precise rules can be given as to the pronunciation of this vowel, for it is often left to the option of the speaker to use either the *o* or the *u* in a great number of words. With the exception of the final *o,* the common characteristic of the masc. gender among the Gypsies, this vowel usually corresponds with the Sr. *u* and *û:* as Sr. *múrti,* 'matter,' G. *morti,* 'leather;' Sr. *dûra,* 'distant,' G. *dur;* Sr. *bhû,* 'earth,' G. *phuv.*

It also represents the Sr. *a:* as Sr. *chandra,* 'moon,' G. *chon;* Sr. *madhu,* 'sweet,' G. *mol,* 'honey:'—or the Sr. *o:* as Sr. *lobhini,* 'desirous,' G. *lubni, lobni,* 'harlot;' Sr. *loha,* 'red,' G. *loló:*—or the Sr. *i:* as Sr. *krimi,* 'worm,' G. *kermó.*

The final *o* of nouns, adjectives, and participles is changed to *i,* whenever abstract substantives are formed by the addition of the particle *pe* or *pen:* as *kaló,* 'black,' *kalipé,* 'blackness, excommu-

---

[*] Pronounced also *gurumni.*

[†] I have heard Gypsies, extremely ignorant of their language, making no distinction between the masculine and feminine of adjectives, saying *kali* (fem.) for *kalo* (masc.), 'black;' *terni* for *terno.* These were all Moslem Gypsies, speaking the Turkish, in which language the adjectives, as in English, have a single termination for both genders. Those in the habit of frequently speaking their language never make such blunders; they are extremely attentive to all their generic terminations.

nication;' *mattó,* 'drunk,' *mattipé,* 'drunkenness;' *tattó,* 'warm,' *tattipé,* 'heat;' *moló,* 'dead,' *meripé,* 'death;' *phuró,* 'old,' *phuripé,* 'old age;' *lachó,* 'good,' *lachipé,* 'goodness, alms;' *piró,* 'foot,' *piripé,* 'gait;' *shuchó,* 'clean,' *shuchipé,* 'cleanliness.'

This rule suffers exception: as in *kamló,* 'perspiring,' *kamlioipé,* 'perspiration;' *bandló,* 'bound,' *bandlioipé,* 'band;' *parnavó,* 'friend,' *parnavoipé,* 'friendship;' *loshanó,* 'rejoicing,' *loshanoipé,* 'joy;' *tattó,* 'warm,' *tabioipé,* 'heat.'

U.—This vowel is extremely common; it is a favorite sound with all the Gypsies, whether Moslem or Christian. It is often pronounced *o.* It represents the Sr. *o* in Sr. *ģo,* 'ox,' G. *gurúv;* Sr. *lobhini,* 'desiring,' G. *lubní:*—the Sr. *u* in Sr. *manusha,* 'man,' G. *manúsh;* Sr. *sukara,* 'benevolent,' G. *sukár,* 'beautiful;' Sr. *pura,* 'former,' G. *phuró,* 'old;' Sr. *uchcha,* 'high,' G. *uchó;* Sr. *pangu,* 'lame,' G. *pankó.*

2. Consonants.

K.—Very common in the Gypsy language. It is often the unaltered representative of the Sanskrit *k:* as in Sr. *kála,* 'black,' G. *kaló;* Sr. *kan,* 'to shine,' G. *kan, kam,* 'sun;' Sr. *káshtha,* 'wood,' G. *kasht;* Sr. *kṛi,* 'to make,' G. *keráva;* Sr. *kṛimi,* 'worm,' G. *kermó.*

It is changed into *f* in *kuri,* 'a colt,' pronounced frequently *furí;* or to *gh,* in Sr. *kal,* 'to sound,' G. *ghelava,* 'to play on instruments.'

It is assimilated to the following consonant, as in Sr. *rakta,* 'red,' G. *ratt,* 'blood.'

It frequently becomes a very gentle aspirate: as in Sr. *kása,* 'cough,' G. *has;* Sr. *kuh,* 'to surprise,' G. *hohaimpé, khohaimpé,* 'a lie;' Sr. *kritta,* 'cut,' G. *hirdó,* 'dwarfish;' Sr. *kand,* 'to itch,' G. *handiováva, hanjiováva,* 'to scratch.'

Ksh.—This compound consonant of the Sanskrit is very constant in its transformation, and may serve as a clue to the true etymology of many Gypsy words. It does not appear in the proper Gypsy language, and the Gypsies never employ it except in *ksilábi,* 'tongs.' In speaking Greek, they pronounce ξ as the Greeks do. This consonant generally becomes a simple *k:* as in Sr. *drákshá,* 'grapes,' G. *drak;* Sr. *aksha,* 'eye,' G. *yak;* Sr. *yaksh,* 'to sacrifice,' G. *yak,* 'fire;' Sr. *rúksha,* 'tree,' G. *ruk;* Sr. *makshiká,* 'fly,' G. *makiá;* Sr. *áraksh,* 'to preserve,' G. *arakáv,* 'guard;' Sr. *çiksh,* 'to learn,' G. *shikáva;* Sr. *kshíra,* 'milk,' G. *kerál,* 'cheese;' Sr. *akshna,* 'time,' G. *akaná,* 'now;' Sr. *naksh,* 'to go,' G. *nakáva,* 'to pass;' Sr. *maksh,* 'to mix,' G. *makáva,* 'to paint;' Sr. *paksha,* 'wing,' G. *pak.*

If my etymology of *bashno,* 'a cock,' as from *pakshin,* be true, then this would be an exception to the above rule.

Kh.—This Sanskrit consonant often retains in the Gypsy its strong aspirated sound, like that of the *kh* of the Arabs and Turks: as in Sr. *khanaka,* 'digging,' G. *khaínk,* 'well;' Sr. *khaṇdin,* 'divided,' G. *khandí,* 'a little;' Sr. *khan,* 'to dig,' G. *khatáva;* Sr. *khani,* 'a mine,' G. *kháv,* 'a hole;' Sr. *khád,* 'to eat,' G. *kháva.*

It is at times dopped, or very gently aspirated: as in Sr. *nakha,* 'nail,' G. *nái;* Sr. *çákha,* 'vegetable,' G. *shah,* 'cabbage;' Sr. *mukha,* 'mouth,' G. *múi.*

It is changed to *k* in Sr. *duḥkha,* 'pain,' G. *duk.*

G.—This retains generally its proper Sanskrit sound: as in Sr. *gaṇ,* 'to count,' G. *ghenáva;* Sr. *gara,* 'poison,' G. *gher,* 'itch;' Sr. *gras,* 'to eat,' G. *grast,* 'horse;' Sr. *angára,* 'coal,' G. *angár.*

It is changed to *k* in *agára,* 'house,' G. *ker.*

Ch.—Is generally retained unchanged: as in Sr. *char,* 'to eat,' G. *charáva,* 'to graze;' Sr. *chush,* 'to suck,' G. *chuché,* 'breast;' Sr. *chumb,* 'to kiss,' G. *chumí,* 'kiss;' Sr. *chik,* 'to obstruct,' G. *chik,* 'mud.'

It is changed to its cognate guttural *k* in Sr. *much,* 'to release,' G. *mukáva;* Sr. *pach,* 'to cook,' G. *pekáva.* It becomes simple *s* in Sr. *chush,* 'to suck,' G. *sut,* 'milk;' Sr. *chatur,* 'four,' G. *ishtár.*

Chh.—This consonant is pronounced like simple *ch:* as Sr. *chhinna,* 'divided,' G. *chináva,* 'to cut;' Sr. *chhurí,* 'knife,' G. *churí;* Sr. *chhard,* 'to vomit,' G. *chattáva;* Sr. *tuchchha,* 'empty,' G. *chuchó.*

J.—This letter retains its genuine Sanskrit sound: as in Sr. *jñá,* 'to know,' G. *janáva;* Sr. *jív,* 'to live,' G. *jiváva;* Sr. *jámátri,* 'son-in-law,' G. *jamutró.*

T, Th, D.—These consonants are pronounced like *t* and *d:* as in Sr. *paṭa,* 'cloth,' G. *páta,* 'garment;' Sr. *káshṭha,* 'wood,' G. *kasht;* Sr. *muṇḍ,* 'to shave,' G. *muntáva;* Sr. *aṇḍa,* 'egg,' G. *vantó;* Sr. *khaṇḍin,* 'divided,' G. *khandí,* 'little.'

N.—This nasal, also, is not distinguished from the common dental *n:* Sr. *gaṇ,* 'to count,' G. *ghenáva;* Sr. *puráṇa,* 'old,' G. *puranó.*

T.—When at the end of a word, this consonant is often dropped: as in *grast,* 'a horse,' also frequently pronounced *gras* and *gra; kasht,* 'wood,' also *kash; vast,* 'hand,' also *vas.* It is distinctly heard, however, when the following word begins with a vowel: as *lachó grast isí,* 'it is a good horse.' When preceded by *r,* it is pronounced like a pure *d,* as in Sr. *púrta,* 'full,' G. *perdó.* At times it is changed to *f,* as in Sr. *tala,* 'earth,' G. *telé* and *felé,* 'downwards.'

D.—This has the sound of the Latin *d:* as Sr. *dram,* 'to go,' G. *drom,* 'road;' Sr. *dárava,* 'wooden,' G. *daravín,* 'pomegranate;' Sr. *dína,* 'distressed,' G. *deniló,* 'fool.'

It is changed into *gh* in Sr. *diva,* 'day,' G. *ghivés.*

Dh.—This Sanskrit consonant I have not been able to hear among the Gypsies. Whenever it occurs in terms of Sanskrit derivation, it is invariably changed to *d* or *t:* as in Sr. *bandh,* 'to tie,' G. *bandáva;* Sr. *dháv,* 'to cleanse,' G. *továva,* 'to wash;' Sr. *dhṛita,* 'held,' G. *tertiováva,* 'to stand.'

N.—Is perfectly similar to the Latin *n.*

P.—This consonant usually has the sound of *p:* as in Sr. *pániya,* 'potable,' G. *pani,* 'water;' Sr. *patrin,* 'winged,' G. *patrin,* 'feather.'

It is frequently changed to *f:* as in Sr. *par,* 'to precede,' G. *furó,* 'old man;' Sr. *pura,* 'city,' G. *forós,* 'market-place;' Sr. *váshpa,* 'tear,' G. *ásfa.*

Or at times to *v:* as in Sr. *apara,* 'other,' G. *yavér;* Sr. *lapa,* 'word,' G. *lav.*

Or it is assimilated to the consonant following it: as in Sr. *tapta,* 'warm,' G. *tattó;* Sr. *supta,* 'asleep,' G. *sottó;* Sr. *svapna,* 'sleep,' G. *sannó,* 'dream.'

It is changed to *b:* as in Sr. *páka,* 'grey-haired,' G. *bakó,* 'bald;' Sr. *pish,* 'to inhabit,' G. *bisháva;* Sr. *prish,* 'to sprinkle,' G. *burshín,* 'rain.'

B.—Has the sound of the Latin *b:* as Sr. *bála,* 'hairs,' G. *bal;* Sr. *balin,* 'strong,' G. *baló,* 'hog;' Sr. *bala,* 'strength,' G. *naisbali,* 'weak;' Sr. *bul,* 'to plunge,' G. *boláva,* 'to baptize.'

Bh.—*Bh* is not a Gypsy sound. In the words of Sanskrit origin containing it it is sometimes changed to *p:* as in Sr. *bhrátri,* 'brother,' G. *pra, pral;* Sr. *bhú,* 'earth,' G. *puv;* Sr. *bhara,* 'much,' G. *paró,* 'great;' Sr. *bhúti,* 'dignity,' G. *puti,* 'business.'

It becomes *b* in Sr. *lobhiní,* 'desirous,' G. *lubni,* 'strumpet;' Sr. *bhañj,* 'to break,' G. *bangáva.*

M.—*M* is mostly pronounced like the Latin *m.* In a few words it is changed to *v:* as Sr. *gráma,* 'a village,' G. *gav;* Sr. *náman,* 'name,' G. *nav;* Sr. *hima,* 'snow,' G. *iv.*

Y.—Is frequently unchanged: as Sr. *yaksh,* 'to sacrifice, G. *yak,* 'fire.'

It is frequently added to words beginning with a vowel: as Sr. *aksha,* 'eye,' G. *yak;* Sr. *eka,* 'one,' G. *yek;* Sr. *apara,* 'other,' G. *yavér.*

R.—The Gypsy *r* often corresponds to the Sanskrit *r:* as in Sr. *rúpya,* 'silver,' G. *rup;* Sr. *rasa,* 'taste,' G. *res,* 'vineyard.'

It is frequently changed to *l:* as in Sr. *dvára,* 'door,' G. *dal;* Sr. *chur,* 'to steal,' G. *choláva;* Sr. *agre,* 'forwards,' G. *anglé;* Sr. *gir,* 'sound,' G. *ghili,* 'song;' Sr. *bhrátri,* 'brother,' G. *plal;* Sr. *mára,* 'death,' G. *moló:* also in Sr. *kram,* 'to go,' united with various prepositions: as *niklaváva,* 'to go out;' *uklaváva,* 'to mount.'

In combinations of *r* with another consonant, the *r* is often dropped: as in Sr. *çringa*, 'horn,' G. *shingh;* Sr. *prachh*, 'to ask,' G. *puchava;* Sr. *çru*, 'to hear,' G. *shunava;* Sr. *çvaçrû*, 'mother-in-law,' G. *shasúi;* Sr. *bhrû*, 'eyebrow,' G. *pov;* Sr. *grâma*, 'village,' G. *gav;* Sr. *krînâmi*, 'I buy,' G. *kinava.*

It is also often assimilated to the consonant following it: as in Sr. *karna*, 'ear,' G. *kann;* Sr. *sarva*, 'all,' G. *savvó;* Sr. *sarpa*, 'serpent,' G. *sapp;* Sr. *chhard*, 'to vomit,' G. *chatâva.*

Or to the consonant preceding it: as in Sr. *râtri*, 'night,' G. *aratti*, 'tonight.'

L.—Requires no remark.

V.—*V* in many words is preserved unchanged, having in the Gypsy the sound of the Latin *v* and Gr. *β:* as Sr. *deva*, 'god,' G. *devêl;* Sr. *nava*, 'new,' G. *nevó;* Sr. *vâi*, 'verily,' G. *va*, 'yes.'

It is changed to *p* in Sr. *vicharâmi*, 'I deliberate,' G. *pincharáva*, 'to be acquainted.'

It is frequently prefixed to Sanskrit words beginning with vowels: as Sr. *uchcha*, 'high,' G. *vuchó;* Sr. *anda*, 'egg,' G. *vantó;* Sr. *oshtha*, 'mouth,' G. *vust*, 'lip;' Pers. *asiav*, 'mill,' G. *vasiáv.*

Or it is changed to *b:* as in Sr. *vinçati*, 'twenty,' G. *bish;* Sr. *varsha*, 'year,' G. *bersh;* Sr. *vaç*, 'to sound,' G. *bashâva*, 'to cry out;' Sr. *vi*, 'without,' G. *bi.*

It is dropped at the beginning of *vâshpa*, 'tear,' G. *âsfa.*

It is omitted, or, with *a*, becomes *o*, in Sr. *lavana*, 'salt,' G. *lon;* Sr. *svap*, 'to sleep,' G. *sováva;* Sr. *çvaçura*, 'father-in-law,' G. *shastró;* Sr. *çvaçrû*, 'mother-in-law,' G. *shasúi.*

Ç, Sh.—Both these Sanskrit sibilants are represented by the Gypsy *sh*, pronounced as in *shall, shore.*

Those Gypsies who live mostly among the Greeks, however, particularly in Roumelia, frequently pronounce this consonant like the Greeks, as *σ:* but the Moslem Gypsies give it its proper sound, on account of their familiarity with the Turkish, where the consonant *sh* is extremely common. It is important to bear this in mind. *Shastó*, 'healthy,' I have heard pronounced very often *sastó*. The modern Greeks experience considerable difficulty in pronouncing this *sh*, excepting those inhabiting the Epirus, particularly the villages near Joannina, who give it its proper sound.

Instances are Sr. *çasta*, 'healthy,' G. *shastó;* Sr. *çru*, 'to hear,' G. *shunáva;* Sr. *çringa*, 'horn,' G. *shingh;* Sr. *çastra*, 'iron,' G. *shastrí;* Sr. *çita*, 'cold,' G. *shil, shilaló;* Sr. *çulla*, 'cord,' G. *sheló*, 'rope;' Sr. *triçûla*, 'trident,' G. *turshúl*, 'cross;' Sr. *çaça*, 'rabbit,' G. *shoshói.*

Ç is changed to *k* in Sr. *driç*, 'to see,' G. *dîkava.*

Sh is dropped before *k* in Sr. *çushka*, 'dry,' G. *shukó.*

S.—This consonant needs no explanation or comparison.

H.—*H* is changed to *k* in Sr. *hansa,* 'goose,' G. *kainá,* 'hen.'
It is dropped in Sr. *has,* 'to laugh,' G. *asáva.*
At times it is commutable with *v:* as in Sr. *hasta,* 'hand,' G. *vast;* Sr. *hima,* 'snow,' G. *biv, viv.*

SECTION V.

GRAMMAR.

The following remarks on the grammar of the Gypsy language are the results of my studies up to the present time, being drawn from my numerous notes and manuscript dialogues. The reader can see an illustration of them in the numerous colloquial phrases scattered through the Vocabulary.

ARTICLE.

The ancient Hindus had no article, and to their demonstrative pronouns correspond the articles of the cognate European languages, which have become separate parts of speech. It was natural, then, that the Gypsies, following the example of other analytical languages, should also acquire an article. In Spain, the article of the Gitanos is the Spanish: here, there is evident the influence of the Greek article; for the Moslem Gypsies use their article very sparingly, since the Turkish, which they mostly employ, possesses no article, properly speaking, The Gypsy article is *o* for the nom. and voc. sing. of the masc. and neut. genders, and *e* for the oblique cases of the singular and for the whole plural. The fem. form is *i* throughout. The *e* of the plural is at times pronounced like *o*.

	Singular.			*Plural.*	
	Masc. and Neut.	Fem.		Masc. and Neut.	Fem.
Nom.	*o*	*i*	Nom.	*e*	*i*
Acc.	*e*	*i*	Acc.	*e*	*i*
Gen.	*e*	*i*	Gen.	*e*	*i*
Voc.	*o*	*i*	Voc.	*e*	*i*

Whoever is acquainted with the variations of the Greek article in the mouth of the common people, cannot be astonished by the indefinite character of the Gypsy article. Some Greeks say τζι ἀνϑρώποι for τοὺς ἀνϑρώπους, τζι γυναῖκες for τὰς γυναῖκας, ἡ γυναῖκες for αἱ γυναῖκες, etc. I am certain that whoever should attempt to investigate the Greek article, as heard in the mouth of the illiterate among our countrymen, would be extremely embarrassed in forming a clear idea of its nature, without referring to the ancient language. How then can we look for accuracy and exactitude from the mouth of this ignorant people, who have not the least idea of anything more perfect than what they constantly use in their every day conversation?

Noun.

The Gypsy noun ends either in a vowel or a consonant.

Nouns ending in Vowels.

A few end in *a:* as *vrehtúla*, 'an extinguisher;' *ásfa*, 'tear;' *makiá*, 'fly;' *vária*, 'weight;' *gúva*, 'pit;' *katúna*, 'Gypsy tent.'

Those ending in *o* are numerous, and are all of the masculine and neuter genders: as *manró*, 'bread;' *bukó*, 'bowel;' *chavó*, 'child;' *moló*, 'death;' *sunnó*, 'dream;' *charó*, 'plate;' *gosnó*, 'dung;' *kurkó*, 'Sunday;' *machó*, 'fish;' *koró*, 'bracelet;' *parnavó*, 'friend;' *rakló*, 'boy.'

Nouns in *i* are less numerous, and are of the masc. and fem. genders.

Masculine nouns in *i* are *nái*, 'nail;' *nilái*, 'summer;' *múi*, 'mouth;' *richini*, 'bear;' *shoshói*, 'rabbit;' *kangli*, 'comb;' *rái*, 'nobleman;' *angustri*, 'finger-ring;' *rashái*, 'priest;' *churí*, 'knife;' *amuni*, 'anvil;' *goti*, 'brain.'

Feminine nouns in *i* are of two classes: 1, those formed from the masculine by the addition of *ni*: as *gurúv*, 'ox,' *guruvni*, 'cow;' *grast*, 'horse,' *grastni*, 'mare;' *kher*, 'ass,' *kherni*, 'she-ass;' *manúsh*, 'man,' *manushni*, 'woman;' *rái*, 'nobleman,' *rani*, 'nobleman's wife;' *rashái*, 'priest,' *rashani*, 'priest's wife:' 2, those which are naturally feminine; as *dái*, 'mother;' *sali*, 'wife's sister;' *shashúi*, 'mother-in-law;' *chái*, 'girl;' *kamni*, 'pregnant;' *nubli*, 'strumpet.'

There are other feminine nouns, formed from the noun by simply adding the ending *i*: as *chukél*, 'dog,' *chukeli*, *chukli*, 'bitch;' *devél*, 'god,' *develi*, *devli*, 'goddess.' As regards such feminine nouns as *romni*, 'woman,' from *rom*, 'a Gypsy, a man,' *dasni*, 'a Bulgarian woman,' from *das*, 'a Bulgarian,' I am inclined to think that they are properly feminine adjectives, from the masculines ending in *ano:* thus *rom*, *romanó*, fem. *romani*, *romni; dás*, 'Bulgarian,' *dasanó*, 'of a Bulgarian,' βουλγαρικὸς, *dasani*, *dasni*, 'a Bulgarian woman;' *grást*, 'horse,' *grastanó*, 'of a horse,' ἱππικὸς, *grastani*, *grastni*, ἱππικὴ, i. e. 'mare;' *manúsh*, 'man,' *manushanó*, 'humanus,' *manushani*, *manushni*, 'humana, woman.' This termination of *i* or *ni* for the fem. nouns has one exception, viz. *pén*, 'sister.'

Nouns terminating in Consonants.

These are by far the greatest number. The final consonants are *g, gh, k, l, m, n, p, r, s, sh, t, v.*

Nouns in *g* are *beng,* 'devil:'—in *gh, shingh,* 'horn:'—in *k, yak,* 'fire;' *drak,* 'grape;' *pak,* 'wing;' *chik,* 'mud;' *nak,* 'nose;' *poshík,* 'soil;' *khaínk,* 'well:'—in *l, prál,* 'brother;' *kerál,* 'cheese;' *turshúl,* 'cross;' *chukél,* 'dog;' *devél,* 'God:'—in *m, rom,* 'Gypsy;' *lim,* 'mucus of the nose;' *drom,* 'road;' *kam,* 'sun:'—in *n, armán,* 'curse;' *kann,* 'ear;' *patrín,* 'leaf;' *chon,* 'moon;' *tan,* 'place;' *len,* 'river:'—in *p, rup,* 'silver;' *sapp,* 'serpent;' *chip,* 'tongue:'— in *r, kher,* 'ass;' *ker,* 'house;' *angár,* 'coal;' *mutér,* 'urine;' *lindr,* 'sleep;' *gher,* 'itch:'—in *s, murs,* 'brave;' *divés,* 'day;' *vus,* 'flax;' *mas,* 'meat;' *res,* 'vineyard:'—in *sh, manúsh,* 'man;' *trush,* 'thirst;' *bersh,* 'year:'—in *t, ratt,* 'blood;' *purt,* 'bridge;' *dat,* 'father;' *grast,* 'horse;' *vast,* 'hand;' *shut,* 'vinegar;' *vent,* 'winter:'—in *v, puv,* 'earth;' *pov,* 'eye-brow;' *giv,* 'grain;' *arakáv,* 'guard;' *suv,* 'needle;' *gurúv,* 'ox;' *gav,* 'village;' *nav,* 'name;' *lav,* 'word.'

The Gypsy noun has no dual number. Its declension I shall attempt in the following remarks to make as plain as possible.

Declension of masculines in *o :*

Sing.	Plur.
Nom. *o chavó,* 'the child,'	*e chavé,* 'the children,'
Acc. *e chavés,* 'the child,'	*e chavén,* 'the children,'
Gen. *e chavéskoro,* 'of the child,'	*e chavénghoro,* 'of the children,'
Voc. *o chavó,* 'O child!'	*o chavále,* 'O children!'

Of masculines in *i :*

Sing.	Plur.
Nom. *o rái,* 'the nobleman,'	*e rayé,* 'the noblemen,'
Acc. *e rayés,* 'the nobleman,'	*e rayén,* 'the noblemen,'
Gen. *e rayéskoro,* 'of the nobleman,'	*e rayénghoro,* 'of the noblemen,'
Voc. *o rái,* 'O nobleman!'	*o rayále,* 'O noblemen!'

Of masculines ending in consonants:

Sing.	Plur.
Nom. *o pral,* 'the brother,'	*e pralé,* 'the brothers,'
Acc. *e pralés,* 'the brother,'	*e pralén,* 'the brothers,'
Gen. *e praléskoro,* 'of the brother,'	*e pralénghoro,* 'of the brothers,'
Voc. *o pral,* 'O brother!'	*o pralále,* 'O brothers!'

Sing.	Plur.
Nom. *o drak,* 'the grape,'	*draká,* 'the grapes,'
Acc. *e drakés,* 'the grape,'	*e draká,* 'the grapes,'
Gen. *e drakéskoro,* 'of the grape,'	*e drakénghoro,* 'of the grapes,'
Voc. *o drak,* 'O grape!'	*o drakále,* 'O grapes!'

Declension of feminine nouns:

Sing.	Plur.
Nom. *i dái,* 'the mother,'	*e daia,* 'the mothers,'
Acc. *e daiá,* 'the mother,'	*e daia,* 'the mothers,'
Gen. *e daiákori,* 'of the mother,'	*e daiánghoro,* 'of the mothers,'
Voc. *e dáia,* 'O mother!'	*e daiále,* 'O mothers!'

	Sing.	*Plur.*
Nom.	*i rakli,* 'the girl,'	*e raklia,* 'the girls,'
Acc.	*e rakliá,* 'the girl,'	*e raklia,* 'the girls,'
Gen.	*e rakliákori,* 'of the girl,'	*e rakliénghoro,* 'of the girls,'
Voc.	*e rakliá,* 'O girl!'	*e rakliále,* 'O girls!'

The above examples are sufficient to show the reader the general declension of Gypsy nouns; but before I make any remarks upon the cases, it may be proper to bring forward an example from Pott's work, in order farther to elucidate the subject. I take an example from Puchmayer as found in Pott (i. 196):

	Sing.	*Plur.*
Nom.	*cziriklo,*	*czirikle,*
Acc.	*czirikles,*	*czirikleu,*
Voc.	*czirikleja,*	*cziriklale,*
Dat. 1,	—— *	—— *
Dat. 2,	*czirikleske,*	*cziriklenge,*
Abl.	*cziriklestar,*	*cziriklendar,*
Soc.	*czirikleha,*	*cziriklença,*
Gen.	*czirikleskero,*	*cziriklengero.*

These forms are identical with those found among the Gypsies of these countries. I decline a noun as pronounced here, following in the cases the order of the above author:

	Sing.	*Plur.*
Nom.	*o rakló,* 'the child,'	*e raklé,* 'the children,'
Acc.	*e raklés,* 'the child,'	*e raklén,* 'the children,'
Voc.	*e rakló,* 'O child!'	*e raklále,* 'O children!'
Dat. 1,	*e rakléste,* 'in the child,'	*e raklénde,* 'in the children,'
Dat. 2,	*e rakléske,* 'to the child,'	*e raklénghe,* 'to the children,'
Abl.	*e rakléstar,* 'from the child,'	*e rakléndar,* 'from the children,'
Soc.	*e rakléssa,* 'with the child,'	*e rakléntza,* 'with the children,'
Gen.	*e rakléskoro,* 'of the child,'	*e raklénghoro,* 'of the children.'

To the reader, at first sight, such a declension must appear wonderfully rich and expressive, and so much the more, as it is in the mouth of a people who have no intellectual cultivation, and who would naturally simplify their language to the utmost. But all this richness, which even the Sanskrit does not possess, is owing merely to the union of particles with the noun in its simplest form; for the Gypsy noun has properly only four cases: nominative, accusative, genitive, and vocative; while to the accusative are joined all these particles, which are similar in both numbers, and cannot be properly considered as forming cases. Before proceeding to speak of the formation of each case separately, I shall analyze a noun, in order to illustrate and make plain the combination of which I have spoken:

---

* These cases, omitted by Puchmayer, are *czirikleste* in the singular, and *cziriklende* in the plural.

	Sing.	Plur.
Nom.	o rakló,	e raklé,
Acc.	e raklés,	e raklén,
Dat. 1,	e raklés-te,	e raklén-te,
Dat. 2,	e raklés-ke,	e raklén-ke,
Abl.	e raklés-tar,	e raklén-tar,
Soc.	e raklés-sa,	e raklén-sa,
Gen.	e raklés-koro,	e raklén-koro.

The occurrence of the liquid *n* in the plural varies considerably the pronunciation of the following consonants, thus:

Dat. 1,	raklén-te	is pronounced	raklénde,
Dat. 2,	raklén-ke	"	raklénghe,
Abl.	raklén-tar	"	rakléndar,
Soc.	raklén-sa	"	rakléntza,
Gen.	raklén-koro	"	raklénghoro.

In this manner the declension of the Gypsy noun becomes extremely clear, and can be reduced to very simple elements. There is no more reason for calling *rakléndar* a case than for giving the name of cases to all those adverbs in Greek which are formed by the ablative particle θεν, or to such Latin words as *mecum, tecum,* which correspond with the so-called social case of the above Gypsy nouns.

The same mode of declension which is followed by nouns ending in *o* holds good also as regards feminine nouns ending in *i,* and the appended particles are not less distinct and clear. As an instance, I give the forms of declension of *romni,* 'woman:'

	Sing.	Plur.
Nom.	i romni,	i romnia,
Acc.	i romniá,	i romnia,
Dat. 1,	i romniá-te,	i romnian-te (romniande),
Dat. 2,	i romniá-ke,	i romnian-ke (romnianghe),
Abl.	i romniá-tar,	i romnian-tar (romniandar),
Soc.	i romniá-sa,	i romnian-sa (romniantza),
Gen.	i romniá-kori,	i romnian-koro (romnianghoro).

This comparison of the declension of masculine and feminine nouns is interesting, as it demonstrates two particulars in the history of the Gypsy noun. First, were it not for the so-called social case of the plural, we should have been at a loss to know whether the final syllable of the singular case was a *sa,* or a simple *a* united to the accusative, since all nouns without distinction have this termination: thus *grast,* 'horse,' *grastéssa,* 'with a horse' ('on horseback'); *rái,* 'a nobleman,' *rayéssa,* 'with a nobleman:' plur. *grasténtza,* 'with horses;' *rayéntza,* 'with noblemen.' In the feminine gender the case is clear, since Gypsies say *rakli,* 'a female child,' acc. *rakliá*; soc. sing. *rakliá-sa,* 'with the female child.' This evidently proves the addition of the syllable *sa* to the accusative, which we shall presently consider. As to the plural social, the fact is palpably evident: thus *piró, piréntza*, 'with feet;' *chavó, chavéntza*, 'with children.'

The second consideration, which is extremely important, is that though in the accusative plural of feminine nouns no final *n* exists, it is to be found in all the compound cases of the plural: a fact which to me amply demonstrates the former presence of this liquid in the accusative plural, although the Gypsies have later entirely abandoned its pronunciation.

I will now proceed to consider more in detail the formation of the different cases, taking them up in their order.

Accusative singular.—This case, in the singular of nouns ending in *o*, is *es:* thus *parnavó*, 'friend,' acc. *parnavés; machó*, 'fish,' *machés; sunnó*, 'dream,' *sunnés; manró*, 'bread,' is often used unchanged: as *khandi manró kháva*, 'I eat a little bread.' Feminine nouns in *i* form the acc. in *a*, with the accent on this vowel: as *romni*, 'woman,' acc. *romniá; buti*, 'business,' *butiá; nubli*, 'strumpet,' *nubliá*. Nouns in *a* generally have the same form in the accusative: as *ásfa*, 'a tear,' acc. *ásfa; katúna*, 'a Gypsy tent,' acc. *katúna*. To me, however, such words, which are few, are properly nouns forming the accusative in *as* or *es*, judging from their genitives etc.: as *katunéskoro*, 'of the tent;' a form of this character presupposes an accusative *katúnas* or *katúnes*, of which, in ordinary usage, the final *s* has been dropped. Nouns ending in consonants, by far the most numerous, form their accusative by the addition of *es:* thus *pral*, 'brother,' acc. *pralés; tan*, 'place,' *tanés; dat*, 'father,' *datés; gav*, 'village,' *gavés*. In nouns ending in *el* and *er*, as *devél*, 'God,' *chukél*, 'dog,' *tovér*, 'axe,' etc., the final syllable drops its vowel: thus *devél*, acc. *devlés; chukél, chuklés; tovér, tovrés*.

Nouns ending in *k*, as *pak*, 'wing,' *yak*, 'fire,' are generally pronounced in the accusative with the vowel *a*: as *paká*, acc., 'the wing,' *yaká*, 'the eye.' The regular accusative form, with its final *s*, is observed in the genitive *pakéskoro*, 'of the wing,' *yakéskoro*, 'of the fire.'

Taking the compound cases, so uniform in their formation, as a guide, it appears to me not implausible to lay down the general rule that the accusative singular of all Gypsy nouns of the masculine gender ends in *s*, and of the feminine in *a*.

Vocative singular.—This case, of which few Gypsies can give any account, is formed, in nouns ending in *o*, by changing this vowel to *e:* as *choró, choré*, 'O poor man!' ὦ πτωχέ; *chavó, chavé*, 'O boy!' In the feminine it is formed by adding *a* to *i:* as *dái, dáia*, 'O mother!' In nouns ending in consonants this case is formed by the addition of *e:* as *manúsh, manúshe*, 'O man!' *dat, dáte*, 'O father!'

Nominative plural.—In this case, the forms are nearly the same with those just given. The nominative of nouns ending in *o* is formed by changing this vowel into *e:* as *chavó,* 'child,' *chavé,* 'children;' *charó, charé,* 'plates;' *rakló, raklé,* 'boys;' *bakró, bakré,* 'sheep.'

Nouns in *i,* whether masculine or feminine, form the nominative plural by the addition of *a:* as *raklí, raklía,* 'girls;' *romní, romnía,* 'women;' *rái, ráia,* 'noblemen;' *rashái, rasháia,* 'priests.'

Nouns in *k,* by the addition of *a:* as *yak, yakú,* 'eyes;' *pak, paká,* 'wings;' *ruk, ruká,* 'trees:'—also those in *v:* as *pov, pová,* 'eyebrows.'

Nouns ending in other consonants, by adding *e:* as *grast, grasté,* 'horses;' *manúsh, manushé,* 'men;' *pral, pralé,* 'brothers.' This vowel is, however, often interchanged with *a:* as *romé* or *romá,* 'Gypsies.'

Accusative plural.—This case, of which I have already had occasion to speak, is formed, in nouns ending in *o,* by changing this vowel to *en:* as *chavó, chavén,* 'children;' *bukó, bukén,* 'bowels;' *parnavó, parnavén,* 'friends.'

In feminine nouns in *i,* it is formed by the addition of *a:* as *romní, romnía,* 'women;' *chái, chaía,* 'girls;' *nublí, nublía,* 'harlots.' The same vowel is added also to masculine nouns ending in *i:* as *rashái, rasháia,* 'priests;' *múi, múia,* 'mouths;' *nái, náia,* 'nails:'—also to nouns ending in *k* and *v:* as *pak, paká,* 'wings;' *drak, draká,* 'grapes;' *triák, triaká,* 'shoes;' *pov, pová,* 'eyebrows;' *gav, gavá,* 'villages.'

In all the numerous class of nouns ending in other consonants, this case is formed by the addition of *en:* as *grast, grastén,* 'horses;' *pral, pralén,* 'brothers;' *shingh, shinghén,* 'horns.'

Vocative plural.—This case is formed, in nouns ending in *o,* by the change of the final vowel to *ále:* as *choró, chorále,* 'O poor men!' *chavó, chavále,* 'O children!' In nouns ending in consonants the same formation is observed: as *róm, romiále* or *romále,* 'O Gypsies!' *manúsh, manushále,* 'O men!' Likewise in feminine nouns in *i:* as *raklí, rakliále,* 'O girls!' and also with masculine nouns in *i:* as *rashái, rashále,* 'O priests!'

The reader must not suppose that there is to be found in the Gypsy the uniformity observed in many other languages, where grammatical usages are more constant, and where even the language of the most ignorant has always had persons of more refinement speaking it. On the contrary, among the Gypsies there is such a difference in pronunciation, and such tendency to alter the vowels in these case-endings, that the subject at times becomes extremely difficult and embarrassing.

There are remnants of the locative case of the Sanskrit, but the case itself does not exist as an independent one: its place is supplied, as in most European languages, by a particle: the remnants referred to are *ratti, aratti,* 'by night;' *telé,* 'under, below;' *anglé,* 'forwards.'

Genitive, singular and plural.—The genitive is formed by the addition of *koro,* in both numbers and genders: as *richiní, richinéskoro,* 'of a bear;' *sunnó, sunnéskoro,* 'of a dream;' *pak, pakéskoro,* 'of the wing;' *richinénghoro,* 'of bears;' *sunnénghoro,* 'of dreams;' *pakénghoro,* 'of wings.' In the feminine, *dái, duiákori,* 'of the mother;'* *chorí, choriákori,* 'of the poor woman;' plur. *daiánghori,†* 'of the mothers;' *choriánghori,* 'of the poor women.' This termination, which is no other than the Sanskrit word *kara* (Gr. ποιος, Lat. *faciens*), from the root *kri,* 'to make,' serves also to form a great variety of nouns, in a way similar to the Greek and Latin terms mentioned. Thus *charó,* 'plate,' *charéskoro,* 'of a plate,' and 'a plate-maker;' *shastrí,* 'iron,' *shastiréskoro,* 'of iron,' and 'a worker in iron;' *butí,* 'business,' *butiákoro,* 'of the business,' and 'a business man, a craftsman;' *bar,* 'stone,' *baréskoro,* 'of a stone,' and 'a stone-cutter;' *mas,* 'meat,' *maséskoro,* 'of the meat,' and 'butcher;' *angár,* 'coal,' *angaréskoro,* 'of the coal,' and 'a collier.' All these terms, and many other similar ones, serve as genitive cases, and are used also frequently as adjectives: thus *katúna,* 'Gypsy tent,' *katunéskoro róm,* 'a Gypsy of the tent,' i. e. σκηνίτης; *katunéskeri romní,* 'a Gypsy woman of the tent.' Like all other adjectives, these nouns take the usual feminine termination in *i:* as *butiákori,* 'a craftswoman;' *maséskori,* 'a butcher's wife;' *machéskori,* 'a female dealing in fish.' In the declension, also, the final *o* of the genitive masculine constantly becomes *i* in the feminine: as *raní,* 'the nobleman's wife,' gen. *raniákori,* and never *raniákoro.*

The confusion resulting from the identity of these terms is somewhat avoided by the use of the masculine article *o: o katunéskoro,* 'the tent-maker,' *e katunéskoro,* 'of the tent;' *o maséskoro,* 'the butcher,' *e maséskoro chavó,* 'the child of the butcher.'

There is no other genitive throughout the Gypsy language than that formed by the termination *koro;* we shall meet it in both adjectives and pronouns, constant and invariable, demonstrating amply that the genitive case is properly a possessive, which in course of time lost entirely this signification.

I come now to consider the other four so-called cases, the first and second dative, the social, and the ablative; and as they are common to the nouns and pronouns, what I offer now is equally applicable to both. As I differ in my view of them from all who have written on the subject before me, it is just to lay before the reader the reasons which have convinced me, and have brought me to an independent conclusion.

---

* Pronounced often *dákori* and *dákeri.* † Also *daidnghere.*

Grellmann appears first to have studied the formation of the cases of the Gypsy noun, and all subsequent writers have more or less imitated him. I have remarked, in speaking of the noun, that it has properly only two cases, the nominative and the accusative, from which latter is formed the genitive, by the addition of *koro*, both in the singular and plural, and both in the masculine and feminine. I have given also the cases of other authors, called dative first and second, social, and ablative. The two datives end in *te* and *ke* respectively, the social in *sa*, and the ablative in *tar;* in the plural, they end usually in *de, ghe, tza,* and *dar,* owing to the preceding liquid *n*, which, though lost at present in the accusative, has been tenaciously preserved in the compounds. The social and ablative are well understood, but the difference between the two datives is not well defined in the grammars of this idiom. The dative ending in *te* means, according to what I have been able to ascertain, 'in, within:' as *me sunnéste,* 'in my dream;' *me tanéste,* 'in my town;' *teráva me sheréste,* 'I have in my head;' *me gotiáte,* 'in my brain;' *me praléskoro keréste,* 'in the house of my brother;' *terávas duk me boriáti,* 'I had pain in my belly;' *te praléskoro biavéste,* 'in the marriage of thy brother.' This is often heard inverted: as *ti pak,* 'in the wing,' for *pakéste; ti biáv,* 'in the marriage,' for *biavéste; ti ker,* for *keréste,* 'in the house.' These examples fully elucidate the meaning of the particle *te,* joined to the noun.

The second dative, ending in *ke,* means 'to, towards:' as *ma pen yavréske,* 'do not say (it) to another;' *machénghe lon chivéla,* 'he throws salt to the fish;' *oghéske,* 'to the soul,' or 'for the soul.' The Gypsies, as in the former case, seem to be abandoning this form, and make use of *ko* and *ke* before the noun. Still the regular form is extremely common in the pronouns, where less license can be taken, and where the meaning of these forms may be still farther explained and clearly understood. Examples of similar inversions we have in modern Greek, where ἰδῶϑεν, ἐκεῖϑεν have been abandoned for ἀπ' ἰδῶ, ἀπ' ἐκεῖ, and the like; and in some parts of Greece, as the Ionian islands, for ἀπ' ἰδῶϑεν, ἀπ' ἐκεῖϑεν, a usage found existing among the Greeks of Homer's time.

In the pronouns, the particle *ke* is never placed before the term to be expressed, as is the case often in nouns: thus *pen mánghe* (for *mán-ke*), 'say to me;' *yavréske,* 'to another;' *aménghe,* 'to us;' *tuménghe,* 'to you;' *túke,* 'to thee;' *léske,* 'to him;' *láke,* 'to her;' *lénghe,* 'to them.' This particle is also often joined to numerals: as *keténghe kinghián les?* *jovénghe,* 'for how much didst thou buy it? for six;' *bishénghe,* 'for twenty;' and so with all the numerals.

The above examples prove the signification which this particle imparts to Gypsy words, and, though less in use than the other particle *te,* it is still extremely clear and definite.

The social case, formed by the addition of *sa* (probably the Sr. *saha,* 'with, together with'), is simple in its construction, and very plain in its signification, both in the singular and plural. It denotes junction, union, and accompaniment, and is united to both nouns and pronouns: as *jáva grastéssa,* 'I go with a horse' (i. e. 'on horseback'); *pindéntza,* 'with the feet' (i. e. 'on foot'); *yavré rakléntza,* 'with other children;' *romniása,* 'with the woman;' *romniantza,* 'with the women.' In the pronouns it is universally found: as *mántza,* 'with me,' Lat. *mecum;* *túsa,* 'with thee;' *améntza, tuméntza, léntza,* 'with us, with you, with them.'

The ablative, formed by the addition of *tar* (probably the Sr. *tas,* which has the same signification, and a somewhat similar use), is found also constantly in both numbers and genders, and in both nouns and pronouns. That it is a particle, independent of the noun, is amply demonstrated by its use in verbs and participles, whenever action from a place is intended to be expressed: thus *nastótar,* 'after he departed' (*nastó,* part., 'departed, gone'); *tapilótar,* 'after it was buried;' *alliátar,* 'after he came;' *kamulótar,* 'after dying;' *pelótar,* 'after falling.' So also in *sostár,* 'because,' formed evidently of *so*—the neut. of *kón,* 'who'—and *tar;* and in the local adverbs, as *até,* 'here,' *attár,* 'from here.' These examples cannot be made to support the opinion of those writers who would make this a case. On such principles we should be compelled to regard as cases all those combinations with particles which impart the idea of direction of action to the noun, or indicate its relation to another object, whether animate or inanimate.

Such are the considerations which have induced me to exclude from the declension of the noun all these forms, which are not cases in the proper sense of the word, and to limit that appellation to the nominative, accusative, genitive, and vocative alone.

Diminutive nouns are formed by the addition of *oro,* and are frequently to be heard among all the Gypsies: thus *grast,* 'horse,' *grastoró,* 'a small horse, a young horse;' *chavó, chavoró,* 'a young child;' *das, dasoró,* 'a young Bulgarian;' *jut, jutoró,* 'a young Jew;' *ternó, ternoró,* 'a youngster. The fem. of these diminutives is regular: as *chavorí,* 'a young female child;' *dasorí, jutorí, ternorí,* etc. They are declined like other nouns in *o* and *i.*

Another class of diminutives ends in *tzo:* as *baló,* 'hog,' *balitzó,* 'a young pig;' *bakró, bakritzó,* 'a lamb.'

ADJECTIVES.

Adjectives end in *o,* plural *e,* and correspond in their declension to nouns in *o.* There are some exceptions to this rule: as *sukár,* 'beautiful;' *naisukár,* 'ugly;' *naisváli,* 'invalid;' *kasukóv,* 'deaf;' *namporemé,* 'sick.'

All adjectives ending in *o* and in consonants are masculine
or neuter. The feminine is formed by changing *o* to *i:* as *kaló*,
'black,' *kalí romní*, 'black woman;' *melaló*, 'dirty,' *melalí chái*,
'dirty girl.'

The feminine of the above mentioned adjectives not ending in
o is formed by adding *i*, often with some variations of the final
syllable: as *sukár*, 'beautiful,' fem. *sukarorí* or *sukarí; naisváli*
serves for both genders; *kasukóv*, fem. *kasukóvi*, 'deaf woman.'

The other adjectives not ending in vowels are declined like
nouns ending in the corresponding consonants.

When adjectives are used otherwise than attributively, they are
thus declined like nouns; but when in combination with substantives, these latter receive the case-terminations, and the adjectives
then change their *o* into *e:* as *e kaléskero*, 'of the black (man),' *e
kalé manushéskoro*, 'of the black man;' *melalén chavén* (acc.) is
pronounced *melalé chavén*, 'the dirty children.' I think, however, we may come nearer the truth in assuming that the adjectives,
in the accusative of both genders, drop the final *s* and *n* in pronunciation.

The comparative degree of the adjective is extremely variable.
It is mostly formed by adding to the positive the particle *po*,
which appears to me to be the Greek πλέον, pronounced by us at
present πιό: as *po lachó*, 'better;' *po kaló*, 'blacker;' *po vuchó*,
'higher.' What inclines me to believe that this is our πιό for
πλέον is the fact that the Moslem Gypsies, less acquainted with
the Greek, adopt the corresponding Turkish word *daha*, which
the Turks universally use to form their comparative degree: thus
daha ey, 'better.' They are not acquainted with the particle *po*,
and only a few use it, who mingle with their fellow-countrymen
the Christian Gypsies. *Po* is not confined to the pure adjective,
but is also used in the adverbial form: as *po lachés*, 'better,' Gr.
κάλλιον, Lat. *melius; po vuchés*, 'higher,' ὑψηλότερον, *altius*.

Though this is the most constant form of the comparative, and
though the Gypsies have in this respect imitated their neighbors,
who have lost in great part the ancient forms of the comparative,
and have substituted in its stead the πλέον, the Gypsy language
has preserved traces of the ancient comparative of the Sr. in *tara*,
the τερος of the Greeks, and which in Persian is regular and extremely common. The Latin has not preserved so universally
as the Greek this original ending of comparison, although it evidently exists in such terms as *exter, inter, alter*, etc.

The Sr. *tara* is evidently to be recognized in such words as
me baredér (*baro*, 'great'), 'my superior;' *me uchedér* (*uchó*,
'high'), 'one higher than me,' ὑψηλότερος ἐμοῦ. In this form the
word is at times to be heard, though it is necessary to remark
that it is not common, and that the Gypsies prefer saying *me po
lachó, me po uchó*. At times, like other ignorant people, they

join the particle *po* to the comparative: as *po kalodér*, 'blacker,' lit. 'more blacker;' *po parnodér*, 'more whiter.' In this they have every day imitators, among the Greeks particularly, who say πιὸ ὑψηλότερος, πιὸ μεγαλήτερος, for simple ὑψηλότερος and μεγαλήτερος. This form of the comparative is, I am sorry to say, fast going out of use. One may hear Gypsies discourse for a long time without suspecting its existence.

As to the superlative, I know of none. Gypsies experience the same difficulty as the common Greeks, when they attempt to express such an idea: thus *lachó*, 'good;' *po lachó*, 'better;' *o po lachó*, 'the best;' *o po kaló*, 'the blackest;' Gr. καλὸς, πιὸ καλὸς, ὁ πιὸ καλὸς, 'the best.'

From the adjectives are formed adverbs, as numerous as the adjectives, and here the Gypsies experience no difficulty. All these terms, extremely common among them, are formed by changing the final *o* into *es*. They are simple and very expressive: thus *lachó*, 'good,' *lachés*, 'well;' *shuchó*, 'clean,' *shuchés*, 'in a clean manner;' *romanó, romanés*, 'in a Gypsy manner;' *dasanó, dasanés*, 'in a Bulgarian manner.' These latter forms correspond to the Greek ἀτζιγκανιστί, βουλγαριστί.

To these adverbs is prefixed the comparative particle *po*: as *po vuchés*, 'higher, *altius;*' *po lachés*, 'better;' *po kalés*, 'blacker.' Also to the proper adverbs of place: as *po anglál*, 'farther ahead;' *po nápalal*, 'still more backwards;' *po andré*, 'farther inwards;' *po avrí*, 'farther outwards.'

The Moslem Gypsies use precisely the same expression, substituting the Turkish *daha* for *po*, as we have already remarked, in treating of the formation of the comparative: thus *daha vuchés, daha lachés.*

PRONOUNS.

Personal.

1st Person.

	Sing.		Plur.	
Nom.	*me*, 'I,'		*amén*, 'we,'	
Acc.	*man*, 'me,'		*amán*, 'us,'	

Gen. { *me, mindó, minró, mánghero,* } 'of me,' { *amaró, amánghoro,* } 'of us.'

2d Person.

	Sing.		Plur.	
Nom.	*tu*, 'thou,'		*tumén*, 'ye,'	
Acc.	*tut*, 'thee,'		*tumén*, 'you,'	

Gen. { *te, tindó, tinró,* } 'of thee,' { *tumaró, tuménghoro,* } 'of you.'

13

3d Person, masc.

	Sing.		Plur.
Nom.	*ov,* 'he,'		*ol,* 'they,'
Acc.	*les,* 'him,'		*len,* 'them,'
Gen.	*léskero,* 'of him,'		*lénghero,* 'of them.'

3d Person, fem.

	Sing.		Plur.
Nom.	*ov,* 'she,'		*o,* 'they,'
Acc.	*la,* 'her,'		*len,* 'them,'
Gen.	*lákero,* 'of her,'		*lénghero,* 'of them.'

Possessive.

1st Person.

Sing. masc. and neut.	fem.	Plur.		
Nom. *mo,*	*mi,*	*me,* 'my,'	*amaró,* 'our,'
Acc. *mo,*	*mi,*	*me,* 'my,'	*amaré,* 'our,'
Gen. *me,*	*me,*	*me,* 'of my,'	*amarénghoro,* 'of our.'

2d Person.

Sing. masc. and neut.	fem.	Plur.	
Nom. *to,*	*ti,*	*te,* 'thy,'	*tumaró,* 'your,'
Acc. *to,*	*ti,*	*te,* 'thy,'	*tumaré,* 'your,'
Gen. *te,*	*te,*	*te,* 'of thy,'	*tumarénghoro,* 'of your.'

3d Person.

Sing. masc.		fem.		Plur.	

léskero, { 'of him, his,' } *lákero,* { 'of her, her,' } *léskere,* 'of his,' *olénghero,* { 'of them, their.' }

Whenever the possessive pronoun is used substantively, *mo* becomes *mindó* or *minró; to* becomes *tindó* or *tinró.* The reader has already seen numerous illustrations of this general usage in the Vocabulary. All the pronouns are declined like nouns in *o* and *i.*

There is another form of the possessive pronoun, which is not common among the Gypsies in these countries, viz. *pes* and *pi.* The first is never used except with the 3d person of the passive verb, and corresponds to the usual *les,* 'him;' the second, *pi,* is a form often found in the place of *léskero,* 'of him, his.' To many Gypsies this latter is entirely unknown.

The perusal of the above pronouns illustrates the general usage of many languages, where the genitive of the personal pronoun seems to form most of the possessives, varied according to their union with the substantive. Compare Gr. ἐγὼ, gen. ἐμοῦ; ἐμὸς, μὸς, ἡμέτερος, etc.

Before comparing these pronouns with those in the Sanskrit, I shall elucidate the use of them by familiar colloquial phrases, by which their meaning and proper employment may be more perfectly understood. The same particles which we have so frequently met in studying the nouns, forming a kind of cases, will be observed also with these pronouns. The reader can easily understand them by simply referring to what we have said on the subject there.

1st Person.—*Kon déla o vutár?* 'who knocks at the door?' *me isóm,* 'it is I,' ἐγὼ εἰμι; *me nastí keráva,* 'I cannot do;' *kon isí? me,* 'who is it? I.' *Kayék jenó na janéla man,* 'no one knows me;' *te des man,* 'that thou shouldst give me;' *de man,* 'give me;' *ma de man,* 'do not give me;' *ma kus man,* 'do not revile me;' *mukéla man,* 'it leaves me.' *Me praléskero keréste,* 'in the house of my brother;' *me grastéskoro i zen,* 'my horse's saddle;' *bi mánghoro,* 'without me.' *Amén isámas otiá,* 'we were there.' *Na dukél' amán,* 'he does not love us.' *Amaró manúsh,* 'our man;' *amaré manushé,* 'our men;' *amari chip,* 'our language;' *diniás amaré chuklés,* 'he struck our dog;' *gurumní amari,* 'our cow;' *amaré gotiáte,* 'in our mind;' *kon diniás amaré peniá?* 'who struck our sister?'

2d Person.—*Tu ghellián ti pólin?* 'didst thou go to the city?' *tu kerghiánles?* 'didst thou make it?' *tu nastí kerésa,* 'thou canst not do it.' *Na reséla tut,* 'it does not suffice thee;' *murdaráva tut,* 'I kill thee;' *allióm ta dikáv tut,* 'I have come to see thee.' *Te gavéskoro manushé,* 'the men of thy village;' *te praléskoro nav?* 'the name of thy brother?' *Nanái tindó,* 'it is not thine;' *isí tindó,* 'it is thine.' *Tumén so penása?* 'what do ye say?' *Tumaró biáv isí?* 'is it your marriage?' *tumaré kheréskoro,* 'of your ass.'

3d Person, masculine.—*Ki ov ki isás otiá,* 'and he who was there;' *méya, túya, ki ov,* 'and I, and thou, and he.' *Kamáva les,* 'I want him;' *astarghióm les,* 'I seized him;' *dikáva les,* 'I see him.' *I romní léskoro,* 'his wife;' *léskoro dat,* 'his father;' *anglé isás oléskoro,* 'formerly it was his;' *isí oléskoro,* 'it is his.' *Ol manushé,* 'those men.' This pronoun is rarely used, and in its stead the Gypsies employ *aklá, akiá,* 'these,' which we have noticed in the Vocabulary. *Na maréla len,* 'he does not beat them;' *dikióm len,* 'I saw them;' *na picharáv len,* 'I do not know them.' *Lénghero vasiáv,* 'their mill;' *lénghero lové,* 'their money.'

3d Person, feminine.—*Ol romní,* 'that woman;' *ol gurumní,* 'that cow.' *Diklióm la yek divés,* 'I saw her one day;' *bighián la,* 'he sold her;' *marélala,* 'he beats her.' *Lákero pral keréla shastrí,* 'her brother makes iron;' *lákeri dat,* 'her father;' *lákeri moskári* (Gr. μοσχάρι), 'her calf;' *lákeri chuchía,* 'her breasts.' The plural is similar to the plural of the 3d person masculine.

Possessives.—These are extremely regular. *Mo dat,* 'my father;' *mo sheró,* 'my head;' *mi dái,* 'my mother;' *mi pen,* 'my sister.' *To rom,* 'thy husband;' *ti romní,* 'thy wife;' *ti gurumní,* 'thy cow.' *Kaléskero isí o ker?* 'whose is the house?' *isí mindó* or *minró,* 'it is mine.' No Gypsy says *isí mo.* The plural does not differ from the declension of adjectives in *o. Me lové,* 'my money;' *me yísmata,* 'my linen;' *te tikné isí melalé,* 'thy children are dirty;' *so keréna te chavé?* 'how are thy children?' *Lénghero* is used both for the masculine and feminine of the 3d person: *lénghero chavé,* 'of these (women) the children;' *lénghero lové,* 'of these (men) the money.' Though these pronouns are pronounced without an initial vowel, it appears to me, judging from the nominative *ov, o,* that they should be written *olénghero, olákero.*

There is a particular form of the 1st and 2d personal pronouns, extremely common among all the Gypsies, and which cannot but strike a person in conversation with them. This form is *méya,* 'I also;' *túya,* 'thou also;' *améya, tuméya,* 'we, ye also.' *Méya pincharávales,* 'I also am acquainted with him;' *isús léskoro, méya kinghióm les,* 'it was his, and I bought it;' *túya kamovés ti gav,* 'and thou wilt be in the village;' *améya, tuméya ki ol t' avén,* 'and we, and ye, and they should come.'

Relative.

The declension of the relative pronoun, which we have already noticed in the Vocabulary, is as follows:

Sing., masc.	fem.	neut.	Plur.
Nom. *kon,*	*kayá,*	*so,*	*so,*
Acc. *kalés,*	*kalé,*	*kalés,*	*kalén,*
Gen. *kaléskoro,*	*kaléskeri,*	*kaléskoro,*	*kalénghero.*

It is extremely difficult to obtain an exact statement of this pronoun; even with all my endeavors, I do not know whether I have set down the proper forms. The feminine *kayá* is rarely heard, and the masculine is often substituted in its place. Both Turks and Greeks have corrupted their relative pronouns. The latter rarely use anything else but their τί, for τίς, τί, τίνες, τίνα, etc. Of course, the Gypsies are no better than their neighbors. It is for this reason that I have not written the feminine and neuter of the plural, as I have been particular in the course of this memoir not to give to the public aught but what I am confident is true.

All the foregoing pronouns are found united to those particles which we have noticed in speaking of the cases of nouns. They corroborate what I have already advanced, that the so-called cases of the Gypsy noun are particles united to the accusative, varying according to the characteristic final consonants *s* or *n.*

For farther illustration of this subject, I shall follow the same plan which I have adopted in other parts of this memoir. *Beshéla bashé mánde, tuménde, lénde,* 'he lives near me, you, them;'

me jáva túsa, 'I go with thee;' *mánja,* 'with me;' *nash améndar,* 'depart from us;' *oléndar,* 'from them;' *nasháva tuméndar,* 'I depart from you;' *penéna mánghe,* 'they say to me;' *sóske puché-sa mándar?* 'why dost thou ask me?' *so kapenés mánghe?* 'what wilt thou say to me?' *kapuchάv léstar,* 'I shall ask him;' *o devél teréla lénghe,* 'God has (care) of them;' *kaléste pashé?* 'near whom?' *bi mángoro nasti kerésa,* 'without me thou canst not do;' *sarnénghe ta penés les, ke tumarénghe, k' amarénghe, sarné parna-vénghe,* 'tell it to all, and to your, and to our, and to all the friends;' *penghiά mánghe mi tái,* 'said to me my mother;' *te penάv túke,* 'that I may speak to thee;' *dikinilό láke,* 'appeared to her;' *te jivél túke,* 'may it live to thee' (a form of salutation when an animal is bought), Gr. *νά σοῦ ζήσῃ; andré lénde,* 'within them.'

The following is the complete declension of the personal pronoun, with its particles.

	Sing.		*Plur.*
Nom.	*me,* 'I,'		*amén,* 'we,'
Acc.	*man,* 'me,'		*amán,* 'us,'
Dat. 1,	*mánde (mán-te),* 'in me,'		*aménde (amén-te),* 'in us,'
Dat. 2,	*mánghe (mán-ke),* 'to me,'		*aménghe (amén-ke),* 'to us,'
Abl.	*mándar (mán-tar),* 'from me,'		*amándar (amén-tar),* 'from us,'
Soc.	*mánja (mán-sa),* 'with me,'		*aménja (amén-sa),* 'with us,'
Gen.	*mánghoro (mán-koro),* 'of me,'		*aménghoro (amén-koro),* 'of us.'

The genitive, of both singular and plural, is never used except in connection with *bi,* 'without:' *bi mánghoro, bi aménghoro,* 'without me, without us.'

	Sing.		*Plur.*
Nom.	*tu,* 'thou,'		*tumén,* 'ye,'
Acc.	*tut,* 'thee,'		*tumén,* 'you,'
Dat. 1,	*tútte,* 'in thee,'		*tuménde,* 'in you,'
Dat. 2,	*túke,* 'to thee,'		*tuménghe,* 'to you,'
Abl.	*tútar,* 'from thee,'		*tuméndar,* 'from you,'
Soc.	*túsa,* 'with thee,'		*tuménja,* 'with you,'
Gen.	——— *		*tuménghoro,* 'of you.'

In a similar way are declined all the other pronouns. The reader has had frequent occasions to observe the cases of the relative *kon,* 'who,' in the Vocabulary.

Though the Gypsies are fond of placing these particles before the noun—as *ti len,* 'in the river,' for *lenéste; ti ker,* 'in the house,' for *keréste*—and though the ablative particle *tar* is found united to indeclinables as often as to nouns, still, in the cases of pronouns, these particles seem to be constant, and so tenacious, that a Gypsy will laugh at your ignorance, if he should ever hear you saying *te man* instead of *mánde, ko man* instead of *mánghe.*

---

* Unknown to me.

Verb.

The Gypsy verbs may be classified in two methods:
1st, Verbs Simple and Verbs Compound;
2d, Verbs Neuter, Active, Middle, and Passive.

Simple verbs are those in which the Gypsy verb is the simple Sanskrit root: as *dikáva*, 'I see;' *shunáva*, 'I hear;' *asáva*, 'I laugh.'

Compound verbs are made up of a primitive word in combination with a verb, such as *keráva*, 'I do,' *aváva*, 'I come,' *dáva*, 'I give.' I have spoken of these verbs in the Vocabulary (see to CHEW), and have shown that the usage corresponds with that of the Persians. *Keráva*, 'I do,' the *kerden* of the Persians (Sr. *kri*), united to the primitive word, serves to form active verbs: as *chamkeráva*, 'I chew,' i. e. 'I make chewing;' *vrakeráva*, 'I talk,' i. e. 'I make speech.' This form of the compound verb is not so common among the Gypsies as among the Persians or the Turks, for the Gypsies have another form of transitive verbs which they prefer, as more congenial to their language: at least, so it appears to me from their conversation. In fact, the reader will observe that in the Vocabulary, in a long list of verbs, there occur few compound ones. By many Gypsies these verbs are never used, since they prefer the other form of the transitive verb, of which I shall presently speak. The second verb, *aváva*, 'to come,' the *ameden* of the Persians, is extremely common, and serves to form a long list of passive verbs, by combination with adjectives and participles: as *phuriováva*, 'to become old,' Gr. γηράσκω, Lat. *senesco ; bariováva*, 'to become great;' *bukaliováva*, 'to become hungry;' *khokhavniováva*, 'to be cheated;' *mattiováva*, 'to become intoxicated;' *shukiováva*, 'to become dry;' *melalio-váva*, 'to become dirty.' So natural and easy is this form to the Gypsies, that they are constantly using it, and with very little variation. *Aváva*, in combination with the adjective or participle, possesses the signification of the Latin *fieri*, 'to become,' and, of course, no other form but an adjective or a participle is ever united to it. The final vowel of the adjective or participle and the initial *a* of the verb are blended in such a manner that they produce *io :* as *mattó-aváva, mattiováva*. This pronunciation is very constant. The reader has seen frequent examples of such compound verbs in the Vocabulary, and will have remarked their signification in the numerous colloquial phrases given under the various verbs.

I do not refer to this class of verbs those which are formed with the auxiliary *isóm*, 'to be,' and more rarely with *teráva*, 'to have,' since these do not differ from similar verbs in other languages.

Neuter verbs are very common, and are formed directly from the Sanskrit root, without any alteration. They are in fact the

Sanskrit verb itself, with its active present, of which the final syllable *mi* is simply changed into *va:* as *charáva*, 'I graze,' Sr. *charámi; asáva*, 'I laugh,' Sr. *hasámi.*

Active verbs.—Besides those formed by the addition of *keráva* to the root, and which are naturally active, the Gypsies form another and very numerous class, whose characteristic sign is the penultimate *ra:* as *taparáva*, 'I heat,' Gr. ϑεϱμαίνω. This formation is so natural, and so usual, that a Gypsy is never at a loss to understand it, or instantly to form it, even were it from a Turkish or Greek root. To his mind it always conveys the idea of a transitive action, precisely as we say ἀγαπῶ, 'I love,' ἀγαπίζω, 'I induce love, I make one love.'

These transitive verbs must not be confounded with such neuter verbs as have the penultimate in *ra*, and which originate from a root ending in *r:* as *choráva*, 'I steal,' *daráva*, 'I fear,' *teráva*, 'I have,' *mutráva*, 'I void urine.' Verbs of this class are of four syllables, while nearly all the Gypsy neuter verbs have three, and a few only two: as *dáva*, 'I give,' *líva*, 'I take.'

These verbs are formed by the addition of *aráva* to the primitive root: as *murdaráva*, 'I murder;' *taparáva*, 'I cause to burn;' *muntaráva*, 'I shave one.' *Tapáva*, 'I heat,' is a striking example of the variation of the Gypsy verb: Sr. *tap*, 'to torment, to heat;' G. *tapáva*, 'I feel warm;' *taparáva*, 'I cause to burn;' *tattiováva*, 'I become hot.'

Middle verbs.—These are extremely simple, formed by the addition to the verb of the accusative cases of the personal pronouns, precisely as the Europeans form their verbs of a similar signification: thus Fr. *je me lave;* It. *io mi lavo.*

Passive verbs.—These are rarely used by the Gypsies, who prefer the active voice, and instead of saying "I was beaten," adopt the expression "one has beaten me." On this account, the passive voice is extremely difficult to describe, and such are the circumlocutions to which the Gypsies have recourse whenever they desire to express a passive idea, that one wonders at the ambiguity and vagueness of their language. Often they differ so much that the hearer doubts whether he has understood them. In a long discourse, the hearer may not meet with a single passive form. Even after satisfying himself that a verb is passive, upon pronouncing it in the hearing of other Gypsies he may meet with contradictions, or his hearers may be unable to understand him. In such cases, a Gypsy may tell you that such an expression is not Gypsy, and that the speaker has no knowledge of his language. In fact, I have written many paradigms of passive verbs formerly, and, upon examining them, I have found that they were at variance with sound grammatical principles. For a long time I thought the Gypsies had no passive voice. Still not despairing, I have made the paradigm of the passive verb, and have finally satisfied myself as to the truth of its grammatical construction.

The reader will see this passive form in the following pages. At times the middle voice is used, with the accusative pronouns constantly joined to the verb. At times the compound form is used for the passive, and the verb which is united is evidently *aváva.* It is united to the Sanskrit root, and not to adjectives and participles, as in the more common compound verbs.

These observations will be better elucidated by paradigms of the verb, after giving which, I shall proceed to speak of the formation of the tenses. I hope that this course, which I have followed in my studies on the subject, will be of service to the reader, assisting him to form a clear understanding of the various forms and significations of the Gypsy verb, and of its intimate relationship to the Sanskrit.

Of the auxiliary verbs *teráva,* 'I have,' and *isóm,* 'I am,' I have little to say. The first is rarely used to form such verbs as we see in modern European languages. Its use is mainly restricted to express the idea of possession: as *teráva duk,* 'I have pain,' i. e. 'I am in pain.' *Isóm* forms a perfect passive, which I shall note in its proper place.

Isom, 'I am.'

Present.

Sing.	Plur.
1. *isóm,* 'I am,'	1. *isámas,* 'we are,'
2. *isán,* 'thou art,'	2. *isána,* 'ye are,'
3. *isi,* 'he is,'	3. *isi,* 'they are.'

Imperfect.

Sing.	Plur.
1. *isómas,* 'I was,'	1. *isámas,* 'we were,'
2. *isánas,* 'thou wast,'	2. *isánas,* 'ye were,'
3. *isás,* 'he was,'	3. *isás,* 'they were.'

Future.

Sing.	Plur.
1. *kamováv,* 'I shall be,' etc.	1. *kamovása,* 'we shall be,' etc.
2. *kamovés,*	2. *kamovéna,*
3. *kamovél,*	3. *kamovéna.*

These are all the tenses used: I have never been able to obtain any knowledge of any other forms.

Chináva, 'I cut.'   Choráva, 'I steal.'

Present.

Sing.	Sing.
1. *chináva,* 'I cut,' etc.	*choráva,* 'I steal,' etc.
2. *chinésa,*	*chorésa,*
3. *chinéla,*	*choréla,*

Plur.
1. chinásas,
2. chinéna,
3. chinéna.

Plur.
chorásas,
choréna,
choréna.

Imperfect.

Sing.
1. chinávas, 'I was cutting,' etc.
2. chinésas,
3. chinélas,

Sing.
chorávas, 'I was stealing,' etc.
chorésas,
chorélas,

Plur.
1. chinásas,
2. chinénas,
3. chinénas.

Plur.
chorásas,
chorénas,
chorénas.

Aorist.

Sing.
1. chinghióm, 'I cut,' etc.
2. chinghián,
3. chinghiás,

Sing.
chorghióm, 'I stole,' etc.
chorghián,
chorghiás,

Plur.
1. chinghiámas,
2. chinghián,
3. chinghiá.

Plur.
chorghiámas,
chorghián,
chorghiá.

Future.

Sing.
1. kamachináva, 'I shall cut,' etc.
2. kamachinésa,
3. kamachinéla,

Sing.
kamachoráva, 'I shall steal,' etc.
kamachorésa,
kamachoréla,

Plur.
1. kamachinása,
2. kamachinéna,
3. kamachinéna.

Plur.
kamachorása,
kamachoréna,
kamachoréna.

Imperative.

Sing.
2. chin, 'cut thou,'
3. me chinél, 'let him cut,'

Sing.
chor, 'steal thou,'
me chorél, 'let him steal.'

Plur.
2. chinén, 'steal ye,'
3. me chinén, 'let them steal.'

Plur.
chorén, 'cut ye,'
me chorén, 'let them cut.'

Subjunctive.
Present.

Sing.
1. te chináva, 'that I may cut,' etc.
2. te chinésa,
2. te chinéla,

Sing.
te choráva, 'that I may steal,' etc.
te chorésa,
te choréla,

14

Plur.	*Plur.*
1. *te chinása,*	*te chorása,*
2. *te chinéna,*	*te choréna,*
3. *te chinéna.*	*te choréna.*

Imperfect.

Sing.	*Sing.*
1. *te chinávas,* 'that I might cut,' etc.	*te chorávas,* 'that I might steal,' etc.
2. *te chinésas,*	*te chorésas,*
3. *te chinélas,*	*te chorélas,*
Plur.	*Plur.*
1. *te chinásas,*	*te chorásas,*
2. *te chinénas,*	*te chorénas,*
3. *te chinénas.*	*te chorénas.*

Participle.

chinavdó, 'cut.'　　　　　　　　choravdó, 'stolen.'

Verbs ending in vowels:

DÁVA, 'I give.'　　　　　　　　LÁVA, 'I take.'

Indicative.

Present.

Sing.	*Sing.*
1. *dáva,* 'I give,' etc.	*láva,* 'I take,' etc.
2. *désa,*	*lésa,*
3. *déla,*	*léla,*
Plur.	*Plur.*
1. *dása,*	*lása,*
2. *déna,*	*léna,*
3. *déna.*	*léna.*

Imperfect.

Sing.	*Sing.*
1. *dávas,* 'I was giving,' etc.	*lávas,* 'I was taking,' etc.
2. *désas,*	*lésas,*
3. *délas,*	*lélas,*
Plur.	*Plur.*
1. *dásas,*	*lásas,*
2. *dénas,*	*lénas,*
3. *dénas.*	*lénas.*

Aorist.

Sing.	*Sing.*
1. *dinióm,* 'I gave,' etc.	*linióm,* 'I took,' etc.
2. *dinián,*	*linián,*
3. *diniás,*	*liniás,*
Plur.	*Plur.*
1. *diniámas,*	*liniámas,*
2. *dinián,*	*linián,*
3. *diniá.*	*liniá.*

Future.

Sing.		Sing.	
1. *kamadáva,*	'I shall give,' etc.	*kamaláva,*	'I shall take,' etc.
2. *kamadésa,*		*kamalésa,*	
3. *kamadéla,*		*kamaléla,*	

Plur.		Plur.	
1. *kamadása,*		*kamalása,*	
2. *kamadéna,*		*kamaléna,*	
3. *kamadéna.*		*kamaléna.*	

Imperative.

Sing.		Sing.	
2. *de,*	'give thou,'	*le,*	'take thou,'
3. *me del,*	'let him give,'	*me lel,*	'let him take,'

Plur.		Plur.	
2. *den,*	'give ye,'	*len,*	'take ye,'
3. *me den,*	'let them give.'	*me len,*	'let them take.'

Subjunctive.

Present.

Sing.		Sing.	
1. *te dáva,*	'that I may give,' etc.	*te láva,*	'that I may take,' etc.

Imperfect.

Sing.		Sing.	
1. *te dávas,*	'that I might give,' etc.	*te lávas,*	'that I might take,' etc.

Participle.

dinó,	'given.'	*liniló,*	'taken.'

All the simple verbs are declined in the same manner. There is some difference in the aorist, which we shall note in speaking of the formation of the aorist. In verbs compounded with *keráva,* 'I make,' *dáva,* 'I give,' the root suffers no alteration in the various inflections: as *cham-keráva,* 'I chew;' *cham-kerghióm,* 'I chewed;' *chumi-dáva,* 'I kiss;' *chumi-dinióm,* 'I kissed.'

Compound verbs, as *mattiováva,* 'to become intoxicated,' *shukiováva,* 'to become dry,' present no difficulty in their inflection, for they differ in no respect from the above paradigms. The aorist of *aváva,* which alone is inflected, is *allióm: mattillióm,* 'I became intoxicated;' *shukillióm,* 'I became dry.'

Verbs of the Middle Voice.

The conjugation of these verbs is very simple, and differs in nowise from the above, except in the pronouns, which form the essential character of this class of verbs.

Indicative.

Present.

Sing.	Sing.
1. *chináva man*, ' I cut myself,'	*továva˙man*, ' I wash myself,' etc.
2. *chinésa tut*, ' thou cuttest thyself,'	*tovésa tut*,
3. *chinéla pes*, ' he cuts himself,'	*tovéla pes*,
Plur.	Plur.
1. *chinása 'men*, ' we cut ourselves,'	*tovása 'men*,
2. *chinéna túmen*, ' ye cut yourselves,'	*tovéna túmen*,
3. *chinéna pes*, ' they cut themselves.'	*tovéna pes*.

Imperfect.

Sing.	Sing.
1. *chinávas man*, ' I was cutting myself,' etc.	*továvas man*, ' I was washing myself,' etc.
2. *chinésas tut*,	*tovésas tut*,
3. *chinélas pes*,	*tovélas pes*,
Plur.	Plur.
1. *chinásas 'men*,	*továsas 'men*,
2. *chinénas túmen*,	*tovénas túmen*,
3. *chinénas pes*.	*tovénas pes*.

Aorist.

Sing.	Sing.
1. *chinghióm man*, ' I cut myself,' etc.	*tovghióm man*, ' I washed myself,' etc.
2. *chinghián tut*,	*tovghián tut*,
3. *chinghiás pes*,	*tovghiás pes*,
Plur.	Plur.
1. *chinghiám 'men*,*	*tovghiám 'men*,
2. *chinghián túmen*,	*tovghián túmen*,
3. *chinghiá pes*,	*tovghiá pes*.

Future.

Sing.	Sing.
1. *kamachináva man*, ' I shall cut myself,' etc.	*kamatováva man*, ' I shall wash myself,' etc.
2. *kamachinésa tut*,	*kamatovésa tut*,
3. *kamachinéla pes*,	*kamatovéla pes*,
Plur.	Plur.
1. *kamachinása 'men*,	*kamatovása 'men*,
2. *kamachinéna túmen*,	*kamatovéna túmen*,
3. *kamachinéna pes*.	*kamatovéna pes*.

Imperative.

2. *chin tut*, ' cut thyself,'	*tov tut*, ' wash thyself.'
3. *me chinél pes*, ' let him cut himself.'	*me tovél pes*, ' let him wash himself.'

---

* Properly *chinghiámas 'men*.

Subjunctive.

Present.

1. *te chináva man,* 'that I may cut   *te továva man,* 'that I may wash
   myself,' etc.   myself,' etc.

Imperfect.

1, *te chinávas man,* 'that I might   *te továvas man,* 'that I might
   cut myself,' etc.   wash myself,' etc.

Passive voice.

Indicative.

Present.

Sing.	Sing.
1. *chinaváva man,* 'I am cut,' etc.	*choraváva man,* 'I am stolen,' etc.
2. *chinavésa tut,*	*choravésa tut,*
3. *chinavéla pes,*	*choravéla pes,*
Plur.	*Plur.*
1. *chinavása 'men,*	*choraváva 'men,*
2. *chinavéna túmen,*	*choravéna túmen,*
3. *chinavéna pes.*	*choravéna pes.*

Imperfect.

Sing.	Sing.
1. *chinavávas man,* 'I was being cut,' etc.	*choravávas man,* 'I was being stolen,' etc.
2. *chinavésas tut,*	*choravésas tut,*
3. *chinavélas pes,*	*choravélas pes,*
Plur.	*Plur.*
1. *chinavásas 'men,*	*choravásas 'man,*
2. *chinavénas túmen,*	*choravénas túmen,*
3. *chinavénas pes.*	*choravénas pes.*

Aorist.

Sing.	Sing.
1. *chintillióm,** 'I was cut,' etc.	*chortillióm,* 'I was stolen,' etc.
2. *chintillián,*	*chortillián,*
3. *chintilló,*	*chortilló,*
Plur.	*Plur.*
1. *chintillámas,*	*chortillámas,*
2. *chintillián,*	*chortillián,*
3. *chintilliá.*	*chortilliá.*

Future.

Sing.	Sing.
1. *kamachinaváva man,* 'I shall be cut,' etc.	*kamachoraváva man,* 'I shall be stolen,' etc.
2. *kamachinavésa tut,*	*kamachoravésa tut,*
3. *kamachinavéla pes,*	*kamachoravéla pes,*

---

* The first person of this tense has a very marked liquid sound of the *ll*. The 3d, *chintilló*, is a simple *l* always.

Plur.	*Plur.*
1. *kamachinavása 'men,*	*kamachoravása 'men,*
2. *kamachinavéna túmen,*	*kamachoravéna túmen,*
3. *kamachinavéna pes.*	*kamachoravéna pes.*

Perfect.

Sing.	*Sing.*
1. *chinavdó isóm,* 'I have been cut,' etc.	*choravdó isóm,* 'I have been stolen,' etc.
2. *chinavdó isán,*	*choravdó isán,*
3. *chinavdó isí,*	*choravdó isí,*
Plur.	*Plur.*
1. *chinavdó isám,*	*choravdó isám,*
2. *chinavdó isán,*	*choravdó isán,*
3. *chinavdó isí.*	*choravdó isí.*

For the imperative I have no certain data: the subjunctive is usually employed in its place.

Subjunctive.

Present.

1. *te chinaváva man,* 'that I may be cut,' etc.   *te choraváva man,* 'that I may be stolen,' etc.

Imperfect.

1. *te chinavása man,* 'that I might be cut,' etc.   *te choravása man,* 'that I might be stolen,' etc.

The pronunciation of the different persons of the verb used by the Gypsies is very peculiar. They are very prone to clip off the final vowel of the tenses: thus, instead of *chináva,* they say *chináv;* for *choráva, choráv,* etc.; in the 2d and 3d persons, likewise, for *chinésa, chinés; chinéla, chinél.* So also with the future, which, more than the other tenses, loses its terminal vowel. In fact, very few Gypsies pronounce it in full, and prefer the word as though written *kachináv, kachoráv,* or *kamachináv, kamachoráv.* So also with the aorist, which, in the 1st person plural, instead of *chorghiámas, chinghiámas,* is commonly pronounced *chorghiám, chinghiám.* Many Gypsies are aware of this, and they tell you that *chivél* for *chivéla, chorél* for *choréla,* is vulgar. In this manner are clipped all their verbs. In general, the verb retains its final vowel whenever it is at the end of a sentence. In their songs the final vowel is generally pronounced. I make these remarks, that the reader may the better understand many of the colloquial phrases, where I have written the words as ordinarily pronounced. To make a paradigm of a verb in this clipped form would be preposterous, and would exhibit a want of judgment in an author, who should take as a standard the constant fluctuations of colloquial use.

TENSES.—*Present.*—This invariably ends, in the first person, in *va:* as *siváva*, 'I sew;' *charáva*, 'I graze;' *kamáva*, 'I wish;' *keráva*, 'I make.' It corresponds with the present active of the Sanskrit, for we have seen, in speaking of the commutation of the consonants, that the *m* of the Sanskrit is frequently changed by the Gypsies to *v:* compare *charáva*, 'I graze,' with Sr. *charámi;* *keráva*, 'I make,' with Sr. *karomi*, etc. The 2d person singular, ending in *esa,* resembles the corresponding person of the Sanskrit, which ends in *si:* compare *charésa,* 'thou grazest,' Sr. *charasi;* *kerésa,* 'thou makest,' Sr. *karoshi.* But the 3d persons singular and plural bear no relation to the corresponding Sanskrit forms.

Imperfect.—The Gypsy language has no augment of any kind in any of its verbs. This tense is a mere imitation of the present, to which it adds a final *s.* It is always pronounced as I have written it, without any clipping of consonants or vowels.

Aorist.—This is of very frequent use, as it expresses action which, among more cultivated nations, belongs to the perfect, pluperfect, and aorist. By this tense is expressed past action, whatever its state or relation to other subjects, or its state of completion with reference to the time expressed. It is formed by adding to the root the syllable *ghióm* or *kióm,* whenever the root ends in a consonant: as *chináva,* aor. *chinghióm,* 'I cut;' *sováva,* aor. *sovghióm,* 'I slept;' *penáva,* aor. *penghióm,* 'I said;' *bisáva,* aor. *bisghióm,* 'I inhabited;' *basháva,* aor. *bashghióm,* 'I cried;' *chiváva,* aor. *chivghióm,* 'I threw;' *shunáva,* aor. *shunghióm* or *shinghióm,* 'I heard;' *meráva,* aor. *merghióm,* 'I died.'

Verbs whose roots end in vowels form the aorist in *lióm* or *nióm:*[*] as *láva,* aor. *linióm, lióm,* or *lilióm,* 'I took;' *dáva,* aor. *dinióm,* 'I gave;' *jáva,* aor. *ghellióm,* 'I went;' *aváva,* aor. *allióm,* 'I came.'

Verbs whose penultimate is *ka* form the aorist in a similar manner: as *dikáva,* aor. *diklióm,* 'I saw;' *chikáva,* aor. *chiklióm,* 'I muddied;' *pekáva,* aor. *peklióm,* 'I cooked;' *nakáva,* aor. *naklióm,* 'I passed;' *makáva,* aor. *maklióm,* 'I painted.'

The passives, and such compound verbs as have *aváva* for their compound verbal element, never can have any other aorist than that of *aváva,* viz. *allióm.* They are always easily distinguished, and form a very prominent part in every Gypsy's conversation: thus *kindiló* is the 3d pers. sing. aor. of the pass. *kinaváva man,* 'I am bought,' *kindillióm,* 'I was bought;' *liniló,* 'it was taken,' from *laváva man,* 'I am taken,' *linilióm,* 'I was taken.' These forms, *liniló, kindiló,* and the like, are used as passive impersonals, and at times, united to the auxiliary verb *isóm,* they form a distinct tense, or rather, enforce the original meaning of the aorist itself.

---

[*] So also, exceptionally, *bandáva,* aor. *bandlióm,* 'I tied.'

Future.—The formation of this tense is extremely interesting, for it originates from another verb, *kamáva*, 'I wish,' Sr. *kam*, which we have already explained in the Vocabulary. It is prefixed to the Gypsy verb without any intermediate term, and it then forms the future. There are three modes of uniting it with the verb. A Gypsy can say *kamajáva, kamjáva,* or *kajáva,* 'I will go;' *kamakeráva, kamkeráva,* or *kakeráva,* 'I will make.' I have heard these various forms used indifferently, and I have put similar questions to different Gypsies, and the word has been pronounced in these various forms. However, the first form, *kamakeráva*, is rarely used: they prefer *kamkeráva*, following their usual habit of clipping the vowels in their conversation. This form of the future is of altogether modern origin. The Modern Greek has also lost the ancient form, and has adopted the auxiliary θέλω, corrupted to θά: as θὰ ὑπάγω, 'I will go.' We say now more generally θέλω ὑπάγειν, though the common people still cling to the θὰ. *Kam* is added to itself to express future wish: as *kamkamáv*, 'I shall wish;' precisely as we now say θὰ θέλω. I do not think that the Gypsies have imitated their neighbors the Greeks in the formation of this tense: they have followed the general analytical spirit, which has so extensively pervaded modern languages. The English makes large use of *will, shall, would, should,* in the formation of its futures.

Imperative.—This mood exhibits in most cases a striking similarity to the primitive Sanskrit root. Were not the different formations of the Gypsy verb so very clear, it would have been extremely easy to recognize the root in the simple form of the imperative: thus *keráva*, 'I make,' imp. *ker; shunáva,* 'I hear,' imp. *shun; dikáva,* 'I see,' imp. *dik; jáva,* 'I go,' imp. *ja; kusháva,* 'I revile,' imp. *kush; dáva,* 'I give,' imp. *de; láva,* 'I take,' imp. *la* or *le.* In the compound verbs, the imperative is formed solely from the second verb: as *vrakeráva,* 'I speak,' imp. *vrakér; chumidáva,* 'I kiss,' imp. *chumidé.* In the transitive verbs, the formation follows the same rule as in the simple neuter verbs, by rejecting the final syllable *ava:* as *taparáva,* 'I make warm,' imp. *tapár; murdaráva,* 'I murder,' imp. *murdár.* As for the imperative of the passive, I have always heard the subjunctive used in its stead.

Subjunctive.—This mood represents both the subjunctive and the infinitive, and the usage of it becomes very clear after obtaining a little knowledge of the language. There is no vestige of the Sanskrit infinitive, and the Gypsies, like the Greeks and modern Slavonians, make use of the indicative mood. The Greeks use their particle νὰ, the ancient ἵνα; and the Slavonians *áko* and *da.* This latter was in use among the ancient Slavonic nations, in the optative and imperative moods, precisely as the particle ἵνα of the Greeks was an optative, and in course of time lost its initial *ι*, and became the *να* of our modern Greek, so common now in the language that it is constantly to be heard wherever the modern Greek is spoken. To us, and to the Bulgarians, the subjunctive of the Gypsies is perfectly intelligible and extremely natural, but to others this is not the case. *Te* is the particle always prefixed, and it is never pronounced *ta;* but, whenever the verb begins with a vowel, *te* drops its own. A few examples will fully illustrate the subject: *alliόm te dikáv,* 'I have come to see,' i. e. 'in order that I may see;' *pen lénghe t' avén,* 'tell them to come;' Gr. εἰπὲ αὐτοὺς νὰ ἔλθωσι, ' that they come.' Again, it is used as a pure optative mood: thus *te jivél túke,* 'may it live to thee;' Gr. ἵνα ζήσῃ, or νὰ ζήσῃ: the whole phrase naturally would be εὔχομαι ἵνα ζήσῃ, 'I pray that it may live;' *kamáva te shikliováva,* 'I wish to learn.' In this example, the subjunctive is evidently a pure infinitive.

I have heard at times the Gypsies using the infinitive as a noun, as the modern Greeks do: τὸ νὰ βλέπω, τὸ νὰ ἔβλεπα.

The aorist is sometimes used in the subjunctive with the particle *te;* more generally the imperfect is employed.

The subjunctive used as infinitive is not altogether devoid of expression, for it possesses number and person, which the ancient infinitives had not. At times it is extremely clear and definite, far more so than the ancient. This form of the infinitive is known both to the Christian and Moslem Gypsies. These latter, many of whom know not a word of Greek or Bulgarian, could not have borrowed it from the Turkish, which has a proper and regular infinitive, and whose verb in richness and variety is not surpassed by that of any language, ancient or modern. Besides this, the Gypsy verb makes but a poor comparison with the various complex moods and tenses of the Turkish verb. To me it appears probable that the natural bent of the human mind, and its progress towards simplicity of expression, have operated with equal force upon the spirit of the Gypsy as upon that of other modern languages, in which such a striking similarity exists in the various forms of their verbal expression.

Participle.—This is not so clear or so well defined as the other parts of the Gypsy verb. Some participles are pure Sanskrit words. Others are formed from the Gypsy verb itself, in a manner altogether peculiar to this idiom. In the first class belong such terms as Sr. *tapta,* 'heated,' G. *tattó;* Sr. *supta,* 'asleep,' G. *suttó* or *sottó;* Sr. *pûrta,* 'full,' G. *perdó.* To the second class belong a great number formed from the Gypsy verbs, pronounced in various ways by different Gypsies, and not always familiar to them all. They seem to take their origin, at times, from individuals who have more or less knowledge of their idiom. The same remark applies to the modern Greek, where one may hear, as participles of λέγω, λεγάμενος, λεγόμενος, and λεγμένος.

15

The following is a list of those Gypsy participles which have appeared to me to be correct, and which I have frequently heard used: *siváva*, 'I sew,' part. *sivdó*, 'sewn;' *charáva*, 'I eat,' part. *charavdó; asáva*, 'I laugh,' part. *asavdó; dáva*, 'I give,' part. *dinó; janáva*, 'I know,' part. *jandó; chináva*, 'I cut,' part. *chindó* or *chinavdó; keráva*, 'I make,' part. *kerdó; piáva*, 'I drink,' part. *piló; mutráva*, 'I void urine,' part. *muterdó; nasháva*, 'I depart,' part. *nashtó; chumidáva*, 'I kiss,' part. *chumidinó; daráva*, 'I fear,' part. *daravdó; shunáva*, 'I hear,' part. *shundó; bisháva*, 'I inhabit,' part. *bishtó; mundáva*, 'I shave,' part. *mundavdó; piráva*, 'I walk,' part. *pirdó; astaráva*, 'I hold,' part. *astardó; jáva*, 'I go,' part. *jadló; mukáva*, 'I let go,' part. *mukavdó; basháva*, 'I cry out,' part. *bashtó; chiváva*, 'I throw,' part. *chivdó; pekáva*, 'I cook,' part. *pekó; továva*, 'I wash,' part. *tovdó; maráva*, 'I strike,' part. *maravdó; resáva*, 'I finish,' part. *resavdó; makáva*, 'I paint,' part. *makavdó*.

From this list the reader can see the great variety of the participles existing in the idiom of the Gypsies. Those formed from simple neuter verbs, as *makáva, makavdó*, 'painted,' *resáva, resavdó*, 'finished,' are of pure Gypsy formation; whilst *pekó*, 'cooked,' is related to Sr. *pakva*, 'baked, heated, cooked,' etc. I have in the course of the Vocabulary noticed such participles as are of indisputable Sanskrit origin.

The reader will observe in the paradigms of the active verb that I have noted the participles *chinavdó* and *choravdó*. These participles have a passive signification, and as such they are constantly used by the Gypsies. As to the proper active participles, I confess that I know of none; the Gypsies seem to make no use of such forms, but in their stead employ the verb, as the modern Greeks constantly do. The Turks, however, are extremely fond of the participle, and are using it constantly.

This want of active participles is another proof of my assertion, that whilst both Greeks and Turks have given many expressions to the Gypsies, they have not influenced their grammatical system, which has followed those natural principles by the operation of which languages of older date have been moulded into their present form, each one by itself, and independent of the others. This holds good with the Gypsy, and if I have remarked in the course of this memoir that the Gypsy language has been thoroughly permeated by the Greek and Turkish languages, it still appears to me true that it has been formed, as to its fundamental principles, independently of both. So also the Modern Greek, which, though constantly imitating the Turkish, has never had any connection with it in its elementary and grammatical forms, for both languages are essentially distinct from each other.

ALPHABETICAL LIST OF GYPSY WORDS.*

abchín, steel.
achdí, yet.
achardva, to sigh.
achdva, to rest; *achardó*, remained.
achíbes, Bor., to-day.
achinelar, Bor., to cut.
akaná, now.
akata (s. within).
akhór, akór, nut; *akhorín, akorín*, nut-tree.
akiarghióm, sighed.
akld, akhíd, this.
allióm (s. come), came (cf. 111).
amáksi (s. up), carriage.
amdl, partner.
ambró, pear; *ambrolín*, pear-tree.
amíni (Bor., *amíñi*), anvil.
andva, to bring.
andré, within; *andrál (andryál)*, from within; cf. behind.
angáli, armful.
angár, coal; *angaréskoro*, collier.
anglé, forwards; *angluinó*, foremost; *anglál*, from the front.
angúst, angrúst, finger.
angustri, angrustí, ring.
anro, Bor., egg.
apdivés, to-day.
aquia, Bor., eye.
arajay, Bor., priest.
arakáv (Bor., *aracate*), guard; *arakáva* (Bor., *arakatear*), to guard.
aratí, Bor., blood.
aratti, night.
armán, curse.
aruje, Bor., wolf.
asán, wheel.
asdva, to laugh.
ásfa, tear.
ashardva, to praise.
astaló, piastre.
astardva, to hold.
astra, Bor., moon.
até, here; *attár*, hence.
avaká, avká, avakhá, avaklíd, this.
avatíd, here.
avdva, to come.
avdivés, to-day.
aver, avel, Bor., other.
avghín, honey.
avkós, first.   [eigner.
avri, out; *avridl*, from out; *avruinó*, for-

bacria (s. sheep), Bor., goat.
bdgnia, bath.
bahtaló, unfortunate.
bahtzé (s. near), garden.
bakó (92), — *pakó*.
bakró, sheep; *bakri*, ewe; *bakrichó (bak-ritzó*, 95a), lamb.
bal, hair.
balamó, Greek; *balamanó*, adj.
baló, swine; *balichó (balitzó*, 95a), dimin.

banddva, to shut, to tie; *bandloipé*, band.
bangdva (92), — *pangdva*.
bar, stone; *baréskoro*, stone-cutter.
baravaló, rich.
baríbu, Bor., much.
baró, great; *baredér* (96a), comp.; *bario-vdva* (s. increase).
baró, heavy.
bas, Bor., hand.
bashdva, to cry out.
bashé, near; *bashál*, from near.
bashipé, habitation.
basnó, bashnó, cock.
bato, batu, Bor., father.
ben, birth.
bendva, to beget.
bendva, to say.
benk (Bor., *bengue*), devil; *beng* (96); *bengaló*, devilish.   [seaman.
beró (Bor., *bero, berdo*), ship; *beréskoro*,
bersh (Bor., *berjí*), year.   [possess.
beshdva (s. habitation), to inhabit, sit, *bestipen*, Bor., habitation; *béstelar*, Bor., to inhabit.
bezéh, pity.
bi, without.
bidv, marriage.
bidva (s. when), to be delivered.
bighián (99), he sold.
bikindva, biknáva (s. buy), to sell.
bísh, Bor., *bis*, (s. numbers) twenty.
bishdva (92), *bisdva* (111), — *beshdva*.
bistó (s. habitation), seated.
biv (Bor., *bífl*), snow.   [hungry.
bokaló, hungry; *bokaliovdva*, to become
boldva, to baptize; *bolipé*, baptism.
bópi, bean.
bor, belly.
bordón (s. ship), — *vordón*.
bov, oven; *bovéskero*, baker.
bracuñi, Bor., sheep.
brakerdva (s. Jew), for *vrakerdva*.
brishundó (Bor., *brijindel*), rain.
buchardó (s. cover), uncovered.
bugló, broad; *bugliovdva*, to spread out.
bukó, bowel.
bunísta, dung.
burda, Bor., door.
burnék, handful.
burshín, rain.
bus, straw.
bus, Bor., much.
busní, Bor., sweet.
but, butló, much.
butí, business; *butiakoro*, day-laborer.
buznó, buzní (s. buck), she-goat; *busnoró*,
búzos, buck.   [kid.

cajuco, Bor., deaf.
callicaste, Bor., yesterday.
calo, callardo, caloro, Bor., black.
cambrí, Bor., pregnant.

---

* Added by the Committee of Publication, as an important, and almost indispensable, appendix to Dr. Paspati's article.

cangri, Bor., church.
cani, Bor., hen.
casian, Bor., wood.
casto, Bor., hammer.
chachipé, truth; *chachipanó*, true.
chái (s. boy), girl.
chaja, Bor., cabbage.
chaliováva, to be sated.
cham, kiss.
chamkerdva, to chew.
chaó, boy.
char, grass; *charáva*, to graze.
charés (s. wing), possible.
charó, plate; *charéskoro*, plate-maker.
chartáva, to vomit; *chartimpé*, vomiting.
chattdva, to vomit; *chattimpé*, vomiting.
chavó, boy-child.
chavory (s. boy), Bor., girl.
chavri, chicken.
chergheni (Bor., *cherdillas*), star.
chíbes, Bor., day.
chik, chiká, mud; *chikáva* (111), to muddy.
chikhandí (s. little), in a little while.
chiktáva, to sneeze.
chimutra, Bor., moon.
chin, till.
chindva (Bor., *chinelar*), to cut.
chinday, Bor., mother.
chiniovdva, to be tired.
chinkerdva, chingherdva, to pierce.
chip, tongue.
chirdo, Bor., dwarfish, small.
chiriklό, bird.
chivdva, chitáva, to throw (also s. poor).
choldva, to steal.
choldva (s. cut), to whittle.
chon, moon, month.
chordva, to steal; *chor, chornó, churnó*, thief; *chordikanό*, stolen.
chori, Bor., knife.
choró, poor; *choripé*, poverty.
chorydl, secretly.
chova, Bor., hand.
chuché, chuchi, breast.
chuchó, empty.
chukél, dog; *chuklí*, bitch.
chukni, tobacco-pipe.   [to kiss.
chumi (Bor., *chupendi*), kiss; *chumidáva*,
chungalό, miserable.
chungdrva, to spit; *chungér*, spittle.
churi (Bor., *chuló*), knife.
churnό (s. steal), thief.
chuti, Bor., milk.
ciria, Bor., passover.
cornicha, Bor., basket.
crallis, Bor., king.
cremen, Bor., worm.
culco, curque, Bor., Sunday.

daha (96a), more.
dái, mother.
dal, door.
dal, Bor., fear.
dant (Bor., *dani*), tooth.
dantáva, dantiláva, to bite.
dar, door.
dar, fear; *daráva* (Bor., *darabar, daraňar*), to fear.   [ate-tree.
darάv, pomegranate; *daravín*, pomegran-
das, Bulgarian; *dasikanό*, adj.

dat, father.
dáva, to give; *de*, imper.
de, mother.
debél, Bor., god.
déla, it rains.
denilό, fool; *deniliovdva*, to become a fool.
dernό, Bor., young.
deryάv, sea.
desh (s. numbers), ten.   [godly.
devél, god; *devli* (89), goddess; *devlikanό*,
dialezáva (s. write), to select.
diar, dicar, Bor., to see.
dikáva, dikháva (*dihάva, didva*), to see.
dini, dimish, pantaloon; *dimialό*, wearing
dinar, Bor., to give.   [pantaloons.
dinelo, Bor., fool.
dinό (107), given.
disilό, day breaks.
divés, day; *diveséskoro*, day's wages.
domúk, fist.
drak, grape.
drom (Bor., *dron, drun*), road.
dua, duga, Bor., pain.
dudúm, gourd.
dui (s. numbers), two.
duk, pain; *dukdva*, to be in pain, to love; *dukhaipé*, love; *dukhani*, mistress.
dulevdva (s. near), to work.
dumó, back.
duquipen, Bor., pain.
dur, afar; *durάl*, from afar.

eftd (s. numbers), seven; *eftavardéri*, sev-
eketané, together.   [enty.
enre, Bor., within.
erajay, Bor., priest.
eresia, Bor., vineyard.
estuché, Bor., sword.

far, time, times.
fάrkia, scythe.
felé, down.
fendo, Bor., good.
fóros, market-place.
furi, colt.
furó, old.

gálpea, gold.
gao, Bor., village.
gardva, to conceal; *garatikanό*, mysterious.
garipé (s. itch), Bor., scab.
gav, village; *gavudnό*, villager.
gel, Bor., ass.
ghamee, Br., ship.
ghantáva, to comb.
gheldva, to play (in music).
ghéles, always.
gheliόm, gherghiόm (s. go), went; cf. 111.
ghendva, to count.
gher, itch; *gheralό*, itchy.
gherdva, to make.
ghermό, worm.
ghili (*ghilό*), song; *ghiláva, ghiliovdva*, to sing; *ghilimpé*, instrument of music.
ghivés, day.
ginar, Bor., to count.
giv (Bor., *gi*), grain, wheat.
give, Bor., snow.
gorbi, Bor., ox.
górko, bad.

gosháva, to cleanse.
goshnó, dung (*gosnó*, 95).
goti, brain; *gotiavér*, intelligent.
grafáva, to write.
grast (Bor., *gras*, *gra*), horse; *grastní* (Bor., *graní*), mare; *grastanó* (*grái*), adj.; *grastéskoro*, horseman.
gris, Bor., cold.
gudló, sweet.
guel, Bor., ass; itch.
guillabar, Bor., to sing.
guriv, *guri*, ox; *guruvni*, *gurumni*, cow.
gustó (s. hen), Bor., goose.
giúva, pit.
guy, Bor., grain, wheat.

handiovdva (90), — *khandiovdva*.
hanló, sword.
hapai, apple.
has, cough; *hasdva*, to cough.
hindovi (s. from), India.
hirdó (90), — *khurdó*.
hohaimpé (90), — *khohaimpé*.

ich (s. come), — *yich*.
iniya (s. numbers), nine; *iniyavardéri*, [ninety.
ishtár (s. numbers), four.
iv, snow.
iv, grain, wheat.

jamutró, son-in-law.
jandva (s. negation), to know.
jangdva, to awake.
jáva, to go; *jadló* (114), part.
jel (s. itch), small-pox.
jeni, Bor., ass.
jenó: kayék jenó, no one.
jeroro, Bor., ass; *jerini*, fem.
jil, *jir*, Bor., cold.
jil, Bor., grain, wheat.
jinar, Bor., to count.
jiváva, to live.
jojana, Bor., lie.
joro, Bor., head.
jov, barley.
jov (s. file), six.
jucal, Bor., beautiful.
juco, Bor., dry.
jumeri, Bor., bread.
junar, Bor., to hear.
jut, Jew; *jutanó*, Jewish.
juter, *juti*, Bor., vinegar.
jutia (s. sew), Bor., needle.
juv, louse.

ka, who, which.
káde (s. early), every.
kaini, *kagni*, *kainá*, hen.
kalipé, excommunication.
kaló, black.
kam (Bor., *cam*, *can*), sun.
kamáva (Bor., *camelar*), to wish.
kamlioipé, *kamnioipé*, perspiration; *kamló*, perspiring; *kamniovdva*, *kamliovdva*, to perspire.
kamni, pregnant.
kándela, it stinks; *kandíniko*, stinking.
kangli, comb.
kann, ear.

kánna, when.
kar, pudendum virile.
karghíri, church.
kárin, where.
kasht, *kash*, *kast*, *kas*, wood.
kasukóv, deaf.
katár, from.
katár, whence.
katáva, to spin.
katúna, Gypsy tent.
kayék jenó, no one.
ke, who, which.
kebór, how many.
keldva, to play (in music).
kelipé (s. because), dance.
ker, house.
kerál, cheese.
keraló (s. wash), — *gheraló*.
kerdva, to make.
kerkó, bitter.
kermó, worm.
keti, how much.
kfur, heel.
khan, crepitus ventris.
khandí, little.
khanínk, *khaink*, well. [*jáva*, neut.
khanjovdva, *khandiovdva*, to scratch; *khankhanló*, sword.
khar, pit.
khasós (s. eat), food.
khatáva, to dig.
kháva, to eat.
khelí, fig; *khelin*, fig-tree. [part.
khidva, *khlidva*, cacare; *khendó*, *khlendó*, *khohaimpé*, lie; *khohavnó*, *khohanó*, liar; *khohavniovdva*, to be deceived.
khokhavniovdva, to be cheated.
kholíterdva, *kholiazáva* (s. write), to be angry; *kholíniakoro*, angry.
khor, deep.
khorakhái, Turk; *khorakhanó*, Turkish.
khristuné, Christmas.
khur, heel.
khurdó, dwarfish, small.
kildv, plum; *kilavin*, plum-tree.
kilavdó (s. rich), fat.
kiló, stake.
kindva, to buy.
kirvó, sponsor; *kirvi*, god-mother.
kisi, sack.
kiustik, girdle.
koch, knee.
kókkalo, bone.
kolin, bosom.
kon, who.
kopána, trough.
kori (s. shut), neck.
korin, root.
koró, blind.
koró (95), bracelet.
koshdva, to cleanse.
kóshnika, basket.
kotór (s. cheese), little.
ksilldbi, *ksillávi*, tongs.
kukudi, hail.
kuri, colt.
kurkó, Sunday.
kurló, throat.
kushdva, to revile (also *kus*, 99).

labelar, Bor., to sing.
lachanó (s. ashamed), shameful.
lachés, well.
lachipé, alms.
lachó, good.
lahtdáva, to kick.
lajdva, to be ashamed.
langar, Bor., coal.
lav, word.
láva, to take, get.
len, river.
lí, Bor., paper.
likhnari (s. sleep), lamp.
lillar, Bor., to take, get.
lim, mucus.
lindr, sleep; *lindraló*, sleepy.
liniló (107), taken.
lir, lil, paper.
lokó, light.
loló, red.
lon, salt; *londardáva*, to salt.
loria, Bor., sea.
loshaniováva, to rejoice; *loshanó*, rejoic-
lové, money. [ing; *loshanoipé*, joy.
lubni (*lobni*, 89), harlot.
luey, Bor., wolf.
luludi (s. similar), flower.
lumi, lumiaka, Bor., harlot.

ma, negation.
macha, Bor., fly.
machó, fish; *machéskoro*, fisherman.
majara, Bor., half.
makáva, to paint.
makiá, fly.
malkóch, a Gypsy tribe. [posite side.
mamúi, opposite; *mamuydl*, from the op-
mang, Bor., meat.
manró, mandó, bread; *manréskoro*, baker.
manukló, mankló, stump (of vine).
manúsh (Bor., *manu, manus*), man; *ma-
nushní* (89), woman; *manushanó* (95),
mára, sea. [human.
mardva, to beat.
marnó, marly, bread.
maru, Bor., man; *marupe*, mankind.
mas, meat; *maséskoro*, butcher.
masék, month.
mashá, tongs. [tween.
maskaré, between; *maskardl*, from be-
mastér, blacksmith. [drunk.
mattó, drunk; *mattiováva*, to become
mel, dirt; *melaló*, dirty; *melaliovdva*, to
become dirty.
meligrána, Bor., pomegranate-tree.
meráva, to die.
merdó (s. die), Bor., sick; see also invalid.
meripé, death.
mermóri, tomb.
milia, Bor., *milan* (s. numbers), thousand.
minch, pudendum muliebre.
mishákos, mouse.
mnemóri, tomb.
mol, wine.
mollati, Bor., grape.
moló, death. [worker in leather.
mortí (Bor., *morchas*), leather; *mortídkoro*,
moskdre (s. beget), calf.
móste (s. shut), from *múi*.

moskovís, Russian.
muclar, Bor., to void urine.
múi, mouth; *muydl, muiydl*, in front.
mukdva, to abandon.
mulanó, ripe; *mulanokeráva*, to ripen.
mulanó (s. dirty), dark.
mulótar (s. die, also 95a), after dying.
muntdva (*munddva*, 114), to shave; *mun-
tardva* (108).
murdardva, to murder.
murs, brave, male, boy.
murtardva (s. die), to murder.
mushó, mouse. [void urine.
mutér, urine; *mutrdva* (Bor., *mutrar*), to

na, negation.
nái, nail.
naisváli (*naisbali*, 92), invalid.
naisukár (s. negation), not handsome.
najabar, najar, Bor., to depart; to lose;
nak, nose. [*najipen*, loss.
nakdva, to pass.
namporemé, invalid; *namporéma*,sickness.
nandí, negation.
nangó, naked.
nao, Bor., name.
napaldí (s. behind), afterwards.
naqui, Bor., nose.
nashdva, to depart.
nashaváva, to lose.
nasti, negation.
nastó, departed.
nasukár, ugly.
nav, name.
ne, negation.
nevó (Bor., *nebo, nebel*), new.
niglavdva (*niklavdva*, 92), to go out.
nildi, summer.
ninelo, Bor., fool.
nubli, harlot.

oghi, heart; *oghéske*, alms. [eighty.
ohtó (s. numbers), eight; *ohtovardéri*,
okaná, now.
okhid, this.
oklistó, mounted.
onghi, heart.
opré, up; *oprdl, oprydl*, from above.
orioz, Bor., wolf.
orobar, Bor., to weep.
ostebel, Bor., god.
ostelis, osteli, Bor., down.
oté (s. negation), for *até*.
otiá (s. why), there.

pachandra, Bor., passover.
pachdva, to ask.
paí, water.
paillo, Bor., Greek.
pak, wing.
pakidva, to believe.
pakó, bald.
palabear, Bor., to shave.
paldl, behind; *palalutnó*, second.
palvál, wind.
panch (s. numbers), five.
pangdva, to break.
pangheráva, to lame; *panghiovdva*, to become lame.

pani, water; *panidáva*, to water.
pankó, pangó, lame.
papai, apple.
papina (s. hen), goose.
paquilli, Bor., silver.
parés, slowly.
parnavó, friend; *parnavoipé*, friendship.
parnó, white.
paró (92), — *baró*.
paroji, Bor., leaf.
parvaráva, to nourish.
parvardó, fat.
pas, pasque, Bor., half.
pashé, near.
páta, clothing.
patranki, passover.
patrin, leaf, feather.
pavi, Bor., nose.
pecháva, to ask.
pekáva, to cook; *pekiló, pekó*, cooked.
pelióm, fell; *pelótar*, after falling.
peló, testicle.
pen (s. brother), sister.
penáva (Bor., *penar*), to say; also for *be-náva* (s. infant).
peninda (s. numbers), fifty.
peráva, to fall.
perdáva, to fill.
perdál, over (the water).
perdó, full; *pertiovdáva*, to become full.
peryúl, peryulikanó, foreign.
pfuv, phuv, earth.   [old.
phuró, phurú, old; *phuriováva*, to grow
pidv, marriage.
pidáva, to drink.   [*va* (s. paper).
picharáva (s. business), to send; *picharár-*
pichiscas, Bor., cough.
pikaló, prop.
pikó, shoulder.
piló, peló, fallen; *piló* (114), drunk.
pincharáva, to be acquainted with.
pindó, pinró, foot.
piráva (Bor., *pirar*), to walk.
pirindós, on foot.
piripé, gait.
pirnangó, barefooted.
piró, pirnó, foot.
pisháva, to grind.
pishót, bellows.
pivli, widow.
piyar, Bor., to drink; *píta*, drink.
plal (Bor., *plan, plano*), brother.
plata, Bor., clothing.
plubi, Bor., silver.
po (s. behind), more.
pol, navel.
polaléste (s. behind), farther back.
pomi, Bor., silver.
pori, tail.
porias, Bor., bowel.
porik, porikin, raisin.
pos, po, Bor., belly.
poshik, soil.
posóm, wool.
pov, eye-brow.
poyicháver (s. yesterday).
práhos, ashes.
pral, brother; *pra* (92).
prasáva, to ridicule.

predál, over (the water).
pucháva, to ask.
pudinó, musket.
puranó, old (ancient).
puró, old; *puripé*, old age.
purt, bridge.
purúm, onion.
pusca, Bor., musket.
pushúm, flea.
putar, Bor., well.
puti, business.
puv, earth.

quer, Bor., house.
querar, querelar, Bor., to make.
querosto (s. house), Bor., August.

rachi, Bor., night.
rái, nobleman.
rakiló (s. night), it is growing dark.
rakló, raklí, child.
ran, cane.
ráni, nobleman's wife.
ráno, early.
rashdi, priest; *rashani*, priest's wife.
rat, ratti, night.
ratt (Bor., *ratí*), blood.
res, rez, vineyard.
resáva, to finish, suffice.
résheto, sieve.
resis, Bor., cabbage.
richini, bear.
rói, spoon.
roi, Bor., flour.
rom, romni, romanó, Gypsy.
romni (Bor., *romi*), wife.
rováva, to weep.
róyi, spoon.
rubli, rod.
ruk, tree.
rukonó, whelp.
rup, silver; *rupovanó*, of silver.
rutuni, nose.
ruv, wolf.

sahriz, tent.
saló, wife's brother; *sali*, wife's sister.
sannó, slim.
sannó (92), — *sunnó*.
sapp, serpent.
sar, similar, like.
sar, Bor., garlic.
saránda (s. numbers), forty.
saro, Bor., all.
sarró, sárrore, sarnó (101), all.
sarvó, sárvolo, all.
sas, Bor., iron.
sashúi, mother-in-law.
saste, Bor., tall.
sastó (s. from and 93), healthy, right.
sastró, father-in-law.
saullo, Bor., colt.
sávvore, savvó (93), all.
semer, pack-saddle.
serka, Br., tent.
sevlia, Br., basket.
shah, cabbage.   [smith.
shastir, shastri, iron; *shastiréskoro*, black-
shastó, healthy, right.

shastró, father-in-law.
shasúi, mother-in-law.
shel (s. numbers), hundred.
sheló, rope.
sheró, head.
shevél (s. cold), hundred.
shikáva (90), to learn; *shikló*, learned; *shikliováva*, to learn.
shil (s. numbers), hundred.
shil, shilaló, cold; *shilaliováva*, to feel cold.
shingh, horn.
shoró, head.
shoshói, hare.
shov (s. numbers), six.
shovardéri (s. numbers), sixty.
shuchó, shuzó, clean.
shukó, dry, emaciated; *shukiováva* (102), to become dry; *shukiaráva, shukiaváva*, to dry.
shunáva, to hear.
shut, shutkó, vinegar; *shutló, shudló*, sour.
sigó, quick.
singe, Bor., horn.
singo, Bor., quick.
sir, garlic.
siváva, to sew.
sivri, hammer.
so, what.
sobelar, sornar, Bor., to sleep.
somnakái (Bor., *sonacai*), gold.
sóske, why.
sostár, because.
sottó (s. sleep), asleep.
sováva, to sleep.
stavros, cross.
sudró, cool.
sukár, beautiful.
sumpacel, Bor., near.
sunáva (s. near), — *shunáva*.
sungalo, Bor., horned.
sunnó, dream.
sut, milk.
suttó (113), — *sottó*.
suv (s. sew), needle.

ta, te, and.
tabioipé, heat.
tahkár, taakár, king; *takarni*, queen.
tái (101), — *dái*.
takhiára, tomorrow.
tam-manúsh, blind man.
tan, place.
taparáva (103), to heat.
tapáva, tap-dáva, to strike.   [feel warm.
tapiáva, to boil, to burn; *tapáva* (103), to
tapillar, Bor., to drink.
tapiováva, to burn.
tardáva, to thirst.
tarshúl, cross.
tato, Bor., bread.
tattipé, heat.   [hot.
tattó, warm; *tattováva* (103), to become
tattó (Bor., *tati*), bath.
tav, thread.
taváva, to boil.
te, and.

telé, down.
teráva (Bor., *terelar*), to have.
terghiováva, tertiováva, to stand.
ternó, young; *ternoro*, Bor., new.
tikng, infant, young.
továva, todáva, to wash.
tovér, tovel, axe; *toveréskoro*, axe-maker.
tránda (s. numbers), thirty.
tragulas, Bor., grape.
trebene, Bor., star.
trésca, fever.
tri, trin (s. numbers), three.
triák, shoe.
trijul, Bor., cross.
trush, trust, thirst; *trushaló*, thirsty; *trushaliováva*, to become thirsty.
trushúl, cross.
turra, Bor., nail.
turshúl (93), cross.
tut, milk.

uchardáva, to cover.
uchó, tall; *uchedér* (96a), one taller.
ukiaváva, uktiaváva, to step.
uklidva, uklaváva (92), to mount.
umdebel, Bor., god.
unga, Bor., affirmation.
ungla, Bor., nail.
uryáva, uryaváva, to dress.
uryoipé, dress.

vá, affirmation.
vanró, vantó, egg.
vaptizdva, to baptize.
var, time, times.
vária, weight.
varó, flour.
vasiáv, mill.
vast (*vas*, 91), hand.
vent, winter.
verni, file.
vesh, ves (s. healthy), forest.
vicha, shoot.
vikó, shoulder.
viv (94), — *biv*.
vlákhia, Wallachian.
vordón, carriage.
vrakerdva, to speak.
vrehtúla, extinguisher.
vuchó, tall.
vudár, vutár, door.
vus, flax.
vust, lip.

yak, fire.
yak, eye.
yavér, other.
yek (s. numbers), one.
yekpdsh, half.
yernó, young.   [terday.
yich, yesterday; *yichavér*, day before yesterday.
yismata, linen.

zámpa, frog.
zen, saddle.
zoraló, strong.

NOTE.—By an oversight, which was discovered too late to be rectified, pp. 97–104 above are repeated. The pages thus occurring a second time, when referred to in the Index, are distinguished by an appended *a*.

Lightning Source UK Ltd.
Milton Keynes UK
UKHW02n1542160218
318016UK00004B/442/P